WITHDRAWN

ROBERT HUNTER, 1666–1734

A New York State Study

Major General Robert Hunter, oil, attributed to Sir Godfrey Kneller. Courtesy of The New-York Historical Society, New York City

ROBERT HUNTER
1666–1734
New York's Augustan Statesman

༽ ༼

MARY LOU LUSTIG

Syracuse University Press   1983

Copyright © 1983 by SYRACUSE UNIVERSITY PRESS
Syracuse, New York 13210

All Rights Reserved

First Edition

This book is published with the assistance of a grant from the John Ben Snow Foundation.

Library of Congress Cataloging in Publication Data
Lustig, Mary Lou.
    Robert Hunter, 1666–1734, New York's augustan
statesman.
    (A New York State study)
    Includes bibliographical references and index.
    1. Hunter, Robert, 1666–1734. 2. New York (State)—
Politics and government—Colonial period, ca. 1600–1775.
3. New Jersey—Politics and government—Colonial period,
ca. 1600–1775. 4. Colonial administrators—United
States—Biography. 5. Colonial administrators—Great
Britain—Biography. 6. Colonial administrators—Jamaica
—Biography. I. Title. II. Series.
E195.H86L87 1983   974.7'02'0924   [B]   83-4750
ISBN 0-8156-2296-1

Manufactured in the United States of America

To my children

MARY LOU LUSTIG is assistant editor of the William Livingston Papers, New York University.

᧞ CONTENTS ᧞

ᑕᔆᖉ PREFACE ᔆᖉᑕ

"The Government of the Plantations"

$\mathscr{R}$OBERT HUNTER (1666–1734) had a long and rewarding imperial career as British governor-general of Virginia (1707–1709), New York and New Jersey (1709–1720), and Jamaica (1727–1734). While Hunter, a man of "Humanity, Justice, and Honour," enjoyed successful administrations in all the provinces he governed, he scored a particular triumph in his New York post. This fulfilled Richard Steele's expectation that Hunter's background and training would produce favorable results in New York. After hearing of his friend's nomination, Steele wrote in the *Tatler* that he "took Part in the Happiness of that People who were to be govern'd by one . . . [who] had read all the Schemes which Writers have form'd of Government and Order, and been long conversant with Men who have the Reins in their Hands. . . . " During the eleven years of Hunter's well-documented New York administration, perhaps the most highly regarded in American colonial history, he brought order and stability to a formerly chaotic society. For Hunter, this period, rich in personal as well as professional associations, was the high point of his American career.[1]

Hunter was given the opportunity to prove his administrative abilities in England's provinces as a reward for a brilliant British military career as a dragoon officer. The impetus of Hunter's public life was the rise of Britain to world power. The events of that Anglo-American career were dictated by imperial centralization, the machinations of politicians, the uses and abuses of power and patronage in the ages of Marlborough and Walpole, the growing intricacies of transatlantic administration, the reactive growth of provincial oligarchies, and, most of all, by fate: "Any man is good while his luck is good, / bad when bad, and for the most part they are best / whom the gods love." Hunter did indeed enjoy good fortune during his lifetime. That he stood well with the governing tendencies of his age, that he was able to adapt when necessary, and that he was fortunate enough to have been born during an era when his particular talents and abilities were needed, is what makes the story of his life exemplary and illustrative.[2]

Hunter's impoverished childhood in the Lowlands of Scotland in-
stilled in him a desire to succeed in the British world. His superior
education in the Scottish school system trained his intellect so he could
accomplish his goal. His innate and acquired abilities permitted him to
rise in the British army. Hunter's background produced a politically astute
and culturally accomplished man who was well suited to be governor-
general of four of England's American provinces. A study of Hunter's
provincial administrations provides organizational dimension and cultural
meaning to the early eighteenth century, a significant, but seldom
explored, period of American history. During this period, America's
political, economic, social, and cultural institutions, as well as that
ambiguous entity known as "the American character," were developed on
the English models provided by governors-general such as Robert Hunter.

While the deliberate transmittal of culture from England to the
provinces brought positive results, Americans and their institutions were
also shaped by their largely negative reactions to subtle shifts in England's
imperial policies. The last half of the seventeenth century had been
characterized by an aggressive military imperialism, as England sought to
extend her physical boundaries by force. Eleven years before Hunter's
birth, a naval expedition, at Cromwell's order, seized the island of Jamaica
from the Spanish. Just two years before Hunter's birth, Charles II and his
brother, James, duke of York, emulated Cromwell and sent another naval
expedition to seize New Netherland from the Dutch. The territory that
would form New York and New Jersey was part of this 1664 conquest.
Hunter, raised in Scotland, a province tamed and disciplined by Cromwellian and Stuart military might, would eventually govern these conquered
New World provinces.

In these North American provinces, Hunter would implement the
techniques of garrison government bred into him as he grew up in Irvine,
Ayrshire. Scotland, like Ireland and England's New World colonies, was
treated as a subordinate province. During the Cromwellian period,
residents of Ayrshire had been governed by the colonel of the local
garrison, appointed by Cromwell, whose function was as much civil as it
was military. Hunter would himself act in both civil and military capacities
as governor-general in America.

Further examples of militaristic imperial rule pervaded Hunter's
childhood when, after the Restoration of Charles II, religious dissidents
were subdued in Scotland so Scots would form a military force for the king.
In 1685, Hunter was aware of James II's repression of the peasant
population in England and Scotland following the aborted coup of Monmouth and Argyll. Hunter also learned that force must be judiciously

applied. In 1688, King James's brutality against the predominantly Whig Lowland Scots caused them to abandon the king and assist the prince of Orange, the future William III, in his invasion of England. Hunter, a Lowland Scot, joined the military coup against King James. Later in Ireland, as a member of a Scottish dragoon regiment, Hunter helped William III secure the Revolution of 1688 by quelling Jacobite rebels.

As part of the British military establishment, Hunter, in 1690, next helped discipline his fellow Scottish countrymen. In 1692, he was still garrisoned in Scotland with the regiment that slaughtered the Highland Jacobites at Glencoe. The Highlands were subdued by this outrage, and almost twenty-five years passed before there was another significant Jacobite uprising in Scotland. Hunter then fought for King William on the continent to reduce France's territorial ambitions. After the conclusion of the War of the League of Augsburg, Hunter, in 1698, helped the English maintain order in reconquered Ireland.

Peace in Scotland and Ireland left Marlborough free to fight the French again on the continent, as England continued in her attempts to expand the empire. Scottish manpower helped England achieve this end during the War of the Spanish Succession (1702–1713), as Marlborough began an amazing string of victories against the formerly invincible French. The French army was demoralized by British martial superiority, particularly after the brilliant 1704 victory at Blenheim in which Hunter and other Scots played prominent parts. Marlborough's victories extended British territory and increased British trade until Great Britain was the foremost power in the European world.

Marlborough's armies were not engaged in continual warfare, however. Between campaigns they had also to govern the subordinate or conquered provinces where they were quartered. As Marlborough's subordinates, Hunter and his dragoons in Flanders and the Netherlands ensured that unwilling civilian populations would supply and house British troops as well as their horses. As a military governor in the Netherlands, Hunter interfered with force in local politics when necessary to preserve in power those men who favored the British cause. Thus, under the tutelage of the later Stuart monarchs and the duke of Marlborough, Hunter in Scotland, Ireland, England, Flanders, and the Netherlands acquired the techniques of intimidation and compromise that he would later use in the American provinces.

In addition to affording examples on the techniques of governance, Marlborough also supplied Hunter with his imperial philosophy of empire. Marlborough heeded Sir Francis Bacon's advice to "let not the government of the Plantations depend upon too many Councellors and Undertakers in the country that planteth but upon a temperate number; and let those be rather noblemen and gentlemen than merchants; for they look ever to the present gain." Marlborough was particularly anxious to prevent the colonies from falling under the influence of mercantilists. Therefore, he staffed the imperial executive at home and abroad with disciplined men, such as Hunter, who were personally loyal to him and were also experienced military administrators. Marlborough insured "that the Queen wou'd not lett any body have Governments but such as have serv'd in the Army, for if the Duke of Newcastel and others can prevail we shall have no other Governors but Parliament men, which I am sure is not for Her Majestys Service. . . ." The "Parliament men" feared by Marlborough were predominantly Whig merchants and traders who invested in and controlled trading companies. Their motivation was primarily consideration of their own profit. Marlborough and other military imperialists, Hunter included, also profitted from commercial investments. Equally aware of the imperial needs of empire to survive and expand, they did not permit economic considerations alone to dictate their official policy.[3]

As a military imperialist, Hunter, along with Marlborough, recognized England's New World provinces were important, not only because of the possibilities they offered for increased trade and profit, but also because they contributed to the stature and power of Great Britain. Hunter also favored the provincial garrison government first implemented by Cromwell because of the strategic placement of the colonies. The French, the Spanish, and the Dutch each zealously protected their own New World possessions and sought to extend their holdings at each other's, and England's, expense. British colonists were repeatedly called upon to fight England's enemies in America. The provincials were also threatened by hostile native Americans and rebellious imported Africans. An experienced military governor, such as Hunter, could organize, direct, and provision not only the provincial militia and regular soldiers stationed in America, but also any additional forces sent from Britain to meet a particular threat.

Garrison government could be effective, as shown by Hunter's New York and New Jersey administrations, but only under certain circumstances. Provincials resented military rule because they rightly saw themselves in oppressed positions comparable to that of Civil War parliamentarians in England. Provincial oligarchs in the assemblies sought to resist military coercion as represented in the person of the governor-general by exercising their control over the raising of money. Governors-general were hindered in their efforts to counter provincial defiance both by their need of money and by their limited ability to make concessions to provincial legislatures. Determination on the part of the governor-general was met with an even greater measure of stubbornness on the part of the representatives. Hunter, for instance, could not at first govern effectively in New York because he adhered rigidly to his instructions. It was only after he ignored the letter of his instructions and permitted limited concessions to the assembly that he won control of the province.

Concessions to provincial oligarchs was not the principal reason Hunter enjoyed successful administrations in New York and New Jersey. This success was achieved because Hunter had the personality, determination, and intelligence to utilize effectively the extensive powers conveyed to him by the crown in his civil and military capacities as governor-general. The result was an end to discord and factionalism in both provinces, at least during Hunter's tenure. Hunter's successes in these provinces proved that garrison government worked, but only if the governor was actually present and as gifted as was Hunter.

Despite its potential for success, garrison government was already on the decline, even as Hunter governed New York and New Jersey. During the 1710s, an obsessive concern with trade and economic prosperity followed Marlborough's victories. The War of the Spanish Succession had not only physically established Britain as a major power, but also compelled commercial concessions to Britain by her European rivals. Thus, armed might increased Britain's share of the world's trade. The concurrent rise of merchants and of capitalism, however, fostered individual economic gain which was distinctly at odds with imperial values. When peace with France was achieved in 1713, England's ruling elite was transformed by the infusion of capital and capitalists. Growing profits fostered an increasingly materialistic attitude among these newly rich Britons.

Walpole, who came to power in 1722 following the deaths of Marlborough and his closest political associates and protégés, contributed to changing attitudes in Britain. Walpole, like Marlborough, favored the expansion of the empire, but Walpole sought to achieve this expansion by peaceful commerce rather than by armed conquest. To maintain the tranquil climate required for trade to flourish, Walpole made state decisions on the basis of commercial considerations, rather than what was best for the empire. By the time Hunter was appointed to govern Jamaica in 1727, Walpole's economically determined provincial policy had supplanted the garrison government of the Cromwellian-late Stuart era.

Walpole's policies fostered an attitude that discouraged home government interference in colonial affairs. Provincials, already irritated by the military rule of the previous era, were now further antagonized by a combination of administrative indifference which was compounded by increasingly inept officeholders. Hunter aside, many military governors in the provinces were now replaced by politicians committed to Walpole's program of economic prosperity. These placemen were given colonial posts not because of merit, but as rewards for political support. Inept officials raised colonial scorn and strengthened the determination of provincial oligarchs to defy the royal prerogative as represented in the person of the governor-general.

Hunter, a holdover from an earlier, imperial era, was one of the best of Walpole's appointees. Despite his competency, however, Hunter experienced serious difficulties in governing Jamaica because the Walpole ministry would not risk alienating mercantile interests in Britain. So much was evident during the Maroon War. Despite the fact that Jamaica faced a serious threat from the rebels and the island's slaves, the home government refused to maintain a sufficient military force on Jamaica because this would raise taxes at home. Neither would they permit the Jamaica legislature to raise money to support troops by taxing British trading companies. Similar examples of administrative blindness were seen in all Britain's colonies. This hardened the convictions and resolves of provincial opposition parties which opposed the governor and his council in virtually every province. During the Stuart era, a few governors-general, such as Hunter in New York and New Jersey, were able to eliminate or control assembly opposition parties. During the Walpolian era, such control became virtually impossible to achieve, even for Hunter. In Jamaica, Hunter found he had to make major concessions which permitted the assemblies increasingly to encroach upon the royal prerogative. Despite assembly opposition and home government ineptness, Hunter was able to protect and preserve his Jamaica command.

These events and situations not only lend human interest and intellectual meaning to a study of Robert Hunter's public life, but also shed light on his multidimensional character. Hunter was more than a competent governor-general and an accomplished army officer. He was an intelligent and dashing man of diverse talents and multiple achievements. He was a realist who had a chameleon quality that permitted him to adapt his own attitudes and beliefs to shifting political and religious currents. He was a man of wit and warmth who gloated unashamedly over the fall of those he despised. His letters give ample evidence of his superior intellect and his well-trained mind. His sense of humor is refreshing and his enthusiasm for life is contagious.

Hunter was also an accomplished poet and playwright who used his literary ability both for the joy of writing and to lampoon his political enemies. In his literary pursuits Hunter was influenced by writers of England's Augustan age. This period was so called because, just as the literature of the Roman Empire reached its peak of perfection during the reign of Augustus Caesar, so did the literature of the British Empire reach rare heights of purity and refinement during the reign of Queen Anne. Hunter included among his friends such literary savants of this era as Jonathan Swift, Joseph Addison, and Richard Steele, all of whom praised Hunter's literary ability and valued his friendship. As governor-general of New York and New Jersey, Hunter, who embodied the virtues, accomplishments, aspirations, and philosophy of statesmen during England's Augustan age, brought the cultural fruits of this era to his provincial commands. In America they helped to shape the thoughts and fix the mold of the provincial character.

As a statesman, Hunter recognized the possible consequences of Britain's inadequate and immature provincial policy. While governor-general of New York, he predicted that this policy would foster provincial rebellion. The long-term effects of the policies reflected by Hunter as an exemplary agent of empire during the late-Stuart and early-Hanoverian periods were at first extraordinarily beneficial, but ultimately staggering, for Britons and Americans alike. This vital era, which set in motion the forces that would determine the separate futures of Britain and America, was shaped by and is reflected in the public life of the Augustan statesman Robert Hunter.

This project would not have been possible without the assistance of many people and institutions. I would like to express my thanks and indebtedness to all who helped me with this work.

I would particularly like to thank the librarians, curators, and clerks of the Ardrossan Regional Library, the British Library, the British Museum, the Burlington Historical Society, the Fort William Museum, the Irvine Public Library, the National Library of Scotland, the National Register of Archives in London, the Newark Public Library, the New Jersey Historical Society, the New-York Historical Society, the Historical Society of Pennsylvania, the Public Record Office in Edinburgh, the Public Record Office in London, the Franklin Delano Roosevelt Library at Hyde Park, the Society for the Propagation of the Gospel in London, the State Library at Albany, and the Syracuse University Library. All offered courteous assistance which was much appreciated.

The research for this work was financed by Syracuse University Fellowships and by the Everett and Marie Kampel Endowed Fellowship.

In addition, funds for travel expenses to Great Britain were provided by the Syracuse University Senate Research Committee. My thanks to the chairpersons and members of these committees.

This study in an earlier form was read by several people, all of whom contributed helpful suggestions. My thanks to Michael Barkun, Michael Flusche, Peter Marsh, James Roger Sharp, Eugene R. Sheridan and William Stinchcombe for their perceptive reading and stimulating suggestions. My particular thanks to Stephen Saunders Webb, who directed the dissertation on which this study is based and has been a constant source of advice and encouragement. Finally, my thanks to my family and friends, who were unfailingly enthusiastic and supportive.

All dates given are Old Style (Julian calendar) except where noted as New Style (Gregorian calendar), but with the year beginning on January 1st instead of March 25th.

Spring 1983   MLL

ROBERT HUNTER, 1666–1734

ନ୍ତୁ INTRODUCTION ନ୍ତୁ

"The High Road"

1666–1688

The noblest prospect which a Scotchman ever sees is the high road that leads him to London.

Samuel Johnson

DINBURGH, where Robert Hunter was christened in October of 1666, was a crowded city of steep, winding streets and dark, narrow lanes, or "closes." The windswept, mist-shrouded cityscape was dominated, as it is now, by a dramatic fourteenth-century castle perched on a hill in the center of town. Edinburgh was built on and surrounded by treeless and stark hills which offered dramatic vistas of the surrounding countryside and the distant Firth of Forth. Despite the Georgian building boom of the eighteenth and nineteenth centuries which created the graceful and elegant "New Town," it is still possible today to see the beautiful and picturesque "Old Town" that surrounded Hunter as a child.[1]

The center of Edinburgh's life in the seventeenth century was its main thoroughfare, High Street, which exists today. This street leads down from the heights of the castle to Canongate, an independent village in the seventeenth century. The most prominent building on High Street is St. Giles's Cathedral, constructed in the fifteenth century and the site of many of John Knox's rousing sermons. Just behind the cathedral is Parliament House, built by Charles I in 1639 to house the Scots Estates. Across from the cathedral and Parliament House is Edinburgh's Tolbooth, in the seventeenth century the site of the courts of law where Robert Hunter's father, James Hunter, practiced law as a writer to the signet seal before the

1

Court of Sessions. In addition to serving as a law court, the Tolbooth, built in the fourteenth century, was the site of city council meetings and also served as a prison and place of execution. Just down the street from the Tolbooth is the town house of the Hay family, close friends to the Hunters, known as Tweeddale House. Not far from Tweeddale House is the Canongate Tolbooth, built in 1591 to serve as courthouse, prison, and the site for municipal meetings. At the end of High Street is the twelfth-century abbey and sixteenth-century palace of Holyroodhouse, royal residence of the Stuarts and all subsequent British monarchs to the present day. This was essentially the core of the city where Hunter spent part of his first years.[2]

Robert Hunter began life in Edinburgh, but his family home was to the southwest in Ayrshire, where both his parents had been born and raised. Hunter's mother was Margaret Spalding of Dreghorn; his father, James, was the third of four sons born to Robert Hunter, twentieth laird of Hunterston, which lies north of Ardrossan. The Hunters' lands were vast, but as younger sons did not inherit estates, James Hunter had been trained as an attorney. He and his family lived in Edinburgh while the courts were in session. The rest of the year was spent in the Ayrshire port village of Irvine, near the family estate of Hunterston.[3]

Hunter's character was shaped by his father's straitened circumstances. Although Hunter's extended family was affluent by Scottish standards, his father was poor and landless in a period when status was measured by the ownership of land. Without any prospect of an inherited estate, Robert Hunter's chances for a successful and profitable career were not very high at the time of his birth. Throughout his life, Hunter sought to overcome his impoverished background through the acquisition of land. Finally, by the time of his own death, his holdings were as extensive as those of his cousin, Patrick Hunter, the twenty-first laird of Hunterston.[4]

As a child, Robert Hunter was also affected by the deep-seated divisions between Highlanders and Lowlanders. The Highlanders, of Indo-European origin, clung to their own Gaelic tongue. The predominantly Norman-descended Lowlanders, the Hunter family included, were closer linguistically and culturally to the English than to the Highlanders. The Highlanders, continually engaged in blood feuds, were a constant source of terror to all of Scotland. The chief delights of these clansmen were to loot Lowland farms and to rob travellers on Scotland's lonely roads. Robert Hunter and other Lowlanders regarded the Highlanders as uncivilized and uncouth, a barbarous people who could only be restrained by the use of force.[5]

Hunter and his fellow Scots were forever marked by their heritage. The continual possibility of violence, the persistent poverty, the bleakness of the treeless landscape, the deep divisions between Highland and Lowland cultures, the rain, mists, and cold damp that lasted year-round and brought rheumatoid arthritis, "the Scottish disease," to those who survived childhood, bred a grim fatalism in most Scots. If fatalism was one aspect of the Scottish character, the other was a persistent sense of inferiority caused by the absence of a culture judged to be worthwhile by the English. The result was that those Scots who succeeded in the English world, such as Robert Hunter, often tended to overcompensate for their presumed cultural inferiority by mastering English values and customs. Perhaps this desire to emulate the English was not unusual in Hunter. Since his earliest childhood, and even before, the English had set the cultural, political, and religious standards of Scotland.[6]

English domination of Scotland began in the decade before Hunter's birth. The defeat of the Scottish royalist forces by Cromwell's New Model Army in 1651 at Worcester was followed by the Union of Scotland with England. After two decades of civil wars and insurrection, Scotland was now brought under control by Cromwell's army. Cromwell kept Scotland in order by employing the same tactics that the Romans had used in that country several centuries before. He promptly established military garrisons of approximately eight thousand men quartered in newly built, or rebuilt, citadels. One such Cromwellian citadel was constructed near Hunter's home in Ayrshire. This fort, built near the harbor between Irvine and Prestwick, was massive enough to contain a marketplace.[7]

Citadels similar to that in Ayrshire were also built in Leith, Inverness, Perth, and at Inverlochy (where Hunter himself would be garrisoned for two years during the War of the League of Augsburg). These garrisons were the bases from which the restless Highland bands were pacified by George Monck, Cromwell's commander-in-chief. "To pacify," in the seventeenth century as in the twentieth, meant to kill as many guerillas as possible and then to destroy their villages and burn their crops. The Highlanders were crushed. For the first time in living memory, the Lowlanders were safe from raids, and it was possible to travel on Scottish roads without fear of robbery and murder.[8]

In addition to subduing the Highland clans, the garrisons also supervised Highland and Lowland politics. The commander of the garrison, who held the rank of colonel, was also named the local governor. His intent was to introduce order, stability, and perhaps a degree of economic prosperity into society. By so doing he hoped to secure the allegiance of local residents. One way this could be accomplished was by instituting agricultural improvements. In Ayrshire, for instance, Cromwellian soldiers "Prompted and encouraged the People to enclose and improve their Lands," benefitting both agriculture and aesthetics. When Daniel Defoe saw these fields early in the next century, he declared that Ayrshire was "the pleasantest County in Scotland, without Exception . . . ."[9]

Cromwellian militarization and modernization were also appreciated by the Scottish historian Bishop Gilbert Burnet, who wrote that during the Interregnum "there was good justice done, and vice was suppressed and punished; so that we always reckon those eight years of usurpation a time of great peace and prosperity." Burnet's attitude, however, was not shared by the majority of Scots in the 1650s. Cromwell had endeavored "To ruin the great work of Time/And cast the kingdom old/Into another mold; . . ." But to Scots, the "new mold" was achieved at the expense of their heritage. Scottish discontent led the Scots to desire the return of a Stuart monarch, who would "deliver them from the yoke of Pharaoh or the Egyptian bondage." They were to be bitterly disappointed, because the king restored would not permit the national interests of Scotland to interfere with his security.[10]

Civil wars and regicide had had their roots in the commitment of the Scots Presbyterians to their Solemn League and Covenant of 1638 and the resistance of the southwestern Lowland shires to the episcopacy that Charles I had attempted to impose on them. With good reason, Charles II regarded the Presbyterian kirk as a breeder of rebels and troublemakers. The king and his secretary of state for Scotland, the earl of Lauderdale, believed that once religious dissidents were subdued, Scotland would be "a citadel for his Majesty's service." The king, determined to subdue the kirk, used as his first weapon the 1661 ecclesiastical settlement. By the terms of this settlement, Presbyterian ministers who had been chosen by their congregations were ordered to accept the authority of Church of England bishops or be ejected from their parishes.[11]

Charles II met the strongest resistance to episcopacy in the southwestern Lowland counties of Scotland, a militant defiance which was especially pronounced in Ayrshire. Robert Hunter's uncle, John Spalding, was but one of the many Ayrshire ministers who chose to defy the

Charles II, c. 1680, by Thomas Hawker. National Portrait Gallery, London. The king's firm control of England and the provinces belies his reputation as the frivolous and idle "Merry Monarch."

king. On November 6, 1662, Spalding was deprived of his ministry. On that date, the minister exhorted his congregation to adhere to "the doctrine and discipline, and the government of the church . . . and not to countenance or consent unto the entrie of any priest in upon them by the bishop or patron as their lawful minister." The congregation heeded their minister's words, and not more than "sixteen or seventeen, and sometimes but six or seven," attended the services conducted by Spalding's replacement, Alexander Bregone, "unless at some time that when souldiers came and forced them there [to church]."[12]

His congregation may have remained steadfast, but Spalding did not. In 1669, an Act of Supremacy was passed which declared the king's authority to be supreme in Scotland even in ecclesiastical matters. That same year, the English government made an attempt at reconciliation with Scotland by issuing a Letter of Indulgence which stated that ousted ministers might be restored to their parishes if they accepted episcopacy and acknowledged the royal supremacy in ecclesiastical matters. To most ministers, the letter was "a comfortless doctrine," but some, the Reverend Spalding included, were eager to grasp the proffered olive branch. On March 29, 1670, the king's privy council gave a chastened Spalding permission to return to his congregation, a lesson in religious compromise Robert Hunter would apply in later life.[13]

While the kirk was Charles II's primary target, steps were also taken at the Restoration to weaken Scotland economically. Scotland, much like England's colonies of Jamaica and New York, both of which Hunter would later govern, was a conquered and dependent province. Therefore, it had no interests that its English conquerors were bound to respect if they competed with those of England. To make this clear, the Cromwellian union between the two countries, which implied a certain equality, was dissolved by the Restoration Parliament. Since English merchants complained they were losing money because of competition from Scottish trade, the Navigation Acts now passed defined Scotland as a foreign country, excluded from English imperial trade. The depressed economy that resulted affected all levels of Scottish society, including the Hunter family. With less business, there was less litigation and less income for attorneys. Robert Hunter's father, James, was evidently hurt by the depression. When he died in Irvine in April of 1671, he left an estate worth only £30 Scot.[14]

James's widow, Margaret, was almost certainly assisted financially by her father-in-law, the laird of Hunterston. Despite his mother's relative poverty, Robert Hunter received a good education in the Scottish school system, held to be one of the best in Europe. The distinctive feature of

Scotland's educational system was that, unlike that of England, it strongly reflected continental influences, since it was a long-established custom for students to travel and study abroad to complete their education. The exposure to continental thought produced a more cosmpolitan, educated elite than that fostered by the smugly complacent insular English educational system. The well-educated Scot was not only expected to be proficient in Latin, Greek, French, Italian, and Dutch, but he also had read history, geography, philosophy, mathematics, and knew how to play the lute, guitar, or violin. Hunter received a solid grounding in the classics, possessed a superior knowledge of foreign languages, and had a deep and abiding interest in science, music, literature, and art.[15]

Throughout Hunter's youth, Charles II accelerated his attempts to destroy Presbyterianism in Scotland, although many Scots continued to defy the king's efforts. By 1678, the king, convinced that southwestern Scotland was in a virtual state of rebellion, sent out a call to the lords of the Highlands to send all the strength they could to assist the king's army. The clansmen, joined by three thousand militiamen, were quartered in the homes of Lowland peasants. The only Lowlanders who were spared from quartering this "Highland Host," who pillaged and destroyed everywhere, were those whom the privy council knew to be loyal. The clansmen stole merchandise and stock worth £200,000 Scot from Ayrshire alone before they made their way back to their Highland strongholds. This was a fact that would be remembered and revenged by Robert Hunter and other Lowlanders in the years to come.[16]

In 1679, such heavy-handed methods as the Highland Host finally sparked open rebellion in the Lowlands and brought the murder of the overzealous Church of England archbishop of St. Andrews, James Sharpe. After killing the archbishop, the rebels marched to Edinburgh with a sizeable army. Charles II sent his illegitimate son, the duke of Monmouth, to quell the rebellion. English soldiers, garrisoned in the north of England for just such an emergency, were joined by the militia of Scotland's loyal counties. On July 2, 1679, the royal army met and defeated the rebels at Bothwell Brig.[17]

Despite the decisive royalist victory at Bothwell Brig, the Lowland radicals remained active. At the king's urging, the Highlander John Graham of Claverhouse, viscount Dundee, raised a force of horse and dragoons to put down the rebels. Shortly after, Sir Thomas Dalziel, a royalist Ayrshire man, raised a regiment of dragoons to assist in the suppression of the Covenanters. As a youth, Hunter must have seen the dragoons terrorize Ayrshire Covenanters. He perhaps agreed with Dundee that "dragoons were the only medicine to be applied to their [Presbyterians'] distempers, and made them more tractable than all the advice he could give them." The sight of these dragoons must have made a deep impression on Hunter. Virtually all his military career, except for a two-year tour of duty in an infantry regiment, was spent with the dragoons, including the regiment Dalziel had raised, later known as the Royal Scots or the Scots Greys.[18]

Dragoons helped to ensure order, but to be certain the kingdom remained subdued, the king sent his brother, James, duke of York, to govern Scotland. The duke had been driven from England by the furor raised by the 1679 Popish Plot. James, because of his Catholic religion, was threatened by the English Parliament with exclusion from the inheritance of the throne of England. Consequently, once he was in Scotland, he immediately took steps to secure his succession to the Scottish throne. Two acts were passed by the Scots Estates. The first ensured that the duke could not be excluded from the Scottish throne because of his Catholicism. The second required a pledge of unlimited submission to the royal prerogative from all Scots who held church or state offices.[19]

The duke's tenure as Scotland's governor marked the turning point of religious defiance by the southwestern Lowland counties. Despite the persistence of such militant sects as the Cameronians, after 1680 southwestern Scots of all ranks finally began to weaken in their opposition to the English. Those who "would do anything to be safe" complied with the parliamentary act and pledged submission to the crown. A few who remained irreconcilable to the new order and refused to submit left Scotland during the 1680s when an exodus ensued to England's colonies, among other places. Many of these exiles settled in Perth Amboy, New Jersey, where Hunter himself would later buy a home.[20]

Some rebellious Scots left their homeland willingly to avoid further persecution by Dalziel's and Dundee's dragoons. Other rebels, such as Hunter's future New York protégé, David Jamison, were sent to America as indentured servants, often against their wills. Hunter reported that Jamison was a member of a radical sect called the "sweet singers," who had renounced "the use of arms, and who were for burning every book except the bible." Jamison and other members of his sect were taken prisoners by the government forces and incarcerated in Edinburgh's Bridewell prison. After being examined by the duke of York and the privy council, Jamison and the other Sweet Singers were summarily put on board a ship bound for America where they were to be sold as indentured servants.[21]

Among other Scots who refused to submit to the crown was Archibald Campbell, the ninth earl of Argyll, whose father had been executed for treason by Charles II in 1661. The earl, also charged with treason, was tried and found guilty. Argyll was sentenced to death but escaped to Holland. The death of Charles II on February 16, 1685, prompted Argyll to assist Monmouth, also in exile in Holland, in his attempt to seize the throne from his uncle, James. After landing near Glasgow, Argyll marched north in the hope of raising his clansmen. James II, however, had anticipated Argyll's plan by billeting troops among the Campbells. They did not stir. Monmouth landed to the south in Lyme Regis on the western coast of England but was not able to coordinate his movements with Argyll. Dalziel's and Dundee's dragoons helped to capture Argyll in Scotland. Monmouth was captured in England, and both were executed. Their followers were chased and captured. Of these, many were hanged, while others were deported to the colonies as indentured servants having an ear cut off so they could never return home.[22]

After the executions of Monmouth and Argyll, and the brutal repression of their followers, the opposition of Covenanters to English rule in Scotland continued to weaken as Scots grew weary of strife. In 1687, James issued a Letter of Indulgence which permitted Presbyterians and other nonconformists to worship as they pleased. All but the most radical were mollified, and religious strife was contained.[23]

By 1687 James II had not only eliminated defiance in Scotland's southwestern counties, he had secured the interests of Lowland leaders to the throne. The Scottish nobility and gentry, of whom the Hunter family were members, formed a closely knit and insular society, connected by ties of kinship and marriage. These Lowland families were at first united in their opposition to Stuart imperialism until Charles II and his brother James, first as duke of York and then as king, systematically broke the will of one family after another. After Argyll's and Monmouth's disastrous invasion attempt and its bloody aftermath, Scottish Lowlanders had no choice but to commit themselves to the crown and to British, rather than Scottish interests. While Lowlanders tendered their allegiance to the crown, they were by no means committed to James II, as were most Highlanders. When a candidate for the throne appeared who was more in sympathy with the predominantly Whig Lowlanders' concept of a limited monarchy, they were quick to abandon King James.[24]

The decision of Lowland Scots to adhere to the British cause was not easily made. Each Scot was faced with personal, religious, moral, ethical, and political compromises. The alternative to compromise was to watch Scotland and themselves sink deeper into poverty and oblivion. In 1688, Robert Hunter was also faced with the alternatives of clinging to a troublesome past or casting his fortune with England and the modern world. Scotland, a poor country with few natural resources and a depressed foreign trade, offered its young people limited opportunities to achieve financial success. A poor Scot of good family could advance by entering the professions of medicine, the law, the church, or the army. Hunter lacked the vocation for the church, and it was at best a notoriously ill-paying profession. So, too, if his father's case was typical, was the law. To the pecuniary liabilities of these professions, add Hunter's physical disqualification. According to the Scot physician Cadwallader Colden (1688–1776), Hunter's New York protégé, Hunter was in his youth a man of "uncommon strength and activity." The impetuous and adventurous nature this suggests would have made him unfit for either law or medicine and a natural candidate for the military. Hunter did not, however, come to his imperial career in the military simply by default. His future life had been shaped in childhood by the visible examples of military control and rule by force provided by Scotland's government, established on Roman models by Cromwell and continued by the Stuart monarchs. The militarization of Scotland made Hunter's choice of the army as a career both logical and obvious.[25]

The military was also the profession most respected by wellborn male Britons, many of whom combined military careers with a pursuit of scholarly interests. The parallel roles of soldier and scholar, seen as unlikely by the modern world, had been established during the late Italian Renaissance. Requirements were codified by the Italian Baldesar Castiglione, born in 1478 and himself a soldier, statesman, scholar, author, and diplomat. In 1529, Castiglione published *The Book of the Courtier*, a handbook for men who wished to succeed. Castiglione told aspiring courtiers they could only rise if they embodied the various attributes possessed by the author himself. The book had an enormous influence in England, even before 1561 when it was translated by Sir Thomas Hoby. Castiglione's image of the courtier was so pervasive and persistent that those British gentlemen who wanted to rise, such as Hunter, patterned themselves on Castiglione's model until the early twentieth century.[26]

Castiglione's courtier was a soldier, because "the first and true profession of the courtier must be that of arms; and this above everything else I wish him to pursue vigorously." The courtier must also be handsome and "well built with finely proportioned members, and I would have him demonstrate strength and lightness and suppleness and be good at all the physical exercises befitting a warrior." Military skill and physical attributes were not sufficient, however. To achieve success, the courtier must be intelligent and well educated, "a more than average scholar, at least in those studies which we call the humanities; and he should have a knowledge of Greek as well as Latin, because of the many different things that are so beautifully written in that language. He should be very well acquainted with the poets, and no less with the orators and historians, and skilled at writing both verse and prose."[27]

Hunter was one aspiring Scottish courtier who had good chances of succeeding in the military. He possessed the firmness of character, clear judgement, intelligence, and ruthlessness that would make him a top flight officer. Hunter also had the necessary physical and mental attributes that would enable him to rise. He was physically attractive. Even when Colden met him in 1717 when Hunter was fifty-one years old, he found Hunter to be an "exceedingly well shaped and well proportioned man." He was also well read, a poet and playwright, a classical scholar, a linguist, an amateur scientist, a mathematician, and a connoisseur of the arts.[28]

Some talented Scots of Hunter's generation also found that military service brought additional rewards such as the governments of England's colonies. Among those military Scots named to govern the plantations during and after the War of the Spanish Succession were Hunter himself as lieutenant governor of Virginia and governor-general of New York, New Jersey, and Jamaica; John Campbell, duke of Argyll, governor of Minorca; George Hamilton, earl of Orkney, governor-general of Virginia; Samuel Vetch, lieutenant governor of Nova Scotia; and Alexander Spotswood, lieutenant governor of Virginia.[29]

All these men were known to one another and all used the military as a stepping-stone by which to advance their careers. All shared similar backgrounds. With the exception of Spotswood, the families of these men had been Covenanters who at first strenuously opposed Stuart rule. All began their British military careers as supporters of William III, either at the time of the Glorious Revolution or immediately thereafter. All, with the exception of Vetch, continued their military service during the reign of Queen Anne. All, again with the exception of Vetch, realized substantial profits from their military and gubernatorial careers. And all who actively governed their colonies extended to provincials the military rule they had witnessed in Scotland during their youth and practiced themselves on the continent during their military careers.[30]

The empire was not held together solely by military force, however. An equally important and perhaps more pervasive cohesive ingredient was provided by shared cultural interests. Each British governor-general carried with him to his post the cultural standards of London, the center of the British empire. In the colonies, governors-general became trend setters and arbiters of taste, as provincials sought to imitate London tastes, fashions, and interests. The cultural unity that resulted helped to bind together formerly diverse peoples.[31]

In 1688, Hunter was prepared by his cultural background and educational training to advance in the British world. All he needed was an opportunity to prove his merit and worth. This opportunity came in November of that year when Hunter proved the truth of Samuel Johnson's expression that "the noblest prospect which a Scotchman ever sees is the high road that leads him to London." Hunter took that high road to seek his fortune. He joined the coup d'etat which deposed James II and placed William of Orange and his wife, Mary, James's daughter, on the English and Scottish thrones.

1

"The Wars' and Fortune's Son"

1688–1706

> But thou the Wars' and Fortune's son
> March indefatigably on,
> And for the last effect
> Still keep thy sword erect:
> Besides the force it has to fright
> The spirits of the shady night,
> The same arts that did gain
> A power must it maintain.
>
> Andrew Marvell, "Horation
> Ode Upon Cromwell's Return"

"What can I expect from those I have done so little for?"

AFTER HIS ACCESSION to the throne on February 16, 1685, James II attempted to impose an even more authoritarian regime on the English people than the absolutism asserted by his brother, Charles II. To accomplish this, he continued Charles's challenges to the privileges of the English nobility and gentry by interfering with the bases of their power at the local level. Charles had accelerated the process in 1681 in retaliation for the Popish Plot by recalling the charters of English cities and towns. James continued it by removing the aristocracy and landed gentry from local offices to control representation in the House of Commons. Removed officials were replaced by upstarts and newcomers, predominantly Dissenters and Roman Catholics, pledged to support James's parliamentary policies of religious toleration and the maintenance of a standing army. James's purges caused the ruling elite, who controlled the church and the army, to withdraw their support from the king. In addition, James's efforts to promote Catholicism lost him the support of the clergy, who influenced the bulk of the population.[1]

Elite disaffection rose even higher when, on June 20, 1688, a son was born to James and his Catholic queen, Mary of Modena. The prince would take precedence over James's two Protestant daughters by Anne

13

Hyde, the princesses Mary and Anne, as well as over Mary's husband, himself a Stuart heir, William of Orange. The prospect of a perpetual Catholic monarchy, revolting to Protestant Englishmen of the ruling class, prompted seven temporal and spiritual lords to send an invitation to William of Orange to invade England. Religious fear spurred the invitation, but the original impetus for revolution was elite apprehension that they would be degraded by Stuart absolutism. King James was "astonished that men of sense did not see that religion was only the pretence and that the real contest was about power and dominion . . . ."[2]

To ensure power remained in their control, members of the gentry and nobility, Whig and Tory alike, were willing to depose the rightful king and substitute in his place the Protestants William of Orange and his wife, Mary Stuart. With the promise of English support for his intervention, William accepted the invitation to invade England. On November 5, 1688, his forces, twelve thousand foot and horse, landed unopposed at Torbay on the coast of Devon.[3]

Within three weeks of William's landing, he won the allegiance of many of England's military officers. Among the first to defect from James's cause was his cousin, Edward Hyde, viscount Cornbury, an officer of the Life Guards. Cornbury and his men were soon joined in William's camp by Prince George of Denmark, James's other son-in-law, and John lord Churchill, James's protégé, "him that I raised from nothing," as the king complained, "on whom I heaped all favours; and if such betrays me, what can I expect from those I have done so little for?" The answer to the king's question was, "very little." These men were only the beginning of the avalanche that would gravitate to William.[4]

After hearing of Churchill's defection on November 24th, James ordered the arrest of Churchill's wife, Sarah, the favorite companion and friend of Princess Anne. On receiving the king's orders to arrest Sarah, Anne sent her to Henry Compton, bishop of London, to arrange their escape. That same night, Compton spirited Princess Anne and Sarah to his residence, London House in Aldersgate. The next day Compton and the women fled northward. When they reached the earl of Northampton's estate, they were joined by forty dragoons who escorted them to Notting-

James II, 1684–1685, by Sir Godfrey Kneller. National Portrait Gallery, London. The nautical background reflects the king's keen interest in the English navy and his own participation in the naval engagements of the Dutch wars. A brave leader, the king fled England in 1688 not from fear but from despair.

ham. The earl of Devonshire added to the size of Anne's escort by giving her two hundred additional dragoons for her protection.[5]

Among the dragoons who formed this royal guard was Robert Hunter. Hunter himself dated his military career as beginning in 1688, when he was "one of the gentlemen who served as a guard under the Bishop of London to the Princess Anne when she retired from her father's court. . . . " Hunter would later serve Anne when she was queen as a subordinate of Sarah's husband, John Churchill, then duke of Marlborough. As governor-general of New York, Hunter would also serve Henry Compton, whose see extended to England's New World colonies. So he did in 1688, when Compton, then fifty-eight years of age, riding in his old cavalry boots, a living embodiment of the church militant, formed the dragoons into a regiment. As its colonel, Compton led formidable forces back to the south and to control of England.[6]

In the few days it had taken Anne to flee northward, the outcome of the crisis had been decided. James returned to London from Salisbury after hearing of Churchill's and Anne's defections. The royal army evaporated after his departure and, by December 1st, William and his advancing army reached Hindon. By December 4th, William was in Salisbury. By December 10th, James, in London, knew all was over and escaped to France.[7]

James's flight meant that Hunter, and the hundreds of other officers and men who had deserted the king, had made a propitious choice. The Glorious Revolution and his role in it propelled Hunter from the oppressive provincialism of Scottish life toward military rank and imperial administration. For Britain, the revolution was a step away from Stuart absolutism toward a constitutional monarchy. Although there was not much immediate diminution of royal power, Parliament had both legitimized the accession of William and Mary and announced its intention to control the royal succession by declaring the throne could not pass to a Catholic or any person married to a Catholic. Parliament had replaced God as the elector of English sovereigns.[8]

"Hunger and Ambition"

The revolution was also accomplished in Hunter's home country of Scotland, although there was Jacobite resistance there. In October of 1688, James had ordered his Scottish-based troops, including the Scots Greys, to march south to help control England, leaving Scotland virtually undefended. In November of 1688, the Scots supporters of William, predominantly Protestant Lowlanders, took over the government in Edinburgh.

William III, 1677, after Sir Peter Lely. National Portrait Gallery, London. Grandson of Charles I, William of Orange considered his claim to the English throne superior to that of his wife, Mary, who was the daughter of James II and the commoner, Anne Hyde.

James, who went to Ireland from France in March of 1689 to organize his Catholic supporters there, sent to the Catholic Highlanders to ask for their help in regaining his throne. They thereupon renewed their raids and attacks on Protestant clans and on Lowland communities. The revolutionary Scots Convention opened in Edinburgh on March 14, 1689, but the next day, the duke of Gordon at the urging of Dundee, seized Edinburgh Castle for James. Major General Hugh Mackay, King William's commander-in-chief in Scotland, took command of the siege of the castle on March 27th. Gordon did not surrender until June 13, 1689, when he marched his men to Castle Hill to lay down their arms. The Scots Convention, however, proclaimed William and Mary as king and queen in April of 1689.[9]

William had to continue the repression of Jacobites in Ireland and Scotland to complete his conquest of Britain. Robert Hunter was one of William's soldiers. Hunter began his military career under William by joining a dragoon regiment raised by a radical Scot Covenanter, Colonel Henry Erskine, baron Cardross, from West Lothian. Cardross, persecuted by the Stuarts, had fled to America where he bought a plantation in South Carolina. When driven out by the Spaniards, Cardross went to Holland and joined William's invasion force. In April of 1689, at the king's urging, Cardross raised a regiment of dragoons for service against the Highland clans under a commission granted by the Scots Estates.[10]

Robert Hunter returned to Scotland after assisting Princess Anne in her escape. On April 19, 1689, he was commissioned an aide major in Cardross's regiment. The usual procedure in the late seventeenth and eighteenth centuries was for officers to purchase their regimental commissions and then buy their way up the promotion ladder, although officers could be promoted for merit. The purchase of a commission was a business investment. In addition to drawing a salary while on active duty and half pay for life after 1706, officers also realized substantial profits from the difference between the amount of money they received from the government for the clothing and subsistence of their troops and what they actually spent. Officers also received allowances for servants, drew extra money for forage, and benefitted handsomely from kickbacks, rake-offs, and booty.[11]

It is possible that Hunter, a poor Scot, did not purchase his commission. Hunter may have received the commission because of his family's associations with the Erskines. Both Cardross and the lieutenant colonel of the regiment, Cardross's son John, were related to John Erskine, earl of Mar, one of Hunter's patrons in later life. The Erskine family was from West Lothian, just to the northwest of Ayr. Lord Cardross may have been inclined to offer a bright young member of the locally prominent Hunter family an opportunity for advancement.[12]

Hunter may also have received his commission from Cardross with the condition that he recruit men to fill the ranks of the regiment. In that case, Hunter and a sergeant would have travelled through the Scottish countryside much like the characters Captain Plume and Sergeant Kite in George Farquhar's 1706 play, *The Recruiting Officer.* Since there was no system of draft, each commander had to depend on volunteers. A few men, like "The warlike Youth," described by Farquhar, who "listens to the charms / Of Plunder, fine Lac'd Coats, and glitt'ring Arms," enlisted eagerly. Most had to be persuaded, tricked, or enlisted only because their present life was intolerable. Men were driven to join the army, as was Sergeant Kite, by "Hunger and Ambition—The fears of starving and Hopes of a Truncheon . . . ."[13]

Once enlisted, the reality of military life, appalling even by the brutal standards of the times, quickly made itself apparent. Sergeant Kite, for instance, was persuaded to enlist by "a Gentleman with a fair tongue and fair Perriwig, who loaded me with Promises . . . he promised to advance me, and indeed he did so—To a Garret in the *Savoy*." The Savoy was a London military prison for mutineers and deserters, also used to house enlistees who were expected to run away. When Kite asked the officer "why he put me in Prison, he call'd me lying Dog, and said I was in Garrison . . . ." Such treatment was only the first of the many unpleasant surprises awaiting enlisted men. Once sent to their regiments, they were literally whipped into shape for war. Brutal treatment of enlisted men was particularly severe in dragoon regiments where the rank and file was often composed of troublemakers, malcontents, and criminals. When Sergeant Kite complained to Captain Plume that one of the recruits was a horse thief, Plume reassured him that "We'll dispose of him among the Dragoons . . . ."[14]

Dragoon regiments, such as that of Lord Cardross, were distinct from the cavalry and were mounted infantry. The unique function of the dragoons in battle was reflected in their training. Dragoons were not only put through the cavalry drill, but then dismounted and were put through the standard infantry drill. The roles in battle of dragoon and cavalry were quite different. The cavalry used only swords and depended for their effect on the massive power of horse and man bearing down on enemy troops. The dragoons, whose horses were smaller (and cheaper) than those of the cavalry, did occasionally make cavalry type charges. Their usual role, however, was to tether their horses and proceed on foot to battle with the infantry. Dragoons were also used as military police, advance scouts, storming parties, and as convoy escorts for artillery or for injured men being removed from the battlefield.[15]

Dragoons were primarily valued for their extreme flexibility and mobility. They were also noted for their cruelty and greed. Brutalized men made brutal soldiers. The dragoons, of all the branches of the military, were probably the most hated and feared by civilians. Seldom restrained by their officers, dragoons plundered, raped, and killed with abandon. When quartered in villages, the dragoons, at their officers' insistence, obtained forage for their horses by taking hay, straw, and oats from civilians who were reluctant to sell. This naturally raised hatred toward the dragoons, as did their reputation for ruthlessness. Dragoons had been employed by Louis XIV of France as part of his terror tactics against the Huguenots after the 1685 revocation of the Edict of Nantes. In England, Cornbury's Dragoons had been used in the merciless suppression of the west country after Monmouth's rebellion. So were they used by William III against Jacobites in Ireland and Scotland. As a result of these and similar usages later, the name is today still associated with the violent and arbitrary use of government force on unarmed and nonmilitary people.[16]

In 1689, Robert Hunter, remembered by subsequent generations as a cultivated Augustan gentleman, began his military career as a ruthless and efficient dragoon officer. Although Cardross's regiment was raised primarily to pacify the Highland clans, they were prevented from doing so immediately when the Protestant defenders of Londonderry were beseiged by the earl of Tyrconnel's Catholic forces. Cardross's regiment was sent to Ireland, one of four British regiments under the command of Major General Percy Kirke, the former governor of Tangier. Kirke was yet another of James's bloody weapons against Monmouth's rebels and governor-general designate of New England.[17]

Kirke's forces arrived at Derry on June 15, 1689. A few days later, Kirke sent three ships up the Foyle River toward the starving city, but the ships were driven back by batteries of Irish guns placed on the river outside of Derry. On July 28th, Kirke's ships finally succeeded in forcing the boom placed across the river by the Irish. That day the first ships laden with food came to the quay in Derry, accompanied by "shouts of joy" from the residents of the town. Derry was relieved by the British on August 19th after 105 days of terror, betrayal, and starvation. The victory gave William III a base in Ulster which was ultimately disastrous for James's cause in Ireland.[18]

Even before the Derry garrison was relieved, Major General Kirke realized that Irish dragoon regiments, loyal to King William, would be needed to help subdue the Irish rebels. One of these regiments, later to be known as the Royal Irish Dragoons, was raised on June 20, 1689. The regiment was at first known by the name of its colonel, James Wynne, father of Owen Wynne, one of Hunter's closest friends. Hunter would eventually join the regiment in 1698 after it had been purchased by Charles Ross. Both Wynne's Dragoons and Cardross's Dragoons would be successful in subduing rebels.[19]

In July of 1689, Cardross and his men were sent back to Scotland to deal with severe Jacobite uprisings in the Highlands. With the establishment of Presbyterianism in Scotland, religious strife between Anglicans and Presbyterians was displaced by dissension between Highland Catholic Jacobites and Lowland Protestant Williamites. Jacobite uprisings, which showed signs of accelerating into civil war, ravaged Scotland in the summer of 1689. The responsibility for quelling the Jacobites was that of Major General Hugh Mackay, in command of a force of three thousand men from foot, cavalry, and dragoon regiments. One of the dragoon regiments under Mackay's command was that of Lord Cardross.[20]

Cardross and his men were in Edinburgh at the time of the July 27, 1689 battle of Killiecrankie, a decisive victory for the Highlanders despite the death of their leader, Dundee. The government forces, comprised mostly of Lowland Scots, were forced to retreat to the safety of Stirling. The Highland soldiers pillaged the fleeing army's stores and then turned their attention to the defenseless farms and villages of their enemies. The MacDonalds of Glencoe and Keppoch were particularly greedy as they made their way through Perthshire. When the MacDonalds reached the farm of their traditional enemy, Robert Campbell of Glenlyon, they laid waste his lands and burned the goods they could not carry away. They then drove Campbell's livestock, worth £8,000 Scot, back to their Highland villages. This was a blow Campbell would not forget and the MacDonalds would long regret.[21]

Hunter and the rest of Cardross's dragoons moved through the Highlands during the summer of 1689 to help subdue the rebels. The Highlanders were incensed by the repressive actions of their fellow Scots. Cardross reported that clansmen often crept to within hailing distance of his campfires to revile his dragoons as "trators and rebells." The English employed Scot against Scot because they had learned that the most effective and ruthless force to use against any enemy was a former foe anxious both to prove his new loyalty and to quell any lingering shame at his own capitulation. Self-justification, when added to a desire to be on the winning side, left little room for sympathy among government soldiers.

The Scot Mackay, for instance, was determined the rebel Highlanders would "feel the foly of resisting the government." He further vowed he would "not leave a hous standing" in the Highlands if the clansmen did not submit.[22]

Mackay, with three troops of Cardross's Dragoons, continued to pursue the enemy, but the Highlanders proved elusive. Mackay adopted Cromwell's method of building and maintaining garrisons at strategic locations in the Highlands. One troublesome area was at Inverlochy, where the Cromwellian garrison had been abandoned since the Restoration. Mackay, along with General John Hill, now suggested to King William that the garrison be rebuilt and used as the center from which the clans could be pacified. The king agreed and Hill was put in command of the garrison. Mackay looked on this as the first step to victory. He believed that "with the help of the garisons which I shall take in possession, they [the Highlanders] can soon and easily be subdued next yeare, and all of the Highlands of Scotland reduced to as peaceable a state as the lower parts . . . ."[23]

John Hill, named to command at Inverlochy, was an old soldier whose experience controlling rebels in Ireland and Scotland went back to the early 1650s when he assisted in the Cromwellian subjugation of Ireland. He remained in Ireland until 1654 when the Highland clans became troublesome. The ancient fort at Inverlochy was then rebuilt and put under the command of Colonel William Brayne, who was also named governor of Lochabar. Brayne's second in command and deputy governor was the then major John Hill. He assisted the colonel in his efficient and successful efforts to pacify the Highland clans with fire and sword. Brayne was so successful in Scotland that Cromwell sent him to Jamaica to work the same miracle with the abandoned military malcontents left behind there to settle and develop the island. Jamaica's pestilential climate killed Brayne in 1657, but not before he established the foundation of garrison government on the island which Robert Hunter would ulimately command. Brayne was succeeded as commander of Inverlochy and governor of Lochabar by Hill, who remained at his post until the Restoration. Hill then returned to Ireland where he lived on his confiscated estates near Belfast and served for several years as constable. Hill returned to Scotland in 1689 and offered to help the king in reducing the Highlanders. He was, after all, eminently well qualified for this task.[24]

The fortress at Inverlochy was rebuilt again and renamed Fort William. Hill was again named commander of the fort and governor of Lochabar, just as he had been in the 1650s. Made colonel, Hill mustered his regiment of foot at Fort William in December of 1690, about the same

time as Cardross's regiment was disbanded. Hunter was out of a job until a
place was found for him in Hill's regiment at Fort William. Hunter was
needed at the fort. With its completion in 1691, the subjugation of the
Highlanders, based on the Cromwellian model, began in earnest.[25]

"A just vengeance"

The government was even more convinced of the necessity of this subjugation in 1691, after reports reached England that Jacobites were making
fresh inroads among the Highlanders. King William ordered several
thousand pounds in bribes to be given to the Highland lords to ensure their
allegiance. Not all clan chiefs were swayed, however, and many Highlanders continued their raids. On February 10, 1691, the unfortunate Cardross complained, "My Lands about Cardross ar now Laid waste by the
heighland rebells." William was aware of the outrages and ordered all clan
chiefs suspected of Jacobitism to take oaths of allegiance before January
1, 1692. All the Highland chiefs submitted except Alasdair MacIain,
MacDonald of Glencoe. MacIain waited until the last day to take the oath
and then went to Fort William to ask Hill to administer it to him. Hill
explained to MacIain the oath must be given by a sheriff or his deputy and
he himself had no authority to do so. MacIain was reluctant to take the oath
from the sheriff of Inveraray, who was a member of the Campbell clan.
Nevertheless, the old chief made his way to Inveraray and took the oath
five days after the deadline.[26]

Despite his submission, tragedy was to strike MacIain and his clan.
One of the secretaries of state for Scotland was Ayrshire-born John
Dalrymple, master of Stair and later second earl of Stair, whose son was
one of Hunter's closest friends. On finding out that MacIain had not taken
the oath before the deadline, Stair, anxious to make an example of a clan,
ordered Colonel Hill to exterminate the MacIains of Glencoe. As Stair
explained to Hill, "for a just vengeance and a public example, the thieving
tribe of Glencoe may be rooted out to a purpose." Stair ordered the
executions with King William's full knowledge and approval, and the
order was signed and countersigned by the king.[27]

On February 1, 1692, 120 soldiers of Argyll's regiment marched to
Glencoe, where they were given shelter by the residents. The blue-
bonneted soldiers were commanded by Captain Robert Campbell of Glenlyon, still grieving for his ruined estate. At five in the morning of February
13th, Lieutenant Colonel James Hamilton, Hill's second in command, was
to meet Argyll's regiment at Glencoe with four hundred men from Hill's
regiment to help in the slaughter. Hamilton's detachment was delayed by a

blizzard and did not arrive until almost noon of the appointed day. They found Campbell had proceeded without them. After living with the MacIains for almost two weeks, Argyll's men had fallen on their hosts and killed thirty-three men, two women, and two children. The rest of the clan had run off to the mountains, ill clothed and without food, where many more died of exposure. The soldiers, at Hamilton's orders, burned the village, collected what booty they could carry, and drove the villagers' cattle and sheep back to Fort William. Survivors were rounded up to be transported to England's colonies as indentured servants. The village no longer existed. The next day, Hill informed the marquis of Tweeddale, "I have . . . ruined Glencoe."[28]

The first public notice of the massacre was sometime in March of 1692, when a letter was published in the *Paris Gazette* describing the murders. An uproar followed in Britain, not so much because a clan had been pacified in proper Highland fashion, as because the slaughter had violated the established rules of clan hospitality, the Campbells having murdered their hosts. Stair absorbed most of the onus, both at that time and from future generations, even though the act was done by the Campbells with the full approval of William III. Stair still held the king's favor and cared little for criticism. On April 30, 1692, he assured a worried Hill he had been right in doing his duty, "in a thing so necessary to rid the country of thieving. . . . When you do right, you need fear nobody."[29]

Hunter may have been involved in this act of repression. Sometime between December of 1690 and July of 1692, he was commissioned a captain in Hill's regiment of foot at Fort William. His name does not appear in any of the published reports of the massacre, however, nor does it appear as witness at the government inquiry and trial held in the spring of 1695 when Hunter was in Flanders. Hunter may have either joined Hill's regiment after the massacre and thus avoided the stigma carried by its perpetrators, or he may have remained at Fort William with Hill and the remainder of the garrison. In any case, Hunter served with Hill's regiment for two years and, like other Scots, absorbed the lesson of Glencoe. Force and terror had prevailed. After the slaughter, the Highlands were quiet for more than two decades.[30]

During the two years Hunter was at Fort William, the strength of the garrison was depleted both by illness and by drafts of its men for regiments sent to join King William in Flanders. The fort, isolated, gloomy, and forbidding, was huddled on a spit of land jutting out into Loch Linnhe at the foot of the barren Ben Nevis and its sister peaks, all equally treeless. The absence of trees meant that firewood was in short supply in the fort.

Indeed, there were few human comforts at Fort William. "There were no blankets, no replacements for worn clothing and shoes, and there was rarely enough food." A neglected and ignored garrison was not the place for an ambitious and bright officer to prove his worth and gain advancement. Hunter looked for a new regiment.[31]

"All mounted on grey and white horses"

On February 28, 1694, Hunter was commissioned as a captain in the Royal Scots Dragoons (Scots Greys), now commanded by Colonel Sir Thomas Livingston, lord viscount Tiviot. The regiment was eventually bought by its lieutenant colonel, John lord Hay, second son of John Hay, marquis of Tweeddale, and grandson of the earl of Lauderdale, the former secretary of state for Scotland, whose desire it had been to turn Scotland into "a citadel for his Majesty's service." The Royal Scots Dragoons began to fulfill Lauderdale's desire as they gathered to assist King William during the War of the League of Augsburg.[32]

In the spring of 1694, the Royal Scots were taken off the Scots establishment and ordered to London. On April 19th, as the five hundred dragoons and their officers were reviewed by the king in Hyde Park where "They made a fine show . . . all mounted on grey and white horses and new clothed and are more like Troopers [Cavalry] than Dragoons." The dragoons were "of large stature, well appointed and disciplined." They were also belligerent, "one of them having reproch'd a Dutchman for cowardice in our late fight, was attack'd by two Dutchmen, when with his sword he struck off the head of one, and cleft the skull of the other to his chin."[33]

Presumably Hunter and his fellow officers knew how to control their men's ferocity, or at least redirect it toward the enemy once the regiment arrived in Flanders in May of 1694. The purpose of this conflict, aptly called King William's War in the North American colonies, was to prevent Louis XIV from seizing the thrones of either the Spanish or the Roman empires. England declared war on France on May 7, 1689. By the time Hunter and his regiment joined the continental fighting, England and the Allies, the Netherlands, Brandenburgh, Saxony, Bavaria, Hanover, and Savoy, had suffered a humiliating string of defeats. The Royal Scots did not turn the tide.[34]

The major action of 1694 was an attack on Brest by seven thousand Allied troops and the combined navies of the Netherlands and England. The French, who had received accurate reports of the planned invasions, heavily fortified the city and repulsed the attack. The Royal Scots remained in Flanders during the winter and in April of 1695 were sent to Dixmude in western Flanders to join the main part of the army. On May 28, 1695, Hunter, at the beginning of the new campaign season, was promoted major of the brigade.[35]

This promotion to brigade major was a significant step for Hunter. He now gained experience as a staff, rather than as a line, officer. The organizational and administrative duties performed by Hunter as a staff officer provided the experience needed to shape him as a colonial governor. Majors were the administrative backbone of the army. The job of brigade major was to organize regimental men and materiel, coordinate the regiments' movements, convey orders to the regiments' commanding officers, assign tasks to these commanders, map out routes for regimental troop movements, and, in general, to do the necessary paper work and handle the administrative detail needed to keep all regiments functioning smoothly. On a personal level, the job was important to Hunter because it brought him into personal contact with high ranking officers.[36]

Hunter was with the Scots Greys during the 1695 campaign season, when on June 30th, King William ordered the city of Namur surrounded. Namur, situated at the junction of the Sambre and Meuse rivers, was protected by a citadel, built on a huge rock, heavily fortified, and defended by sixteen thousand French troops. The city held out, despite heavy shelling by Allied artillery and a brilliant series of attacks by the Scots Greys and the Seventh Fusiliers. On August 3, 1695, the city finally capitulated. The surrender followed the Allied attack on the counterscarp of St. Nicholas gate, made famous in fiction by Laurence Sterne in *Tristram Shandy*. It was during the attack on the counterscarp, in which "the Dutch lodged themselves upon the counterguard, — and that the English made themselves masters of the covered way before St. Nicholas's gate," that Uncle Toby received his unfortunate wound. The character of Uncle Toby was probably patterned on a distant cousin of Laurence Sterne's, Robert Stearne, who served under William III in Ireland and on the continent and was present at the taking of Namur. Laurence Sterne's father, Roger Sterne, was also a soldier, but too young to have fought at Namur. Roger Sterne, who had a remarkably unsuccessful army career, served in Marlborough's wars and concluded his military service and his life in 1731 in Jamaica under the command of Robert Hunter.[37]

The citadel at Namur, located in the south of the city, was thought by the French to be impregnable. The garrison continued to resist until September 1st, when worn down by continued Allied assaults, the commanding officer surrendered. On September 5th, the five thousand survivors of the original sixteen thousand defenders, marched out of the fort and laid down their arms. The victory was a particularly bright spot for the Allies in an otherwise fruitless war, Namur being the only great victory in William's sixteen campaigns. It was also the first time in more than three decades that the French had been beaten.[38]

The War of the League of Augsburg ended with the signing of the Treaty of Ryswick in October of 1697. For William III, the most important part of the treaty was Louis XIV's recognition of him as king of England. William wished to maintain an army in England even after the signing of the treaty. Parliament, however, refused to maintain a large army on English soil and voted to disband all troops raised after September 1680, a time at which the army was at a low point of only sixty-five hundred men. In 1698, Parliament finally compromised with the king on the troop issue by agreeing to maintain ten thousand men in England and twelve thousand men in Ireland, which had to pay for their support. The Royal Scots were sent to Ireland on March 10, 1698, reduced from 8 to 6 troops and from 590 officers and men to only 294 officers and men. Hunter may have been superfluous because he changed regiments that year. On April 23, 1698, he was commissioned a major in Colonel Charles Ross's (formerly Wynne's) Irish Dragoons and a captain of a troop in that same regiment.[39]

Hunter now began an extended stay in Ireland where he developed a loathing of Irish Catholics which would become more pronounced in later life. The Irish were of the same ethnic origin as Highland Scots and, like most Highlanders, were predominantly Jacobites. Hunter scorned both Highlanders and Irish Catholics for what he considered their backwardness and stubborness. His attitude toward Irish Catholics was shared by virtually all members of the politically dominant but miniscule Anglo-Irish ruling elite. The total population of Ireland in 1732–1733 was estimated at 1,407,000, of whom 527,000 were Protestants. Most of the Protestants, however, were Ulster Presbyterians who could neither vote nor hold public office, another political truth that could not have failed to impress the Presbyterian Hunter. Ulster Presbyterians, along with other Protestants, owned land, however, unlike most Irish Catholics. After the 1691 Treaty of Limerick, Catholics retained only 14 percent of the land in Ireland, as compared to 50 percent in 1641.[40]

A predominantly landless and politically mute population was, however, only part of Ireland's problem. Although Ireland was "called a kingdom, it was both politically and economically an English colony," much like Scotland or any of England's New World colonies. There was an Irish Parliament, but its decisions could be overruled by the British privy council and Parliament. Like any colony, Ireland's economic interests were subordinated to the needs of the mother country. The Anglo-Irish accepted English political and economic domination because they needed protection. They realized they could only keep Catholics landless and Presbyterians voteless "by relying on the metropolitan power of royal and parliamentary rule from London to supply military force. . . ." Robert Hunter and the 361 other officers and men of Ross's Irish Dragoons were part of this military force. In the four years that Hunter remained in Ireland, detachments of dragoons were quartered throughout the province in potentially troublesome areas. Their presence prevented any further threats to the security of either the Anglo-Irish elite or William III. Conditions remained relatively stable in Ireland, so that in 1702, when British military forces were once again needed on the continent, most of Ross's Dragoons could be relieved of their peace-keeping tasks in Ireland to join the main army in Flanders.[41]

The renewal of hostilities between the English and the French was directly related to the question of who would inherit the English throne. The question of the succession had at first caused little concern in England. At the accession of William and Mary, Anne had agreed to renounce her claim to the throne in favor of William in the event of Mary's death. When Mary died in December of 1694, William continued to rule alone. Anne was to succeed William after his death, and her heir was her son, the duke of Gloucester, born in July of 1689. The young duke died on July 30, 1700, and the question of the succession assumed major importance. Tories had to again question their belief in divine right when they realized the legitimate king was still the Catholic, James II, and the legitimate heir was his son, the baby of 1688, James Edward. Most Tories could not tolerate the return of a Catholic king. By necessity, they acquiesced in the passage of the 1701 Act of Settlement to assure the succession of a Protestant, George, the prince of Hanover, descended from James I's daughter, the princess Elizabeth.[42]

Two other deaths, which occurred shortly after that of the young duke of Gloucester, were also to have far-reaching consequences for Britain. In September of 1700, Charles II of Spain died. His death caused Louis to attempt to seize and control the Spanish Empire. As a result of this, representatives of England, the Netherlands, and the Holy Roman emperor met in September of 1701 to sign a treaty of grand alliance by which they agreed that the French and Spanish thrones would not be united and that France would have no share in Spain's colonial trade. The course of England into war was confirmed in that same month when, on September 16, 1701, James II died in St. Germain and the French king proclaimed James II's son, James Edward, king of England. The immediate effects of this pronouncement were to create resentment in

England at France's meddling in her internal affairs and to raise fears that James Edward would attempt to seize the English throne with Louis's help.[43]

King William was determined to keep the British throne and decided to challenge France's military supremacy once more. Dutch and English forces began to gather in the Netherlands. The king named John Churchill, now earl of Marlborough, ambassador to the Netherlands and commander-in-chief. One of the British regiments under Marlborough's command was Ross's regiment of dragoons. On March 16, 1702, Ross's Dragoons left Dublin for England, the first step of a journey that would take them to Holland. Three days later, King William died and the Princess Anne, Marlborough's patron, ascended the throne. A month later, Marlborough was appointed generalissimo of the confederate armies with headquarters in The Hague. In May, war was declared by England and her allies, the Netherlands and the emperor, against France, Spain, Savoy, the elector of Bavaria, and his brother, the prince-bishop of Cologne and Liege. During one of the first actions of the war, Marlborough, with Ross's Dragoons, captured Liege, but the allies lost ground in Germany.[44]

In the winter of 1702–1703, Marlborough's troops remained quartered in the Low Countries. Training recruits in the elaborate firing orders and drill of the day was the chief task in winter quarters. Yet another vitally important job for mounted regiments was the securing of sufficient fodder to keep horses alive through the winter. As a major, Hunter was responsible for supervising the collection of hay, straw, and oats. In 1702, Hunter complained to Marlborough that he was having trouble collecting fodder requisitioned from the surrounding villages. Adam de Cardonnel, Marlborough's secretary, told Hunter he should secure the fodder "by sending out Parties to fetch it in if the Village don't comply." The people in the town of Weert were particularly obstinate and known to have a "great quantity of Hay & Oats. . . ." They were, therefore, "order'd to deliver two hundred Rations of oats and one hundred of Hay & Straw," and Hunter was ordered to seize it from them. Methods of obtaining fodder were often arbitrary and even cruel. The earl of Stair in 1708, for instance, annoyed because supplies were not being received as quickly as he wished, promised the villagers of Furness that he would have "no mercy for those [who] did not deliver grain." He told Cardonnel he had ordered "a house or two [to] be burnt where they had been most defective."[45]

The village people among whom Marlborough's armies were quartered were treated as subordinate populations under military control. One winter, Hunter was commandant of the troops quartered in a Dutch

John Churchill, first duke of Marlborough, by John Closterman after Sir Godfrey
Kneller. National Portrait Gallery, London. This early portrait of Churchill shows
the intelligence, grace, and character that brought him to the attention and won
him the favors of five British monarchs.

village. The magistrates of the town were unpopular because they were sympathetic to the British, so the people decided to hold elections to replace them. Hunter asked the duke of Marlborough how he should proceed. The duke did not order Hunter to stop the elections, but implied he would be pleased if they did not take place. When the people met in a church to vote, Hunter marched his regiment to the church "and when he was near it ordered all the drums to beat the grenadiers march. This so frightened the people in the church that they rushed out by the doors and windows in the greatest fright and confusion. Many were bruised and lamed and an end thereby put to the attempt for a new election. Colonel Hunter marched the regiment past the church (without taking the least notice of what passed) to the place where the Regiment usually performed their exercise." Such experience in the military control of civilian populations in the Netherlands was later applied by Hunter in New York, New Jersey, and Jamaica.[46]

Hunter, although still attached to Ross's Dragoons, was also on the administrative staff of the duke of Marlborough as an aide-de-camp. This role brought Hunter into close contact not only with the duke, but also with the leading men in Europe. The duke apparently was pleased with Hunter's services. On January 1, 1703, Hunter was promoted to lieutenant colonel by the duke's brevet. Such commissions were given only at the discretion of the commander-in-chief and were not purchased.[47]

As a lieutenant colonel, Hunter looked forward eagerly to the 1703 campaign season, but it did not bring any major victories to the Allies. Indecision among the Allied leaders caused Marlborough to abandon the thought of capturing either of his major objectives of Ostend or Antwerp. Marlborough instead took Huy and Limburg and then closed the campaign season in October to return to England. Once there, he secured parliamentary funds for men and supplies for the next summer. Marlborough returned to Holland in the spring of 1704 to conduct the march into Bavaria that ended in the battle of Blenheim on August 2, 1704.[48]

"A Glorious Victory"

At two o'clock in the morning, Marlborough's army of fifty-six thousand men, began their advance westward from their camp at the Kessel between Kessel Ostheim and Munster on the Danube toward the villages of Blenheim and Oberglau. The French, slightly superior in number, did not at first believe the Allies would attack. When it was apparent Marlborough planned to seize the initiative, the French hurriedly formed battle lines. The French commander, Marshal Tallard, sent twenty-seven battalions of infantry into the small village of Blenheim as a garrison for the center of the French line. The soldiers were so crowded they could scarcely fire their weapons.[49]

Marlborough's main advance was on the plain between the villages. In the afternoon, the Allied foot and horse swept down on the French on the plain. The French were finally driven back to the Danube. Thirty squadrons of horse, two thousand men, were forced over the steep embankment. Most of them drowned. For days after, the corpses of men and horses were washed ashore along the course of the river, grim and silent bearers of the news of France's defeat.[50]

The battle lasted all day long. In the evening, the French still held the village of Blenheim. Lord George Hamilton, the earl of Orkney, in command of a brigade of infantry, and Lieutenant General Charles Churchill's Buffs kept Blenheim under attack. Orkney and Churchill were joined by two dragoon regiments, Hay's Scots Greys and Ross's Irish Dragoons. The dragoons surrounded the village to prevent the escape of the French infantry. The French tried to break out on one side but were headed off by the Scots Greys. They then attempted escape from the other side but were driven back by the Irish Dragoons. Bottled up inside the village with a powerful enemy without and no hope of succor, the French finally yielded to Orkney's demands that they surrender. At 9 P.M., Orkney took prisoner twelve thousand men and thirteen hundred officers from the village.[51]

Allied casualties at Blenheim were forty-five hundred killed and seven thousand wounded. Approximately forty thousand Frenchmen were either killed, wounded, or taken prisoner. That same day, Marlborough sent word to his wife, Sarah, by his aide-de-camp, Colonel Daniel Parke, "I have not time to say more, but to beg you will give my duty to the Queen, and let her know Her Army has had a Glorious Victory." The next day Marlborough in another letter to Sarah referred to the victory as being "greater than has been known in the memory of Man."[52]

Rewards for participating at Blenheim were quickly forthcoming. The official booty collected by the government was considerable and included cannon, mortars, colors, standards, kettle drums, tents, coaches, mules, boats, pontoons, and twenty-four barrels and eight casks of silver. Unofficial booty was taken from French prisoners and stripped from French corpses. In addition, a cash bounty was distributed by the government to participants in the battle. Hunter, who either served Marlborough directly as aide-de-camp, or was with his regiment, received £61 10s 0d as a regimental major's share of the £64,013 bounty. Hunter was further rewarded on January 1, 1705, when he was promoted to full colonel.[53]

Offices and sinecures, governments and pensions, were also given to their subordinates by Marlborough and Treasurer Sidney Godolphin, who now tried to control many military and civilian appointments and promotions within the British Isles. Their intent was "that the Queen wou'd not lett any body have Governments but such as have serv'd in the Army . . . ." The Blenheim victory had been secured primarily because of the dedication and bravery of officers and men from England's provinces, and some of these men were suitably rewarded. The Virginian, Daniel Parke, who brought news of the victory to the queen, was given the governorship of the Leeward Islands. The Scottish earl of Orkney, hero of Blenheim, was given control of the governor-generalship of Virginia. Henceforward, until his death in 1737, all the serving commanders of Virginia, including the Scot Robert Hunter, whether commissioned as governors-general or as lieutenant governors, were in fact Orkney's deputies. Hunter's successor as Orkney's deputy was another Scot, Alexander Spotswood, lieutenant quartermaster general, who had been wounded at Blenheim. All of Orkney's deputies, including Hunter and Spotswood, were former staff officers of the duke of Marlborough, whose design it was to organize the empire along military, imperialist lines.[54]

As a military imperialist, Marlborough also favored the reunion of Scotland and England, as did many other Britons. A firm step was taken toward union in 1705, when the English Parliament authorized the queen to appoint commissioners in England to effect such a measure. Parliament, to assure a peaceful succession, put pressure on Scotland through the Aliens Act, which stated that the crown of Scotland must be settled on the successor to the crown of England. If this was not done before December 25, 1706, all Scots would be considered aliens and barred from holding any government office. By the autumn of 1705, the Aliens Act was beginning to have its desired effect. Although some Scots, such as Argyll and Stair, had long been in favor of union, others, such as Hamilton and Mar, were not. Both of the latter changed their positions as a result of the act and made a motion to the Scots Parliament to ask the queen to name the Scots commissioners to effect the union. Since the queen favored the union, it was a foregone conclusion that the ministers she chose would support it. The union cause was also helped when a group of about twenty-four men, led by the marquesses of Tweeddale and Montrose and the earls of Haddington, Marchmont, Roxburgh, and Rothes, all previously against the union but now converted by the Aliens Act, formed the squadrone volante to work for its passage through the Scots Parliament.[55]

While the unity of Great Britain was being guaranteed, that of the unionist ministry was shattering. The war had been financed through the parliamentary leadership of the Junto Whigs. In 1706, as a reward for

Queen Anne, by the studio of John Closterman. National Portrait Gallery, London. The queen gave birth to seventeen children, all of whom died. She may well have preferred the succession of her half-brother, James Edward, rather than her distant cousin, George of Hanover.

their services, they demanded that Marlborough's son-in-law, Charles Spencer, second earl of Sunderland, be named secretary of state in place of Charles Hedges. Godolphin and Marlborough supported the Junto's decision because of the latter's prowar position. Harley, however, did not believe Junto support was necessary for the successful continuation of the war. In addition, Harley disliked Sunderland and supported the queen in her opposition to the appointment. The queen held out for a time against the combined assaults of the duke and duchess of Marlborough and Godolphin, but finally yielded to their bullying in November of 1706. The control of government by the Junto seemed assured with Sunderland's appointment, but the Junto had pushed the queen too hard. Anne particularly resented Sarah's heavy-handed methods, and a breach began to widen between the two women.[56]

"The victory of Ramillies"

While personal and political enmities and negotiations for union paradoxically progressed in London and Edinburgh, Marlborough continued his continental wars. His next major victory was at Ramillies on May 12, 1706. In this campaign, Hunter served as one of Marlborough's aides-de-camp. During the battle, Marlborough ordered eighteen squadrons of horse to move from the right to the left to reinforce the cavalry charge of the Dutch and Danish squadrons. After Marlborough left to lead the massive charge himself, William Cadogan, later first earl of Cadogan, acting as Marlborough's liaison officer, ordered Hunter "to go to the General of the Horse on the right and order him to carry all the [remaining] horse on the left and immediately attack the French horse." Such a move would leave Orkney's foot, which was advancing through a morass on the right toward the French-held village of Autreglise, without any mounted protection and exposed to enemy assaults. Hunter thought the order irresponsible and even asked Cadogan to repeat it in the presence of other officers. Cadogan did so, and Hunter reluctantly delivered the order to the general of the horse.[57]

Cadogan, rough and unpolished, was resented by many officers for his rapid rise in the army and the favor shown him by the duke. Hunter undoubtedly believed his own military experience and tactical judgement were equal to Cadogan's. Consequently, he questioned the wisdom of Cadogan's order, particularly since Marlborough was nowhere near since "the Duke about that time was born down dismounted and for some time in great danger so that he was not in a capacity to give orders." Marlborough had fallen off his horse while leaping a ditch during the cavalry charge and was for several minutes in imminent danger of being captured or killed by the French. Hunter managed to convey his skepticism as to the wisdom and authenticity of the order to the general of the horse, who also "seemed surprised and after a little hesitation swore he would leave one regiment, which he did, and then put the orders he had received in execution." Twenty-one additional squadrons of horse, with the exception of seventeen squadrons of English cavalry and dragoons, moved to the left to join the attack on the French. Soon twenty-five thousand horsemen were engaged on the plain between the villages of Ramillies and Taviers.[58]

At the same time, the battle also proceeded on the right, where Orkney continued to lead his foot across the morass to Autreglise. Marlborough, or perhaps Cadogan, now realized that with the withdrawal of the cavalry to the left, there was not sufficient protection for Orkney's men and so ordered their retreat. Orkney, who had crossed the morass and was at the very walls of the village, refused to retreat at first, despite the urgent appeals of ten aides-de-camp sent by Cadogan. He agreed only when Cadogan himself came to him and explained the lack of cavalry support. Orkney's men, with much bitterness and complaining, withdrew with only the English horse providing cover.[59]

The French cavalry, including the elite Maison du Roi, were routed by the Allied dragoons, led by Hay's Royal Scots and Ross's Royal Irish. Orkney's foot were regrouped and joined the main attack against the French infantry. The English horse now joined the Allied horse to mount a final assault on the exposed French flank. The French fled from the plain of Ramillies with the Allied army in pursuit until early morning when they reached Meldert. Small wonder that "Mr. Hunter that day tired out four horses in the execution of his duty."[60]

Hunter believed the victory at Ramillies had been achieved only because he had urged the general of the horse not to move all the cavalry to the left, as Cadogan (or Marlborough) ordered. Marlborough has been criticized by some military strategists for the decisions to transfer all the cavalry to the left and to have Orkney retreat. But whether the decisions were right or wrong, and whether they originated with the duke or with Cadogan, were moot points. The Allies won the battle of Ramillies.[61]

Marlborough, as general, accepted the credit for the victory. He was nevertheless willing to reward competent subordinates and gave Cadogan the honor of taking Antwerp. Cadogan was given command of the foot forces that would form the siege, while Hunter, perhaps in acknowledgement of his role at Ramillies, was given command of six squadrons of horse. Hunter's mounted forces arrived at Antwerp well before Cadogan's foot. "When Mr. Hunter came before the town some of the French officers came out to parley. While he was in discourse with them and persuading them to surrender as they could hope for no relief, a merchant of the town came behind Mr. Hunter and pulled him by the sleeve. Mr. Hunter turned and went aside with the merchant." The merchant arranged an interview between Hunter and the Spanish governor. Hunter, who was fluent in Spanish as well as French, secured the surrender of the city from the governor who asked "to be continued Governor of Antwerp under King Charles [III] . . . . Mr. Hunter informed the Duke, by express, of these terms and he readily confirmed them," after sending Orkney with reinforcements of horse. The French were convinced by this show of strength and surrendered on June 6, 1706, "before the army under Mr. Cadogan could come up to form the siege."[62]

Unfortunately, what may have been the most triumphant moment in Hunter's career was to be spoiled, because he had unwittingly stepped on Cadogan's toes. In doing so, he also offended the duke of Marlborough, who greatly admired the large Anglo-Irishman, later described by Bishop Atterbury as "a big, bad, bold, blustering, bloody, blundering booby." At the conclusion of the arrangements, Hunter "went to wait on the Duke but was surprised to be received very coolly. Sir, said the Duke, I think you might have trusted to me to publish the service you have done." Hunter responded that he had not told anyone of his deeds but that other officers knew what had happened and they might have talked. "But as the Duke hereby was disappointed in the honour he designed for his favorite, Mr. Cadogan, he resented it on Mr. Hunter. Perhaps the Duke thought that Mr. Hunter was too much in the secret of what gained the victory of Ramillies and was chagrined on that account."[63]

Cadogan was rewarded by Marlborough for his alleged activities at Ramillies and Antwerp and his loyalty to his commander by being promoted to major general. Later that same year, Marlborough also had given to Cadogan the lieutenancy of the Tower of London, with an income of £1 18s 4 ½d per day. These signs of favor from Marlborough must have been particularly galling to Hunter, who was nine years Cadogan's senior, equalled him in nimbleness of wit, excelled him in culture and breeding, but who had failed to win the duke's favor. Later that summer when Cadogan was captured by the French, Marlborough secured his release on parole only three days later, and he was soon after exchanged. Hunter was to remember this with particular bitterness when he himself was captured and held prisoner of war by the French for more than a year and a half.[64]

Besides glory and the duke's favor, Hunter suffered an additional loss the summer of 1706, when on August 15th his friend, John lord Hay, died at Courtrai. The next day, Marlborough in a letter to Godolphin mentioned that Hay "colonel of the royal regiment of Scots dragoons, died of a lingering fever, after about twenty days illness, being generally regretted through the whole army," and even more regretted by his young wife of less than a year. Hay was succeeded as colonel of the Royal Scots by another of Hunter's friends, John Dalrymple, now master of Stair.[65]

As the 1706 campaign season came to a close, Hunter realized that, out of favor with Marlborough and Cadogan, he had little future in the army. After almost two decades of service, he "left the army in the winter and went over to London."[66]

Hunter had changed considerably during his military service. At the age of forty, his life and interests were now more British oriented than Scots oriented. The friends Hunter made since 1694 were members of the intellectual and professional elite, whether Scottish, Irish, or English, who played an ever larger part in British political and cultural life. His personal charm and keen personality had won and kept him the friendship of influential men of affairs who would continue to favor his interests. Hunter would need their assistance, because he did not return to England to fill a comfortable, well-paying post in the central government bureaucracy. He returned to begin a new career and another phase of his life. Perhaps it was with more anticipation and hope, than regret and defeat, that Robert Hunter returned to England in the winter of 1706–1707.

❧ 2 ❧

"Thro' Th'Extended World"

1707–1710

Then, sit no more, as dreaming Fools at home:
But thro' th'extended World, with Boldness roam.

Daniel Defoe,
"A Scot's Poem"

"The money was the thing"

COLONIAL GOVERNORSHIPS were political plums dispensed by
Marlborough and Godolphin to military officers as rewards for
exceptional service. As Marlborough reminded Godolphin in 1707, "I
must again beg you to intercede with the Queen not to give way to the
sollicitation of 17 [Newcastle?] but that Governments may be filled with
such officers as have serv'd since Her Raine." Marlborough wanted only
men of his own making to defend the empire's interests against the French
and Spanish in the New World. Among the rewards given to these men for
loyal service were the governments of England's empire.[1]

One such imperial plum, with an official yearly salary of £2,000
sterling, was the governorship of Virginia, which Marlborough had given
to the earl of Orkney in 1705. Orkney, who continued his highly successful
military career, had no intention of actually governing Virginia in person.
Instead he made arrangements with subordinate officers to govern on his
behalf and split the salary with them. The first "lieutenant and Governor-
Generall" of Virginia during Orkney's tenure was Major Edward Nott,
chosen by Orkney with Marlborough's approval. Nott was at his post less
than a year when he died in August of 1706. Orkney's next choice was his
friend and fellow Scot, Robert Hunter.[2]

39

Presbyterians could not hold state office and so Hunter's acceptance of this post followed his decision to join the Church of England.
Church membership was but one precondition of the gubernatorial post;
the other was obtaining the approval of the duke of Marlborough. Since few
colonial appointments were made without Marlborough's knowledge, it is
almost certain that the duke approved Orkney's choice, despite his annoyance with Hunter after the surrender of Antwerp. Nevertheless,
Marlborough did throw unnecessary obstacles in Hunter's path by preventing Hunter from selling his commission as captain of a troop of dragoons.
Orkney interceded with the duke by pointing out that this placed a
financial burden on Hunter who had not as yet begun to receive his salary
as governor-general of Virginia. Orkney urged Marlborough to grant
Hunter permission to sell promptly. Failing that, he asked if the duke
would at least "let him [Hunter] Continue his [full army] pay, till he Enter
in pay in Virginia . . . ."[3]

Despite Orkney's concern, Hunter was not without a steady source
of income. The acquisition of empire during the Marlborough era brought
the professionalization of the army, with the maintenance and support of a
permanent cadre of trained officers. Hunter was still in the army. He and
other officers continued on the army lists, collecting half pay and advancing up the promotion ladder until they died. Hunter's finances also
improved in 1707 because he married a rich woman. His choice was the
widow of John lord Hay, Elizabeth Orby, Lady Hay.[4]

Elizabeth, scarcely more than twenty at the time of her marriage to
Hunter, was well educated and charming. She was the only daughter and
heir of Sir Thomas Orby. She was also the heir of her childless uncle, Sir
Charles Orby. The Orby land in Lincolnshire and Surrey had been granted
to the family by James I sometime prior to 1624. Elizabeth's grandfather
Thomas Orby, was a staunch royalist whose loyalty to the crown earned
him a baronetcy in 1658. In the 1680s, Elizabeth's father and uncle both
served Charles II and James II as officers in the Life Guards and the Royal
Regiment of Fusiliers. The Orbys were ardent Anglicans as well as
royalists, however, and so in 1688 quickly transferred their allegiance to
the Protestant prince of Orange.[5]

At the time of his marriage to Elizabeth, Hunter took possession of
part of the Orby land. The 6,599 acres at Croyland, Lincolnshire, were
part of Elizabeth's dowry, which she retained after the death of Lord Hay.
The estate was transferred to Hunter at the time of his marriage. In
addition to Croyland, the Orby estate, which Hunter would eventually
inherit, included 1,506 acres at Burton Pedwardine, Lincolnshire, three
houses in the Savoy, and an estate at Chertsey, Surrey. After maintenance

expenses and payment of rent to the crown, the Lincolnshire estates yielded a pretax income of £3,357 a year. Almost £2,800 of this sum came from the Croyland estate, a tidy income for Robert Hunter, whose father had died leaving an estate worth only £30 Scot.[6]

Hunter's wife was also heir to property in Jamaica. Sir Charles Orby's second wife was Dame Anne Hopegood Beeston, widow of the late governor-general of Jamaica, Sir William Beeston, one of the wealthiest men on Jamaica. Beeston left only £3,000 to his daughter, Jane. The bulk of his estate was left to his wife. Beeston had taken his will and other personal papers with him to London, where he died in 1701. His daughter, who claimed Beeston had never drawn a will, took possession of Beeston's plantations, houses, furnishings, and money in Jamaica. Dame Anne, now married to Sir Charles Orby, promptly sent Beeston's will back to Jamaica. A trial, held in August of 1706, upheld the inheritance of Beeston's daughter. Dame Anne now filed an appeal with Jamaica governor-general Thomas Handasyde and waited to hear the decision.[7]

The prospect of eventually inheriting such profitable land must certainly have increased Hunter's estimation of Lady Hay, as she was known throughout her life. It was undoubtedly a love match on Elizabeth's part. At the time of their marriage, Hunter was twice her age and landless. Although Hunter had bright prospects of future financial success as a governor-general, he had little else to offer a young and wealthy widow. Hunter probably returned Elizabeth's love, but he had waited until middle age to marry in the hope of making a profitable match. Elizabeth, as an heiress, had the prerequisites necessary in the early eighteenth century to attract a mate. Defoe was a severe, but accurate, critic of his time. His observation "that money only made a woman agreeable," was probably true. "Men chose mistresses indeed by the gust of their affection, and it was requisite for a whore to be handsome, well shap'd, have a good mein, and a graceful behaviour, but that for a wife, no deformity would shock the fancy, no ill qualities the judgement; the money was the thing. . . ." Hunter might echo Captain Plume's remark when he resigned from the army to marry an heiress, "farewel Subsistance and welcome Taxes."[8]

"The men of wit and pleasure"

Hunter's marriage to an English heiress, along with his acceptance of the governor-generalship of an English colony and his decision to join the Church of England, marked the final steps in his Anglicization. This process had begun for Hunter, and many other Lowland Scots, in the early

1680s when the Stuarts' brutality toward Presbyterians overcame their defiance. Many privileged Scots, Hunter included, cultivated a new cosmopolitanism, as they identified culturally, economically, politically, and socially with the English. Like Hunter, these Scots fought Britain's, rather than Scotland's wars, substituted French wine and brandy for Scots ale, replaced Presbyterianism with Anglicanism, acquired English land and wives, and, in London, saw English plays and Italian operas.[9]

Shared tastes among British courtiers included an attachment to learning. The commitment to lifelong education produced multifaceted men of affairs, present in Britain since at least the sixteenth century. The most prominent soldiers-scholars-statesmen of the Tudor and Stuart eras were Sir Walter Ralegh, Sir Francis Bacon, King James I, Sir Henry Wotton, John Milton, Sir Andrew Marvell, John Wilmot, earl of Rochester, John Locke, Charles Montague, earl of Halifax, John Sheffield, duke of Buckingham, Joseph Addison, and Richard Steele. Neither did a religious vocation preclude a literary avocation. Perhaps the two most accomplished poets of their respective eras were John Donne, dean of St. Paul's and Jonathan Swift, dean of St. Patrick's. While the ability to write well was much admired throughout all this period, the intelligentsia of the first decade of the eighteenth century particularly valued, and often rewarded, those of its members who composed poetry. Consequently, many Britons, including Hunter, turned to writing verse.[10]

As Hunter well realized, his cultural attainments helped him to rise in the British world. Learning, as well as an ability to write, were the factors that brought three of Hunter's friends, Joseph Addison, Richard Steele, and Jonathan Swift, to fame. These men, like Hunter, began life as impoverished members of the lesser gentry. All were "men from the periphery making their way by exercising a talent for writing." Their desire to succeed led them to become courtiers and to adopt "the propriety of good society, of the court, as a means of becoming accepted at the centre." In time these men would seek to extend their cultural standards to other self-made men both in England and the provinces of empire.[11]

Hunter probably made the acquaintance of Addison, Steele, and Swift in the early 1700s at one of London's many coffee houses. Men of affairs met in coffee houses for intellectual stimulation and entertainment, as well as to gather political information. The coffee houses of this era were also the sites where business affairs were conducted, auctions were held, petitions were circulated, and letters were received. They were, in a sense, the equivalent of the modern-day London business office, auction gallery, lobbyist office, pub, and drawing room, all in one. Coffee houses usually catered to clienteles with specific interests. Hence, there was a

Jamaican coffee house for those who wished to further that province's economic or political interests. St. James's Coffee House was a favorite of the literary elite. It was there and to Will's and Button's that Hunter and his friends would often stroll "after the Play . . . in hope of meeting some new poem, or other entertainment, among the men of wit and pleasure. . . ."[12]

Joseph Addison was one of these men of "wit and pleasure." Statesman, poet, essayist, and playwright, Addison was the son of a minister, born in 1672 in Milston near Amesbury, Wilts. He was educated at Queen's College, Oxford, and was soon translating classical works and writing poems of his own in Latin. Addison's literary work brought him to the attention of statesman and poet, Charles Montague, later earl of Halifax, who helped him launch his political career. Addison helped his own career along after the 1704 battle of Blenheim, when he composed a commemorative poem, "Campaign." The poem was so well received that in 1705 Addison was rewarded by being named undersecretary of state to Charles Hedges, a post he retained when Hedges was replaced by the earl of Sunderland in 1706.[13]

Richard Steele, playwright, poet, and essayist, was Addison's house guest in the summer of 1706. Perenially in debt, Steele moved in with Addison following the death of his first wife to save expenses while he looked for a second (wealthier) wife. Steele was born in Dublin in 1672, the son of a poor English attorney. One of the quickest roads to success for a bright, impoverished young man was military service. Steele, like Hunter, joined the army. Steele began his military career in 1694 as a gentleman volunteer in the second troop of Life Guards. He advanced his army career through his poetic talents. In 1694, Steele dedicated a poem to John lord Cutts, colonel of the third regiment of Foot Guards, who took Steele into his household, employed him as secretary, and promoted him to the rank of captain in his regiment. In September of 1706, Steele became gentleman waiter to Queen Anne's consort, Prince George. In the spring of 1707, Steele, a staunch Whig, was "appointed by the Secretaries of State to write the Gazette with a Salary of Three Hundred pounds."[14]

Steele's duties as gazetteer were to edit and publish official government despatches in the government newspaper, the *London Gazette*. The gazetteer was not permitted any editorial comment in the restricted format of the paper, which was published thrice weekly during the time of Steele's appointment. The *Gazette* existed primarily for the purpose of bringing the literate public information the government wanted it to know, including a highly selective account of military news, all approved beforehand by the duke of Marlborough. It also contained announcements and advertise-

ments similar to those found in a modern newspaper. Steele soon looked for relief from the restrictive format of the *Gazette*, but until he was able to start his own newspaper, he diverted himself with his new (rich but demanding) wife and his circle of friends.[15]

Steele, along with Hunter and Addison, shared the friendship of the Anglo-Irish clergyman Jonathan Swift, essayist, poet, and pamphleteer. Born to an English family in Dublin in 1667, Swift was educated at Trinity College in that city. He then became secretary to the statesman and writer Sir William Temple. Swift entered the church in 1694 and two years later rejoined Temple's household, where he remained until Temple's death in 1699. He then became domestic chaplain to Ireland's lord justice, the earl of Berkeley, and returned with Berkeley to Ireland. At the same time, Swift received a cathedral stall in St. Patrick's, Dublin.[16]

Hunter was also in Ireland with Ross's Dragoons during this period, but it is unlikely the two men met until after 1701, when Swift returned to England with Berkeley. That same year, Swift published his first political tract for the Whigs. He followed this in 1704 with the publication of *A Tale of a Tub*, a satire on corruptions in religion. Lord Somers and other Junto Whigs were delighted to use Swift's talents for the Whig cause. Swift eagerly wrote proadministration propaganda pieces with the expectation that he would be rewarded with a high church post. Yet, in 1707, at the relatively advanced age of forty, Swift's only post was the modest one of rector of Laracor and Rathbeggan in Ireland.[17]

"Governors in subordinate precincts"

Hunter had been far more successful than Swift in parlaying his own considerable talents and his political contacts into a potentially profitable career. In addition to future wealth from official salaries and allowances and unofficial fees and presents, colonial governorships carried power and prestige. In a colony, a royal governor-general (or the lieutenant) had more power than the monarch at home. He was accountable for the exercise of that power only to the monarch and her ministers, who were three

Joseph Addison, by Sir Godfrey Kneller. National Portrait Gallery, London. Staunch Whig and loyal friend to Hunter, the brilliant essayist and poet eventually became Hunter's superior when he was named secretary of state with responsibility for the American colonies. He died on June 17, 1719.

thousand miles away and biased in his favor. The governor-general's authority came directly from the crown. In the colony he was the prime supporter and principal interpreter of the royal prerogative.[18]

The nature of the gubernatorial office as it existed in the early eighteenth century proved the truth of James Harrington's assertion that "governors in subordinate precincts have commonly three functions: the one civil, the other judicial, and the third military." As part of his civil function, Hunter as governor was head of the legislature. He could summon, prorogue, or dissolve the assembly and could veto its acts. Acting with his council, the governor-general granted lands and recommended quit rents. Hunter's judicial responsibilities included the appointment of judges, commissioners of oyer and terminer, and justices of the peace. With his council, the governor acted as the highest court in the province. Hunter, and other governors, could also create courts of chancery and preside in that court as chancellor. Hunter held a separate commission as vice admiral by which he could create vice-admiralty courts, and appoint the presiding judge and other court personnel. The governor-general also commanded the militia, whose officers he could appoint or dismiss at will. As governor, Hunter was also in command of any regular forces stationed in his province, either permanently or temporarily.[19]

The prestige of the gubernatorial office was commensurate with the power. As the chief executive and representative of the royal prerogative, the governor-general and his wife took precedence over all other people in the province, were the acknowledged social leaders of the colony, and set its cultural standards. Hunter and Lady Hay would interpret English culture for the provincials. They would teach colonists how to dress, how to act, what books to read, and what music and art to admire.[20]

As a representative of the bishop of London, the governor-general was also the defender of the state church. He recommended and installed ministers and supervised ecclesiastical affairs in his province. Both the ecclesiastical and lay authority of the governor-general were confirmed by the Church of England's clergy and acknowledged within the physical church where, during services, the governor and his family sat in a raised, ornately decorated, enclosed, and canopied pew. The presiding minister included the governor in his prayers, along with members of the royal family. Hunter may not have been a zealous convert to Anglicanism, but he recognized the importance of the state church, both in furthering a cultural unity among diverse peoples and in maintaining the authority of the government.[21]

"The end o' an auld sang"

Hunter's future career as a governor-general, like the careers of many Scots, depended on the revocation of the Aliens Act and the confirmation of the Union. The Aliens Act was revoked by the English Parliament in December of 1706, just before it was to take effect, when it became apparent Scots leaders were amenable to Union. By the time the Union's principal architect, the earl of Stair, died in January of 1707, it was a foregone conclusion. The Scots Parliament was dissolved by proclamation on April 28, 1707. It was, as the earl of Seafield was led to comment, "the end o' an auld sang." The Union was officially proclaimed on May 1, 1707. By its terms, Scotland accepted the Hanoverian succession. In return for the loss of her independence, Scotland gained freedom of trade with England and her colonies and the security of her Presbyterian church.[22]

Despite the religious tolerance promised by the Union, efforts were made by the English government to promote conversion to Anglicanism among Highland Scots. It was believed that binding the Highlanders to the English with the shared cultural ties of religion would help to destroy their provincialism and clannishness. In 1708, by order of the queen, proselytizing mission centers, similar to those established by the English among New World Indians, were set up throughout the Highlands and islands of Scotland. The schools met with limited success, and most Highlanders continued to cling to their old religions.[23]

The Highlanders were particularly resistant to conversion overtures because they resented the Union, which they saw as threatening traditional Scottish values. Discontent caused Jacobitism to bloom again in the Highlands. The Scottish Jacobites, eager for the return of the exiled Stuart, expected both French and papal assistance to restore him. Indeed, less than a year after the Union was officially declared, a French fleet carrying five thousand men made an unsuccessful attempt to bring the Old Pretender to Scotland.[24]

"I drank your Health yesterday with Colonel Hunter"

During this period of heightened imperial tension and continued war, Hunter prepared to sail for Virginia. The official notice of his appointment to succeed Nott was transmitted to the Board of Trade by the earl of Sunderland on April 3, 1707. On August 12, 1707, Hunter was on board the *Dover*, Captain Matthews commanding. Lady Hay presumably planned to join Hunter later, as she would when he sailed for his New York governorship in 1710. Hunter's fleet was ill fated, although Hunter could not have known that in port. The ships were attacked by French privateers, perhaps off the coast of Virginia. The *Dover* was taken, with Hunter and his entire equippage. The governor-general of Virginia was a valuable prize, so Hunter was carried to Paris as a prisoner of war and waited there to be exchanged.[25]

Hunter's exchange was delayed for two reasons. First, as he rightly suspected, Marlborough was still annoyed with him and so did little to facilitate his exchange. Second, the French were themselves holding up the exchange of prisoners because the English had captured Jean Forquet, bishop of Quebec, and some other clerics. The French wanted to exchange lower ranking English prisoners for the bishop, much to Queen Anne's annoyance. The queen refused to release the bishop except for a cleric of equal rank. On April 22, 1707, the English Commission for the Exchange of Prisoners proposed to the French that the bishop be exchanged for the baron of Mean, dean of Liege. The French opposed this exchange, and on November 26, 1707, shortly after Hunter's capture, Monsieur l' Empereur, the French commissary at Saint Malo, wrote to the English commissioners to propose the exchange of Hunter for the bishop. The French thought this exchange might be agreeable to the English because Hunter was the "governor of a province on the same continent, where Monsieur de Quebec is bishop . . . ."[26]

The French permitted Hunter to return to England on parole during the winter of 1707–1708, shortly after he was captured, to arrange this exchange. The queen again refused, although she was willing to exchange Hunter for any French prisoner of equal rank. On April 21, 1708, Sunderland asked the commission if they had any objections to exchanging Hunter for the marquis le Meux, colonel of the Regiment of Aginot. The exchange was approved by the commission and the queen.[27]

While on his extended parole in London, Hunter again made the rounds of coffee houses and visited his old friends, Addison, Steele, and Swift among them. Addison, on September 11, 1708, reported to an unknown correspondent, "I drank your Health yesterday with Colonel Hunter and Dr. Swift." Swift had a high regard for Hunter and his literary ability, at least according to Anthony Henley, who, in September of 1708, wrote to Swift, "I hant the Honour to know Coll: Hunter But I never saw him in so good Company as you have putt him, ld Hall[ifax]: Mr Add[ison]: Mr Cong[reve]; and the Gazettier [Richard Steele]: Since he is there lett him stay there."[28]

Hunter and his literary friends were all Whigs at this time and dependent on the ministry for patronage. The ministry itself, however, was beginning to weaken from internal dissension. In February of 1708, Anne, who had never been reconciled to the Junto Whigs, dismissed Godolphin, who had consistently favored Junto Whig policies. The queen now favored a government led by the moderate Whig, Robert Harley, afterward earl of Oxford and Tory "prime minister." Harley was a relative of the duchess of Marlborough's cousin and the queen's favorite, Abigail Hill, later Lady Masham. Marlborough's adherence to Harley might have made the new government succeed, but he would not abandon Godolphin and resigned as commander-in-chief in protest. Harley alone did not as yet have a sufficient following among moderate Whigs and high Tories to remain in power. Less than a week after Marlborough's resignation, Harley was himself forced to resign as secretary of state, and Marlborough and Godolphin came back to power. Harley went into opposition with other moderate Whigs and, with the queen's approval and encouragement, began to unite all the dissident anti-Junto Whig elements within English society. For the moment, however, the Junto Whigs were supreme. Godolphin and Marlborough, who wanted to continue the war to destroy France's power, had no other choice but to support the policies of the pro-war Junto.[29]

"The poor Palatines"

One of the problems encountered by the Junto Whigs was that of resettling the Palatine refugees. In the spring of 1707, France's Marshal Villars had led his troops across the Rhine where they terrorized and laid waste the Palatinate. Many German vintners and farmers left their homes in the following spring to go to England, the first step of a voyage some hoped would bring them to America. The English government was receptive to the idea of sending "the poor Palatines" to the American colonies. In the fall of 1708, fifty-two Palatines were sent to New York with the new governor-general, John lord Lovelace, baron of Hurley, to produce naval stores. The Palatines were to settle on five hundred acres provided in New York at the queen's expense.[30]

Colonel Lovelace had been named governor of New York and New Jersey on March 28, 1708, to replace Lord Cornbury, one of the first of James's relatives to defect in 1688. The decision to replace Cornbury had been made by Marlborough and Godolphin as early as June of 1707. Cornbury was recalled after the home government was regaled with reports of his improvidence and lack of propriety. The governor not only ran up a debt of more than £8,000 to New York shopkeepers and merchants alone, but his entire administration was notorious for its corruption. Cornbury was also a transvestite, as New Jersey and New York landowner Lewis Morris informed John Chamberlayne, secretary for the Society of the Propagation of the Gospel. "He [Cornbury] rarely fails of being drest in Womens Cloaths every day and almost half his time is spent that way and seldom misses it on a Sacrament day[. He] was in that Garb when his dead Lady was carried out of the fort and this not privately but in the face of the Sun and in sight of the Town . . . ." The complaints against the governor became so persistent that not even the fact that Cornbury was cousin to the queen could prevent his recall. On hearing of his removal, Cornbury's New York creditors had him taken into custody by the sheriff and thrown into the common jail on Wall Street. There he continued to affect his bizarre attire "in Women's Cloths," although, perhaps out of condescension for the changing fashions, "now 'tis after the Dutch manner." Cornbury was released from prison only when elevated to the earldom of Clarendon following the 1709 death of his father.[31]

Clarendon's successor, Lord Lovelace, arrived in New York on December 18, 1708, after a nine-week passage. The North American continent was experiencing the same bitter cold weather that would drive many thousand more Palatines to England the coming spring. Lovelace landed in the middle of a snow storm and found "the Ports and Rivers are full of Ice. . . . This Coast is so terrible in the Winter I think no Ship ought to be sent hither from England after August . . . ." Lovelace was so weakened by the bitter cold that he remained ill through the winter and into the spring.[32]

Human frailty also weakened the rule of the Junto Whigs when Anne's husband, Prince George of Denmark, died on October 28, 1708. The prince had been a strong supporter of Godolphin and Marlborough, even after the queen grew disenchanted with them. His death crippled the duke of Marlborough's influence, particularly when the duchess found herself displaced in the queen's affections by Harley's cousin, Abigail Hill.[33]

"Le plus honnête garzon"

In 1708, Hunter's primary concern was not high level politics, but rather his own freedom. According to the terms of his parole, Hunter had to return to Paris in the late fall or early winter of 1708, still a prisoner of war. Hunter travelled back to France with some good news, at least. The

Virginia council, acting on instructions from the queen, agreed to pay him £1,418 5s from quit rents for the equippage taken by the French privateers and £500 per year for his gubernatorial salary from July 1, 1707.[34]

Hunter's captivity was also eased by correspondence with friends such as Jonathan Swift. At this time, Swift's connections with prominent government rulers were still tenuous. He was, therefore, anxious to secure Hunter's patronage. Hunter was close to the center of Whig power and knew influential ministers. In the winter of 1709, after Hunter had returned to Paris to wait for his exchange, Swift wrote two letters meant to cheer the captive. Aside from their humor and lighthearted tone, which makes them a delight to read, these letters provide an invaluable insight into the cultural interests and pursuits of the Augustan world and into Swift's personality.

In his letter of January 12, 1709, Swift told Hunter, "I know no People so ill used by your Men of Business as their intimate friends." Swift's playful complaint was not directed at Hunter, but at Joseph Addison, who had been tardy in forwarding one of Hunter's letters to Swift. The opening was by way of apology for Swift's delayed reply. Swift continued in a light tone and next teased Hunter about his recent activities in Paris. Swift commented that "Tis a delicate Expedient you Prisoners have of Diverting your selves in an Enemyes Country, for which other men would be hanged." Swift went on to acknowledge that Hunter had apparently made a social success of his imprisonment, for he reminded Hunter to "be very tender of Your Honor, and not fall in Love because I have a Scruple whether you can keep your Parole if you become a Prisoner to the Ladyes. At least it will be a scandal for a free Briton to drag two Chains at Once. I presume," Swift continued, "you have the Liberty of Paris and fifty miles round, and have a very light pair of Fetters, contrived to ride or dance in and see Versailles, and every Place else except St Germains—I hear the Ladyes call you already Notre prisonnier Hunter, le plus honnête garzon du monde . . . ."[35]

After dealing with Hunter's personal affairs, Swift went on to discuss his own interests. Sometime before Hunter left for Virginia, Swift, the perennial office seeker, had exhibited an interest in an American bishopric. Hunter, as governor-general of Virginia, could be useful to Swift in securing the post. To achieve this honor (and Hunter's support), Swift was willing to make some compromises with his essentially antimilitaristic nature. Swift, therefore, dwelt with apparent delight on the military matters beloved of Colonel Hunter: will the French "owe us Brittons to be a brave People? will they allow the D. of Marlborough to be a great Generall?" after so many, shocking, defeats at the hands of

Marlborough's armies. Then referring to a former single combat of Hunter's, Swift asked, "Have you yett met any French Collonell, whom you remember to have formerly knockt from his Horse, or shivered at least a Lance against his Breastplate? Do you know the Wound you have given when you see the Scars!"[36]

To military speculation Swift added political reports, the characteristic concern of Augustan gossips. Addison, Swift reported, had recently been named secretary to Thomas Wharton, lord lieutenant of Ireland. Swift promised (or threatened) to accompany Addison back to Ireland if Hunter did not hurry back to resume his governorship "and get me my Virginian Bishoprick." Swift next commented upon the continued political successes of the radical Junto Whigs, who "Carry all before them, and how far they will pursue their Victoryes, we moderate Whigs can hardly tell."[37]

Social gossip followed political news. Swift boasted of "writing Verses to Mrs Finch," the celebrated beauty and poet, who was later Countess of Winchelsea. For relief from business in this hard-drinking age, Swift admitted "Mr Addison and I steal to a pint of bad wine, and wish for no third Person but you, who if you were with us, would never be satisfied without three more . . . ."[38]

According to Swift, the new cultural obsessions of Augustan gentlemen were opera and its performers. "We are here nine times madder after Operas then ever, and have gott a new castrati from Italy calld Nicolini who exceeds Valentini I know not how many Bars length." Swift concluded his letter by asking that Hunter let him know "what hopes we have of seeing you, and how soon . . . ." In a postscript to the letter, Swift presented Richard Steele's compliments to Hunter. He then commented on Hunter's speculation that Swift was the author of Shaftesbury's celebrated "lettr of Enthusiasm." Swift disclaimed authorship but returned the compliment nicely by stating that "I have some good Reasons to think the Author is now at Paris."[39]

This letter to the talented and sociable Hunter may have miscarried, because on March 22, 1709, Swift again wrote to Hunter after the latter had mildly scolded him through Addison for failing to write. In the

Jonathan Swift, c. 1718, by Charles Jervas. National Portrait Gallery, London. As Swift himself acknowledged, "Had he but spar'd his Tongue and Pen, / He might have rose like other Men. . . ." He spared neither, offended the queen, and lived out his days in Dublin in virtual exile. He died there, deaf and insane, in 1745.

second letter, the equal of the first in charm and news content, Swift sympathized with Hunter on his captivity and then teased him on his absence from his Virginia governorship: "I hear your good Sister, the Queen of *Pomunki* waiteth with Impatience until you are restored to your Dominions . . . ." Swift then reported on the activities of mutual friends. Ambrose Philips, the poet who was to be Hunter's agent for the colony of New York, was in Copenhagen, where he "writeth verses in a Sledge, upon the frozen Sea, and transmits them hither to our warmer Clime. . . ." Moving from climate to personal news, Swift reported he had "fallen out" with Anne Long, the toast of the Kit-Cat Club, (a disagreement that apparently was quickly resolved, because Swift remained a devoted friend to Mrs. Long), but that Catherine Barton, Sir Isaac Newton's niece, was "still in my good Graces." Swift assured Hunter he would get Mrs. Barton to ask her lover, Lord Halifax, "when you are to be redeemed, and will send you Word." As Swift told Hunter, women were his most reliable sources of information and gave him "the best intelligence I get of publick affairs . . . ."[40]

Cultural news followed personal and political gossip. Opera was still in fashion, Swift said, but he and other literati, such as Addison, were already weary of Italian imports. Swift promised "to set up a Party among the Wits to run them down by next Winter . . . ." Military news was next. Swift told Hunter that the duke of Marlborough had been delayed by bad weather from sailing to Holland to begin the coming campaign season.[41]

Swift had yet to receive any rewards from the Junto Whigs for his propaganda services. He still wanted a bishopric but, he told Hunter, "being not able to make my Friends in the Ministry consider my Merits, or their Promises, enough to keep me here," he was returning to Ireland in the coming summer. Swift apparently had more than a passing interest in the colonial post and told Hunter "that all my Hopes now terminate in my Bishoprick of Virginia . . . ." Swift ended his letter by reminding Hunter that he held "fast my Claim to your Promise of corresponding with me . . . ." He told Hunter he was writing the letter in Addison's presence, "with whom I have fifty Times drunk your Health since you left us . . . . I cannot write longer in so good Company, and therefore conclude . . . ."[42]

Hunter left Paris shortly after receiving Swift's second letter. On April 2, 1709, the mayor of Hythe wrote to Sunderland to tell him he had seized a man who said he was Colonel Robert Hunter as he landed from a French boat. Hunter may have been exchanged for the French colonel marquis le Meux, but he was certainly not exchanged for the bishop of Quebec. There had, of course, been discussion about the French-proposed exchange of Hunter for the bishop, but the queen remained opposed to such an arrangement. The bishop was returned to France, but the agreement to exchange him for the dean of Liege was not reached until April 24, 1709, almost three weeks after Hunter landed in England.[43]

"Some elegant little pieces in poetry"

After his return to England, Hunter was caught up in the cultural excitement of the day. By 1709, Hunter's literary friends had achieved enough worldly success and gained enough self-confidence in their own taste and judgement to assume their roles as cultural arbiters. In the eighteenth century, England and Englishmen were entering a new and better-ordered world. It was a time when men "were determinedly turning their backs on a barbarous past. They were simplifying language, ordering knowledge, refining literature, making politics scientific and philosophy rational, and generally civilizing mankind in accordance with the laws of nature and reason."[44]

In April of 1709, just a week after Hunter returned to London, the efforts of the literati to civilize mankind began in earnest. That month, Richard Steele published the first issue of the *Tatler*. The intent of the thrice-weekly news-sheet, stated in the very first issue, was to educate. Steele was determined "to expose the false facts of life, to pull off the disguises of cunning, vanity, and affectation, and to recommend a general simplicity in our behaviour." Steele, a self-made man, used the *Tatler* to instruct other self-made men, who unlike himself and his friends, lacked the sensitivity to adopt society's standards of elegance and virtue. Steele's friends believed their roles were that of reformers, and their intent was "to mend the World as far as they are able."[45]

The *Tatler* was divided into sections, so that "All accounts of Gallantry, Pleasure, and Entertainment, shall be under the article of *White's* Chocolate-house; Poetry, under that of Will's Coffee-house; Learning, under the title of *Grecian;* Foreign and Domestic News, you will have from Saint James's Coffee-house; and what else I have to offer on any other subject shall be dated from my own Apartment." The news-sheet, with its attractive format, was an almost immediate success, particularly when Steele's friend, Addison, began making anonymous contributions. Swift also contributed to the *Tatler,* as did Hunter, who some time in 1709 "wrote some elegant little pieces in poetry which never appeared in his name."[46]

Hunter's friends were determined that the influence of the *Tatler* would reach the provinces. It certainly reached Lincolnshire, where

Hunter now owned property. In 1710, the Gentleman's Society was founded in Spalding, Lincolnshire, at the urging of Addison, Steele, "and others of Button's club." The purpose of the Spalding Society was to examine current literary works such as "the Tatler, then a new periodical paper; and the reading of such and other publications as well as of MSS. intended for the press . . . ." Members eagerly awaited the arrival of the *Tatler* by mail, and the paper was read aloud in the Spalding coffee house. The members would then "sit and talk over the subject afterwards." Besides discussing literature and current events, the members of the society extended their "enquiries into the History and Antiquities of this kingdom," particularly the extensive ruins of Croyland Abbey Church near Hunter's estate and the Roman fortifications and ancient houses found throughout Lincolnshire. The society's members also investigated "Natural History, and improvements in Arts and Sciences in general." Distinguished members of the Spalding Society eventually included Robert Hunter, Isaac Newton, Hans Sloane, John Evelyn, Alexander Pope, and John Gay.[47]

"Eboracensis"

Cultural pursuits took only part of Hunter's time after his return from Paris. He had to decide whether to assume his post as Orkney's Virginia deputy or whether to seek a new assignment. Hunter's interests now centered more and more on Lincolnshire and the Orby family. In the summer of 1709, the Orbys' suit to recover Beeston's Jamaica estate was still unresolved. The Jamaica appeals court had been unable to reach a decision because its presiding officer, Governor-General Thomas Handasyde, could not obtain a disinterested quorum among the councillors who comprised the court. In the summer of 1709, Handasyde returned to England, and the Jamaica post was available. If Hunter became governor-general of Jamaica, instead of Virginia, he could control the nomination of that province's council. He would also sit as presiding judge

Sir Richard Steele, by Sir Godfrey Kneller. National Portrait Gallery, London. The intensely loyal and invariably good-natured Steele was overjoyed when Hunter was named governor-general of New York. He was also a strong defender of the duke of Marlborough, even when the latter fell from favor with the queen. Steele died in 1729.

in the appeals court. The Orbys would then have little concern about the outcome of their petition. The Jamaica post also held the promise of being more profitable than that of Virginia.[48]

Hunter asked Queen Anne for the Jamaica governorship through his friend the Scots-born Dr. John Arbuthnot, physician and favorite of the queen. Arbuthnot, who was a poet and essayist, as well as a physician, agreed to approach the queen who approved the reassignment. Hunter, however, learned that the Junto Whig ministry, which was still in power, "Had designed that government [Jamaica] for another . . . ." The new governor-general was Orkney's brother, Lord Archibald Hamilton, a Scot who used naval service as a route to a colonial governorship. Hunter realized it would be foolish to defy the ministry and withdrew from consideration for the post. Fortunately for the Orby family, Hunter's intercession in Jamaica was not needed. The Orbys petitioned the privy council, and in 1710 that body ruled in their favor. The Orbys took possession of Beeston's Jamaica estate and increased Hunter's potential wealth.[49]

Hunter's immediate future was settled on August 17, 1709, when Godolphin told Marlborough that word had just been received in London that New York's governor-general Lord Lovelace had died May 7, 1709, less than five months after taking office. On hearing of Lovelace's death, Godolphin told Marlborough he wanted "to joyn the two governments of New York & new England into one, to give these to Coll: Hunter, if you approve the Scheme & the person & to send him thither immediately with instructions to raise about 1500 men in those governments and transport them to Jamaica," for a planned invasion against the French and Spanish West Indian colonies. The next day, Godolphin repeated his plan to Marlborough in another letter.[50]

The West Indian expedition was cancelled, but Marlborough nevertheless approved the choice of Hunter for New York. He so informed Godolphin on August 22nd (New Style). The duke further assured Godolphin that he considered Hunter "a very honest man, and a good officer." Marlborough signified his approval of Hunter's appointment to New York and New Jersey throughout the autumn of 1709. By September 6th, the queen had agreed to appoint Hunter governor of New York and New Jersey. Hunter accepted the assignment, and the decision was officially announced on September 9th. By Saturday, September 17, 1709, the news was already common knowledge in London. Richard Steele's *Tatler* carried a congratulatory announcement on that date:

> Turning my Thoughts as I was taking my Pipe this Evening after this Manner, it was no small Delight to me to receive Advice from Felicia.

That Eboracensis [he who is of York] was appointed a Governor of one of their Plantations. As I am a great lover of Mankind, I took Part in the Happiness of that People who were to be govern'd by one of so great Humanity, Justice, and Honour. Eboracensis had read all the Schemes which Writers have form'd of Government and Order, and been long conversant with Men who have the Reins in their Hands; so he can very well distinguish between chimaerical and Practical Politicks. It is a great blessing, when men have to deal with such different characters in the same species as those of freemen and slaves, that they who command have a just sense of human nature itself, by which they can temper the haughtiness of the master, and soften the servitude of the slave—"Hae tib erunt artes." This is the notion with which those of the plantation receive Eborancesis; and, as I have cast his nativity, I find it will be a record made of this person's administration; and on that part of the shore from whence he embarks to return from his government, there will be a monument with these words: "Here the people wept, and took leave of Eboracensis, the first governor our mother Felicia sent who, during his command here, believed himself her subject.[51]

The announcement must have been much prized by Hunter, who later made a point of mentioning its appearance to his New York friend Cadwallader Colden. It was, first of all, an acknowledgement of Hunter's ability as well as his readings of politics and government and his acquaintance with the leaders of empire. From Hunter's experience, Steele could predict that after a long period of misgovernment in New York and New Jersey, Hunter would justify England's claim to be "Felicia," or the benificent mother. The article also showed an acute awareness of colonial concerns, while its references to "chimaerical" politics was a thrust at Hunter's predecessor, Lord Cornbury, whose behavior in New York had become cause for scandal in London. The article also proved prophetic. Hunter's departure from New York in 1719 prompted an official address from that province's assembly which was indeed a monument in words to the governor-general.[52]

While awaiting his assignment, Hunter took two formal steps to further define his cultural attachment to England. In June of 1709, Hunter joined the Society for the Propagation of the Gospel in Foreign Parts. The society was the missionary arm of the Church of England, whose interests Hunter was sworn to protect as governor of New York and New Jersey. Shortly after, in 1710, Hunter joined the prestigious Royal Society, whose members were committed to scientific inquiry. The president of the society was Isaac Newton. Hunter's friend John Arbuthnot was a member of the society's council and probably urged Hunter to join. Other distinguished members of the council at that time were physician and naturalist Hans Sloane, architect Christopher Wren, and astronomer Edmond Halley. Among the statesmen who comprised the society's 137-man membership were the future New York governor-general William Burnet; New Jersey proprietor and physician Daniel Coxe; the past or future governor of New York, Virginia, Maryland, Virginia, Nova Scotia, and South Carolina Francis Nicholson; the Junto Whig John lord Somers; and Hunter's friends, writer and statesman Charles lord Halifax and the Scots James, duke of Montrose, and John, duke of Roxburgh. The society did indeed have a diverse and illustrious membership. Hunter was in distinguished company and remained a member of the Royal Society until his death in 1734.[53]

Hunter also had to deal with more practical concerns while he prepared to travel to New York. At his suggestion, the English government was preparing to establish a more extensive naval stores program in that colony. London was overrun with Palatines in the summer of 1709. The Germans, who had not recovered from Villar's 1707 raids, were further devastated by the severe winter of 1708–1709, which killed their vines, fruit trees, and livestock. In the spring of 1709, many Germans decided to emigrate, as had their friends and relatives the previous year. Ten thousand or more sold farms, equipment, furnishings, and remaining livestock, packed what little supplies and clothing they could carry, and waited for transportation down the Rhine to Rotterdam and from there to England, the first steps of a journey most hoped would take them to America.[54]

One of the primary concerns of Sunderland, as secretary of state, and John lord Somers, as lord president of the privy council, was the resettlement of the Palatine refugees. Lord Somers served on a board of trustees set up to supervise the collection and disbursement of funds donated to help the poor Palatines. These funds, with more than £20,000 from London alone, came from all over Great Britain. No matter how generously people gave, however, the money could only provide temporary relief. The Palatines' poverty frightened England's poor, who did not want to share charity with them. Wealthy Englishmen resented the extra burden of having to provide for so many indigent people. The immigrants had to be placed somewhere on a permanent basis so they could become self-supporting. On October 19, 1709, Hunter suggested to Lord Somers that a large group be moved to New York to produce naval stores. Both Somers and Sunderland approved Hunter's plan and put him in charge of moving three thousand Palatines to the province.[55]

Much of the organizational planning involved in the movement of the Palatines was handled by Colonel Hunter, whose army experience qualified him to transport, provision, and govern large bodies of people. At a Board of Trade meeting, he requested that cauldrons, ladles, funnels, and hatchets be purchased. He also asked that four people skilled in the production of naval stores be sent with the Palatines to supervise and direct their work. Tents were also needed to shelter the refugees until permanent housing was constructed.[56]

Hunter suggested to the board that the Palatines work as indentured servants to the crown until they paid back the money the government spent for their maintenance and settlement. To ensure the Palatines fulfilled their part of the bargain, Hunter urged they be asked to sign contracts, as did other indentured servants. The board agreed, and the queen approved Hunter's proposal. By the terms of the contract, the Palatines acknowledged they had been "subsisted, maintained and supported" in England and would be transported to New York and maintained there at government expense. They agreed they would produce sufficient naval stores to repay these expenses. When the money was repaid, Governor-General Hunter was to give each person forty acres of land, free from taxes and quit rents for seven years. The Palatines further promised to settle where they were directed in New York.[57]

With this document, the official planning for the Palatine emigration was concluded. In December, 2,814 Palatines were loaded on board 10 ships. The government expected that they would sail with Hunter for America before the end of the month. Their departure was delayed, however, until Hunter arranged financing for the expedition. He did this by establishing a line of credit with the treasury for £8,000 sterling.[58]

The Palatine migration was a planned effort to provide the naval stores which Great Britain bought from the Baltic at considerable expense. In addition to being expensive, the Baltic supply was often cut off during wartime, just when most needed by the navy. In the past, colonial emigration had been haphazard, the establishment of profitable or necessary exports almost a matter of chance and circumstance. There were, of course, some small groups, such as the fifty-two Palatines who accompanied Lovelace to New York, which had been transported for a specified purpose. The 1710 migration was the first time that an entire community of people, indeed the largest single civilian migration to America in colonial history, were deliberately transplanted to provide commodities urgently needed in Great Britain.[59]

In addition to preparing the Palatine migration during the winter of 1709–1710, Hunter also planned for the military security of New York and New Jersey, both threatened by the French in Canada. Hunter believed in direct action and recommended to the ministry that the British attack Canada which was not very highly prized by the French. Nor did

Hunter think France would "be at a very considerable charge to relieve
Canada" if the British attacked. While a prisoner of war in France, Hunter
had "heard some of good sense and Interest at that [French] Court Say that
Canada was no otherways worth their Care then it was a Thorn in our Side."
Canada cost France fifty thousand livres a year to maintain and brought in
nothing in return. The colonel believed a strong land attack launched from
New York, "under the Conduct of one officer of known zeal[,] courage and
Experience, of which her Matie has not a few [himself, of course], might
meet with a prosperous Issue."[60]

Military concerns were paramount in Hunter's thoughts as he prepared to leave for New York. In addition to commanding the New York
garrison, Hunter was also commissioned as captain of one of the four
independent companies there. In a memorial to Sunderland, Hunter
suggested that the size of the four hundred-man garrison be increased.
Hunter proposed drafting an additional two hundred men to form two new
companies. He further requested additional arms and ammunition.[61]

The "Wonder Fleet"

Hunter's military preparations were completed by February of 1710, when
the admiralty advised Hunter that the New York bound fleet was ready to
leave. After a farewell visit to the queen, Hunter travelled from London to
Gosport. The departure of the fleet was delayed for several weeks, however, by bad weather. Hunter was still at Spitshead on March 17, 1710,
when the Sacheverell trial was held in London.[62]

On November 5, 1709, the minister, Dr. Henry Sacheverell,
preached the Guy Fawkes Day sermon before the mayor and aldermen of
London. In this sermon, Sacheverell denied the lawfulness of resistance, a
statement which shook the foundations of Whig philosophy and seemed to
undermine the revolutionary settlement of 1689. Sunderland, supported
by Godolphin and Marlborough, decided to press for Sacheverell's im-
peachment, and the minister was brought to trial. The persecuted priest
became popular with London mobs as an antiwar and anti-Whig symbol.
Despite the rioting in support of Sacheverell, he was condemned by the
House of Lords by a vote of sixty-nine to fifty-two. The margin was so
slight, however, that it was interpreted as a Tory victory. Sacheverell, who
was forbidden to preach for three years, was acclaimed as a national hero.
This seemingly unimportant trial, when added to the discontent produced
by endless wars, heavy taxes, and the Palatine immigration, eventually
brought down the Whig ministry.[63]

The full impact of the weakening of the Whig ministry could not as yet be assessed as Hunter and the Palatines prepared to sail for New York. The ten ships and their convoy had been termed the "Wonder Fleet" by the emigrating Palatines. The Atlantic crossing, finally begun on April 10, 1710, was another step in their long and tedious journey, which for many had lasted more than a year. The Palatines were crowded into the holds of the transports, with as many as three hundred passengers on board each vessel. Hunter travelled on board the *Lowestaffe,* one of the two men-of-war which convoyed the fleet. The governor-general's accommodations were private and much more comfortable than those of the Palatines. His food, which he brought on board for his personal use, was infinitely more palatable than the salted meat given to the refugees. Nevertheless, Hunter shared something of the Palatines' trauma. Like them, the governor-general was leaving behind the European continent for the uncertain comforts of an uncivilized, uncultured, and distant wilderness. Like them, he was beginning a new life in a new land. Prospects were promising, however, both for the governor-general and the immigrants.[64]

"The Land of Canaan"

June 1710–June 1711

When ye come into the land of Canaan, this shall be the land that shall fall unto you for an inheritance, even the land of Canaan according to the borders thereof.

Numbers 34:2

...the tract intended for them [the Palatines] *is, in their minds, a Land of Canaan . . . .*

Jean Cast to Robert Hunter
March 27, 1711

*R*OBERT HUNTER and the Palatine refugees who sailed with his fleet to New York hoped to find in America the biblical land of Canaan. As governor-general of New York and New Jersey, Hunter expected to demonstrate his executive abilities and to make money. The Palatines, landless and penniless refugees, hoped to pick up the threads of their lives, tragically torn by Villar's armies, by obtaining land of their own in New York. As the fleet carrying the hopeful immigrants approached New York in June of 1710, governor-general and refugees looked at the late spring landscapes visible from the ships with a mixture of apprehension and anticipation.

The ships sailed through the Narrows to the Upper Bay and Manhattan Island. The city of New York, with a population of less than six thousand, was situated on a small hill at the very tip of Manhattan Island, where the East and Hudson rivers meet Upper New York Bay. In 1710, most of the city faced the East River rather than the Hudson, the former being the safer mooring and less exposed wharfage. A 1717 sketch of New York done by William Burgis and engraved on copper by I. Harris, illustrates a colonial metropolis, far removed from the country town of houses, fields, and orchards that had been preconquest New Amsterdam. A 1716 visitor, John Fontaine, described New York City as being "com-

View of New York 1717, by William Burgis, Section 1. Courtesy of The New-York Historical Society, New York City. This view was sketched from Brooklyn. The fort with its chapel, armory, and governor's house is visible across the East River at the tip of Manhattan Island. Beyond is the Hudson River and New Jersey.

pact, the houses for the most part built after the dutch manner, with the gable ends toward the street."[1]

The most prominent structure in the city was the fort, currently "Fort Anne," so-called for the queen whose authority it manifested. This substantial, square, bastioned complex stood near or on the site of present-day Battery Park. A similar fort, built by the Dutch in 1642 had been demolished by Governor-General Benjamin Fletcher in 1693, and the new fort was completed by 1696. The fort would have reminded Governor-General Hunter of the Cromwellian garrisons of Scotland. Its twenty-foot-high curtain walls contained the governor's house, a stone and brick chapel, a secretary's office, officers' quarters, enlisted men's barracks, and an armory which in 1697 contained "1500 excellent fire armes." The governor's study was "lined on one part with pistolls set in Rondellos after the manner of ye guard chamber at Whitehall or Windsor . . . ." From the fort there was "a most lovely prospect to ye water," but the fort's main entrance was on the north side. This gate opened onto the garrison's parade grounds from which the main thoroughfare, the Broad Way, ran to the north.[2]

The first transport of the Wonder Fleet arrived in New York on June 13, 1710. The next day, the *Lowestaffe* docked, and Robert Hunter was welcomed to the city by its mayor, Ebenezer Wilson. The garrison and militia of New York City, all under arms, formed a guard on both sides of the street from the landing to the fort with drums beating and hautboys playing, while the governor-general was escorted to the fort by the leading gentlemen of the city. The sound of drums and the sight of soldiers were to be as familiar to Hunter in New York as they had been while he was in Britain or Flanders. He and his family not only shared the fort with two of the four companies of Independent Fusiliers garrisoned in New York, but the governor never left the fort without a military escort, with "the droms beating a march, as often, as he goes out or coms in . . . ."[3]

When Hunter reached Fort Anne, he had the queen's commission read appointing him captain-general and governor-in-chief of New York. He then directed his commission be published, took the oath of office, and assumed the powers of government from Gerardus Beekman, president of the council. The seal of the province and the public records were then turned over to Hunter. A few days later, Hunter travelled to Perth Amboy in New Jersey where, with similar ceremonies, he assumed the goverment of that province.[4]

"If not supported at home I am undone"

Only seven of the ten Palatine transports had reached New York by June 16, 1710, when Hunter wrote to notify the Board of Trade of his arrival. The *Bercley Castle*, left at Portsmouth for repair, sailed later in the spring. The *Herbert* was also missing, but finally word was received that the vessel had gone aground on the eastern end of Long Island when caught in a storm. The terrified Palatines were all saved, but the tents and arms on board were damaged. The *Bercley Castle* arrived in New York in late July, more than a month after Hunter took command of the colony and of the Palatine experiment in social engineering.[5]

The Palatines were not permitted to set foot in New York City. The immigrants would have increased the city's population by more than a third and could not possibly have been sheltered in New York's 800 houses. Moreover, New York's mayor and the governor's council feared contagion from the sickly Palatines, 470 of whom had died during the voyage. Even before Hunter's arrival, the council ordered the surviving Palatines, who were "in a deplorable sickly condition," landed directly on Nutten (now Governor's) Island. Carpenters were dispatched to the island to fit up temporary houses and hospitals for the ailing people who were looked after by three of New York's physicians.[6]

After their debt to the queen for transportation, food, and clothing was paid, many of the migrants hoped to establish themselves as farmers and vintners on land of their own in the Schoharie Valley. The Palatines later claimed this tract had been promised to them by four Mohawks who visited London in April of 1710 with General Francis Nicholson and New York's Indian agent, Peter Schuyler. John Conrad Weiser was one of the Palatine immigrants. His son inaccurately recalled that "the Indian deputies who were in England at the time the german People were lying in tents on Blackheath had made a present to Queen Anne of this schochary that she might settle these People upon it." The migrating Palatines were already on board ship when the Iroquois arrived at Portsmouth on April 2nd and could not possibly have met.[7]

Hunter may himself have been the first to mention the possibility of settling in the Schoharie to the Palatines. This area was one of two possible sites suggested by the Board of Trade and was the first considered for the project by Hunter. The tract, about forty miles north of Albany, was fifty miles long and four miles wide. It had once belonged to Colonel Nicholas Bayard, who in 1696 "bought" it from six drunken Mohawks for thirty beaver skins. The grant to Bayard was confirmed by Governor-General Fletcher, who issued a patent to Bayard for this land. The tract reverted to the Mohawks, however, when Governor Bellomont annulled the Bayard patent with the 1699 Vacating Act. This act was passed by Bellomont for the specific purpose of vacating his predecessor's extravagant land grants. Both Hunter and the Board of Trade knew the land had reverted to the Indians, but the board assured the governor it could be obtained cheaply. Hunter, prompted by considerations of both personal profit and public patronage, wanted the land vested in the crown where its disposition, either to the Palatines or to other settlers, would be under his control. Land was scarce in New York. Hunter was aware that a part of his potential income would come from fees for approving land grants. Grateful land owners would also give their political support to the governor-general who approved their patents. Hunter, perhaps in an effort to bluff the Indians, ignored their title and ordered surveyors to the site in July. The Mohawks promptly reminded the surveyors that the land belonged to them and ordered them to leave. Hunter feigned surprise on hearing of the Indians' objections but indicated he would discuss the issue with them if they permitted the surveyors to work. The Mohawks reluctantly agreed.[8]

In early August, Hunter, accompanied by John Bridger, sailed up the Hudson River to Albany. Bridger, her Majesty's surveyor-general of the American colonies, had been put in charge of the naval stores project by the queen. Bridger went on to inspect the Schoharie Valley while Hunter remained in Albany to meet with the Mohawk sachems and with sachems from the rest of the Five Nations (the Onondaga, the Seneca, the Oneida, and the Cayuga), along with leaders of the River (Algonkian) Indians. When the Mohawks pursued the Schoharie land issue, Hunter made a pretence of investigating their claim. After the commissioners who handled Indian affairs in Albany confirmed their right of ownership, Hunter acknowledged the Mohawks' title. Hunter's ploy worked because the Iroquois needed English trade goods and the governor-general's goodwill, as much as the English needed their armed assistance against the French. The Mohawks decided to give the land to the queen as a present, despite opposition to this plan from within their ranks. Hunter accepted the land in the queen's name and gave the Mohawks a "suitable present" in return. After acquiring the land from the Mohawks, Hunter heard from Bridger that the Schoharie Valley was fertile farmland but had few pine trees. This, and the fact that the tract was at least twenty miles from a navigable river, led Hunter to reject the Schoharie for the naval stores project. Bridger now turned his investigation to sites near the Hudson River.[9]

With the conclusion of the Indian conference on August 20, 1710, Hunter returned to New York City to meet the first session of the thirteenth provincial assembly which he had summoned to meet on September 1st. While the assembly was in session, Hunter, with Bridger's advice, arranged to establish the Palatines on the Hudson River on two tracts, both heavily wooded with pine trees and near other large stands of pine. More than two thousand Palatines prepared to move once more. In late September, Hunter adjourned the New York assembly for ten days to supervise the movement of the Germans one hundred miles up the Hudson.[10]

Some of the Palatines settled on sixty-three hundred acres, part of a sixty-thousand-acre tract of crown land on the west side of the Hudson, south of present-day Catskill. This land was part of Fletcher's grant to Captain John Evans, which had also reverted to the crown with Bellomont's Vacating Act. In the spring of 1711, Hunter secured an additional eight hundred acres, to the north of Evans's tract, from Thomas Fullerton. Hunter also bought six thousand acres on the east side of the river, south of present-day Hudson, from Robert Livingston for £400 New York (£266 English). As the Palatines arrived at these sites, they were greeted by Livingston, who was awarded the Palatine victualling contract by Hunter.[11]

Robert Livingston, one of the wealthiest landowners and merchants in New York, had been brought to Hunter's attention by Livingston's son-in-law, Samuel Vetch. Vetch, professional soldier, colonial entrepreneur, and eventually the first governor of Nova Scotia, was an old army friend of Hunter's. Born in 1668, the Scot Vetch began his army career in 1688, as did Hunter. Vetch fought in Flanders for William III. In 1698, he was part of the Scots-backed colonization attempt at Darien. After Darien was abandoned in 1699, Vetch and other survivors sailed to New York to ask Bellomont for supplies and provisions to enable them to return to Scotland. Bellomont let them buy supplies on credit, but Vetch did not return to Scotland. Robert Livingston, Vetch's uncle by marriage, had extensive land and extensive influence in New York. Livingston also had a daughter, Margaret, who was unattractive, rich, and of marriageable age. Vetch married Margaret and embarked on a colonial career in New York and Massachusetts. When Hunter arrived in New York, it was natural that Vetch should introduce his friend to his father-in-law.[12]

Despite minor altercations, Hunter and Livingston remained closely allied during the nine years Hunter was in New York. Born to the family of a Presbyterian minister in Scotland in 1654, Livingston migrated to America after his father's death in 1673. He built his fortune on the Albany fur trade and a successful marriage to Alida Schuyler Van Rensselaer in 1679, which allied him with the most powerful families in New York. In 1686, Livingston was issued a patent by Governor-General

Thomas Dongan for twenty-six hundred acres, the lordship and manor of Livingston. No additional patents were granted to Livingston after 1686, but in 1710 he was able to sell six thousand acres to the crown. When Livingston Manor was surveyed on October 20, 1714, it was found to encompass more than 160,000 acres.[13]

Livingston was a strong political supporter of Hunter who, in turn, extended favors to his fellow Scot. One such favor was the potentially profitable Palatine victualling contract. Livingston Manor, equipped with grist mill, brew house, and bakery, was well suited for the purpose of preparing food for large numbers of people. Alida Livingston obtained the raw food and other provisions the Palatines needed from local farmers or New York City merchants. Payment to Livingston was to be approved by James DuPré, commissary of stores for the Palatines. The actual transfer of funds was to be made by George Clarke, secretary of the province and treasurer to the commissary of stores, from funds allocated by Parliament.[14]

The day-to-day supervision of the Palatine project was the responsibility of a staff appointed by Hunter. These supervisors included Robert Lurting, deputy commissary, and two assistants, Jean Cast and Andrew Bagge. There were also a physician, two surgeons, two overseers, and two clerks or schoolmasters. Hunter then employed military organization to form the Palatines into six companies. The governor-general commissioned six captains and six lieutenants from among the Palatines to head the companies. The system effectively opened lines of command from Hunter to the rank-and-file Palatines, but the Palatines now had an efficient network by which to formulate and state grievances.[15]

In September of 1710, Hunter found out that grievances both on his part and the Palatines were quite likely. That month word reached New York that on June 14, 1710, the very day Hunter landed in New York, Sunderland had been forced to resign his office as secretary of state. Sunderland's appointment to this office had been the symbol of the Junto Whigs' ascendancy. As the Tories returned to power, Harley, who had left his moderate Whiggism behind to become leader of the Tories, decided Sunderland's dismissal would be a fitting signal for the Whigs' expulsion. Sunderland's fall presaged the collapse of the Whig ministry which had sponsored the Palatine migration. Unknown to its participants in New York, the Palatine experiment, which could only succeed if assured of continuing financial support from the Junto Whig government, had been doomed to failure even before it began.[16]

Hunter's first tangible warning that the political unrest at home would lead to difficulties with the naval stores program came in a letter from London merchant, Micajah Perry. The merchant told Hunter he could not get money from the treasury to cover Hunter's Palatine bills. After receiving Perry's letter, Hunter quickly wrote home to the Board of Trade. As he pointed out, once the £8,000 line of credit was gone, he "must see poor people starve or subsist them upon what credit I can make here, which if not supported at home I am undone." Hunter needed more money to ensure the success of the program. The trees would not begin to yield any significant amounts of tar for two years, and the Palatines had to be supported during that time. To do this, Hunter told the board he needed an additional £15,000 a year. After two years, tar would be in full production, the Palatines could begin repaying their debt to the queen, and in the future would be self-supporting.[17]

"The more general interests of the country"

The Palatine affair was but one of Hunter's concerns during his first year in America. The governor-general had also to provide for the governance of his colonies, as well as to establish new enterprises in them. Hunter, well travelled, sophisticated, knowledgeable, and urbane, was well equipped to deal with the problems of the thirty thousand people he governed in the province of New York. By the standards of the time, New York, unlike most other English colonies was a hodge-podge of nationalities, religions, and economic interests.

The colony had first been settled by the Dutch but was captured in 1664 by Colonel Richard Nicolls for his patron, James, duke of York. At the time of the conquest, most residents were Dutch, but there were also many French, Germans, Swedes, Flemish, English, and Africans. The polyglot population worshiped in the Dutch Reformed Church as well as in those of the Presbyterian, Lutheran, Anglican, and Quaker. The economic interests of the province were almost as diverse as its religions: merchants, landowners, and fur traders controlled the three most lucrative spheres. National and economic differences corresponded with geography. Fur trading was centered in Albany and was the legal monopoly of the still Dutch-dominated city corporation. Large landowners, mostly English and Dutch, were located along the banks of the Hudson River, their vast estates worked by tenant farmers. Small independently owned farms were on Long Island, inhabited by New Englanders from Connecticut. The wealthy trading class of mercantile New York was mostly Dutch, but the city also contained a resentful plurality of English, French, German, and Swedish artisans, traders, and small merchants.[18]

The colony also had a degraded slave population of four thousand, almost half of whom were in New York City. In the country, slaves were used to work the fields. In the cities, slaves were used as house servants and in virtually all crafts and trades in which indentured servants were employed. Since the Dutch era, most affluent New Yorkers owned slaves, including the governors-general. Slaves were usually imported to New York from the West Indies, but a few came directly from Africa. Algonkian Indians had also been enslaved by the Dutch and the English until 1679, when Governor-General Edmond Andros prohibited the practice. There were, however, still Indian slaves on Long Island at the time of Hunter's tenure of office. Slavery was lifelong and inherited. Manumission aside, virtually the only hope of freedom for New York's slaves was escape to the Indians of the Five Nations, who welcomed slaves into their tribes.[19]

Slaves and Indians were only two of the problems Hunter faced in New York. He also found that the colony was rent by political discontent which had been rampant since the Dutch era. Before the 1664 conquest, the English on Long Island had been continually at odds with the restrictive Dutch government in New Amsterdam. These Long Islanders had expected the introduction of more liberal English political forms after the conquest. They were disappointed because Nicolls in 1665 proclaimed the Duke's Laws over Long Island and Westchester. There were no provisions in the laws for an assembly, nor were the communities permitted any control over taxes or the disbursement of provincial monies.[20]

Nicolls acquired control of the province by forming political alliances with the existing Dutch ruling class, many of whom were continued in office. Far from being the enemies of the English royal executive, Dutch city merchants allied with governors throughout the seventeenth century. Nicolls's successors continued to advance the interests of this still predominantly urban Dutch elite by extending to them monopoly privileges and profits of office, often at the expense of outlying districts. In 1670, for instance, the Assize Court, acting for city interests, regulated Long Island's commerce for the benefit of New York City. The orders issued by the court established grain prices for milling and bolting, for which New York City was given a monopoly. The orders also required that livestock be slaughtered in New York City by tax-paying butchers and imposed taxes on furs shipped to Europe by Albany traders. Furs exported, as well as all imported goods, had to be unloaded in New York City. There, taxes on exported furs and all imported goods were collected by the government and handling charges assessed by the city merchants. In return for these privileges, the urban oligarchs supported the governors in their efforts to administer the colony and to increase their own wealth.[21]

In the mid-1670s, the ruling oligarchs' ranks were invaded by the New York-based factors of London merchants. These factors resented Dutch mercantile control of the colony and resented even more the favor shown to this group by the governor-general, Sir Edmund Andros. In 1680, the English merchants brought so much pressure to bear on the duke of York, temporarily weakened by the 1679 Popish Plot, that he recalled the governor. Andros, who lost the governorship of New York, but not the duke's favor, was replaced by Thomas Dongan. Under Dongan, the English merchants quickly joined the oligarchs.[22]

Government in New York changed under Dongan. At the duke's orders, Dongan yielded somewhat to the colonists' demands. In 1683, a representative assembly was instituted which lasted just two years until the duke ascended the throne as James II in 1685. The assembly was then dissolved and the province lost its 1683 "Charter of Liberties." In 1688, King James established the Dominion of New England which incorporated all of New England, New Jersey, and New York under one centralized government based in Boston under the leadership of Sir Edmund Andros. Long Islanders, again excluded from the colony's government, agitated for a representative assembly in New York. Their cries of discontent were swelled by members of the voting population who remained shut out from the power and privileges enjoyed by the ruling elite. Some political outcasts, such as the German-born merchant Jacob Leisler, were often as wealthy and successful as the elite, but were nevertheless excluded from its ranks because they lacked the political connections or the social polish that would make them acceptable. Also excluded from power were yeomen and tenant farmers from Long Island and the Hudson River Valley, as well as craftsmen, artisans, and small merchants from New York City. These people, the "middling sort," constituted the bulk of the voting population in New York.[23]

In April of 1689, New York's malcontents were excited by news of the overthrow in England of James II and in Boston of his governor-general, Sir Edmund Andros. In June, the Long Island English farmers and the Dutch city artisans and merchants united as militiamen under the leadership of Jacob Leisler, who was also a militia captain. They forced the lieutenant-governor, Captain Francis Nicholson, to flee to England. Then, the rebels with Leisler at their head as governor, not only removed the oligarchs from office, but threw several of them into prison. Robert Livingston was one of Leisler's targets. Soon after seizing power, Leisler ordered Livingston's arrest. Livingston fled to Connecticut, but Leisler had all Livingston's goods, lands, and houses seized by the sheriff and then approved an assembly act to confiscate Livingston's estate.[24]

The Leislerians were triumphant against oligarchs such as Livingston only until William Blathwayt, Francis Nicholson, and Sir Edmund Andros lodged complaints against them with the new king. William III ordered the expulsion of Leisler and appointed Colonel Henry Sloughter as governor-general. Sloughter, who arrived in 1691, soon formed alliances with members of the old elite. The oligarchs began their revenge for the indignities they had suffered during Leisler's regime by having Leisler tried and executed as a traitor. Leisler's martyrdom perpetuated factionalism, bitterness, and hatred between his followers, the Leislerians, and their opponents, the Anti-Leislerians.[25]

Leisler's Rebellion had done little to forward the economic interests of its supporters, but one political concession was achieved when William III ordered Sloughter to establish a representative assembly. The oligarchs nonetheless remained in control of the colony's politics. Despite the vociferous protests of Long Island farmers and Albany fur traders, New York City retained its control over the export and import of merchandise on which the government continued to collect substantial taxes. The only economic concession made to rural interests was that the city lost its monopoly of bolting, baking, and transporting wheat, but this was not sufficient to soothe rural discontent.[26]

Strife continued to mount in the 1690s, even within the ranks of the oligarchs where merchants vied for dominance with the landed elite. This enmity escalated following the re-establishment of the assembly when two political parties became active in New York. These parties were roughly equivalent to the court and country factions of the English Civil War era. The first consisted of those members of the elite, usually merchants, but an increasing number of landowners of large holdings, who aligned with the governor-general to form the court party. The second group was made up of those oligarchs, whether merchants or landowners, temporarily excluded from the court party. These men usually ran for the assembly. Once elected, they used their assembly seats to protect their own interests and to weaken the influence of the court faction with the governor and the home government. The wealthiest members of both the court and the country factions were usually Anti-Leislerians. There remained a numerically superior, enfranchised, third group in New York composed of the middling sort who were usually, but not always, Leislerians.[27]

The affiliation of the governors-general with the Leislerians or the Anti-Leislerians followed Anglo-American party lines, that is, Tory and Whig. The Tory governors-general, Sloughter, Fletcher, and Cornbury, allied with the Anti-Leislerian merchants and landowners. Bellomont, the sole Whig governor before Hunter (Lovelace's five-month term excepted), cultivated the support of Leislerians and New Yorkers of the middling sort. Bellomont won the support of the latter by his attacks on the privileges and power of both wealthy landowners and merchants: he revoked land grants, repressed piracy, and restricted illegal trade. The result was the allegiance of a broad electoral base which gave Bellomont a relatively successful and popular administration. Bellomont's solution was also used by his fellow Whig, Robert Hunter. As Cadwallader Colden recalled:

> Sloughter, ye first governor [after Leisler's Rebellion], fell in with the landed men, and his administration was as inglorious as it was short. Col. Fletcher fell in with the merchants. He had a perpetual struggle all his time and was at last recalled in disgrace. The Earl of Bellomont employed the third sort, or the most numerous, and succeeded in all his devices. The Lord Cornbury turned to the landed men and the merchants, who led him into such measures that the Queen, his own cousin, was obliged to turn him out. After such examples, Brigadier Hunter followed ye Earl of Bellomont in joining with the more general interests of the country, and he went through a long administration with more honour and advantage to himself than all his predecessors put together.

In 1710, such honor for Hunter was in the future. When he took office, quick solutions were impossible because the colony remained rent by ethnic, religious, geographic, social, economic, and political divisions. Each of the factions, kept alive by the political favors of one or more of a half dozen successive governors, remained strong and determined.[28]

Factionalism had worsened during seven years of maladministration under Cornbury. This debt-ridden and morally bankrupt governorgeneral believed the colonists existed merely to be fleeced. His misappropriation of £1,500, slated by the assembly for the colony's defense, to build a "pleasure palace" on Nutten Island was a repeatedly recalled example of his peculation. When released from New York's debtors prison in 1709, Cornbury, now earl of Clarendon, sold off his household goods to pay his creditors. The money raised was insufficient, however, and Clarendon was still in New York when Hunter arrived because of a £200 debt to Captain Paston. Hunter, anxious to be rid of the embarrassment of Clarendon's presence, paid the debt. Clarendon finally sailed for England on July 31, 1710, after sending Hunter his "hearty thanks" for his financial assistance. He also sent Hunter promises of future help in London. The memories of Clarendon's avarice and corruption did not leave with him, however. By 1710, New York's politicians were wary of potentially greedy governors-general who were all tarred with Clarendon's dirty brush.[29]

The internal turmoil Hunter found in New York was compounded by the news of the fall of the Junto Whig ministry at home. Hunter realized the fall of the Junto might also bring his own recall and that of other prominent Whigs. Many changes had already occurred in England, where, on August 8, 1710, Sidney Godolphin was forced to resign his office as treasurer. Although this resignation disturbed Hunter, it delighted Jonathan Swift. Swift deeply resented Godolphin's failure to procure him a high church office. In addition, he was offended that Godolphin had treated him with disdain on a recent visit. Swift was so hurt at Godolphin's rudeness that he published a satirical poem, "The Virtues of Sid Hamet the Magician's Rod," in which Godolphin was scolded for casting his rod of office into the fireplace when ordered to return it by the queen.[30]

Swift's attack on Godolphin marked his conversion to the Tory cause. He soon was writing anti-Whig propaganda for Robert Harley and Henry St. John. Swift, of course, still hoping for promotion in the church, courted the Tory leaders for their support. Both Harley and St. John valued Swift's writing skills, but Swift would never achieve the bishopric he wanted because the queen hated him. "The royal prude," as Swift termed Queen Anne, had been deeply offended by Swift's *Tale of a Tub*, which she considered an irreligious work. Swift, as yet unaware of the depth of the queen's hostility, worked on for the Tory cause as editor of the party paper, the *Examiner*. Both within the context of the paper and in anonymously published pamphlets and poems, Swift turned his attack against his former patrons, the Whigs, proving the truth of Rochester's observation that *"Women* and *Men of Wit,* are dang'rous Tools, / And ever fatal to admiring Fools."[31]

Despite Swift's 1710 prediction that "every Whig in great office will, to a man, be infallibly put out," Hunter was not in any immediate danger of losing his post. It would take the ministry several months to think about purging colonial officeholders. The Tory ascendancy did, however, have an immediate effect on Hunter's administration because the lack of government backing in England weakened Hunter's bargaining position in the colony and permitted his provincial opponents to gain ground.[32]

"A very indifferent humour"

Hunter began to identify his New York opponents during the first session of the thirteenth provincial assembly, which began in September of 1710. The governor-general, obedient to his instructions, requested the merchant-dominated assembly to enact fundamental laws for the financial support and military security of the province. The assembly, whose members were heirs of the political upheavals of the past two decades, "met in a very indifferent humour." Despite their collective bad temper, the assembly was willing to consider military matters and passed an act for continuing the militia until November 1, 1711, as well as various acts to raise money. None of these money acts, however, were "sufficient for the support of Government." The assembly refused to consider further fund-raising bills at this session because Hunter insisted the queen's receiver-general disburse the province's funds. The representatives demanded that the money be given to the treasurer of the province, the only person they would trust with the disposition of funds. The assembly's demands for monetary control were rejected by the governor-general. The assembly retaliated by refusing to consider either a short- or long-term revenue for the province.[33]

After a ten-day recess, which permitted Hunter to supervise the Palatine movement up the Hudson in October, the assembly reconvened. One of their first actions was to "resolve that 2500 ounces of Plate should be levied for the Governor's necessary expences for one year." Hunter was at a loss as to what to make of this offer. He decided the amount, which was worth only a little more than half the salary of £1,200 set by the queen, was meant as a gift (or bribe). He informed the assembly he could not accept the money since he was prevented from doing so by his instructions. The assembly then claimed it could not pay either salary or establish a permanent revenue. The colony, they said, was sunk into debt because of the "misapplication of former Revenues" by Clarendon.[34]

In addition to stolen former revenues, the assembly was also irritated over the question of fees. On May 24, 1709, after the death of Lovelace, the assembly passed a bill to regulate and establish fees of officeholders. The act was repealed by the crown, which considered it an attack on the royal prerogative. Hunter was instructed to establish a schedule of fees with his council on his arrival. Hunter proceeded to do so only to find that the assembly was preparing another bill to establish fees. The governor won this skirmish with the assembly the next spring when he put a new table of fees into effect by executive ordinance.[35]

Hunter may have been able to establish fees for other crown employees, but he was less successful in convincing the assembly they should pay him the salary set by the queen. In 1708, Queen Anne had raised the yearly salary of the governor-general of New York from £600 sterling to £1,200 sterling. The assembly resented the fact that the queen had usurped their power to set the governor's salary and justified their resentment by pointing out that the queen could as easily establish a salary of £12,000 as £1,200. Hunter, of course, defended the queen's preroga-tive power to set "such salaries for Her Governors as she should think fit, out of the subsidies granted Her for the support of Her Government...." Hunter's defense infuriated the assembly, as did representative Lewis Morris's attempt to defend the governor-general's position and the royal prerogative. The assemblymen seized the money bill, and, as Hunter told the board, they "went on striking out some articles intirely, which had formerly been allowed for these purposes, and retrenching others to less than one half...." Despite the pleas of Morris and others "that what I said to them might be taken into consideration," the assembly refused to yield on the salary issue. Finally, Morris's defense of Hunter raised the ire of the house to such an extent that they charged Morris with "falsly and scandal-ously vilifying the honour of their house [and Morris] was expelled the same."[36]

Lewis Morris, of Welsh Quaker descent, was a good friend and political ally of Hunter. Morris, born in New York City in 1671, was the son of a Cromwellian captain. He was orphaned in New York at the age of one and raised by his uncle, Lewis Morris of Barbados, who moved to New Jersey in 1674 and died there in 1691. Lewis Morris inherited two thousand acres in New York's Westchester County and thirty-five hundred acres in New Jersey's Monmouth County. On December 21, 1709, Hunter had asked the Board of Trade to restore Morris as a New Jersey councillor, a post he had lost because of his enmity to Cornbury. Soon after his arrival, Hunter urged Morris to expand his political activities to New York. In 1710, Morris was elected representative from Westchester to the New York assembly. Morris also continued his political career on the New Jersey council.[37]

Hunter and Morris shared provincial backgrounds which placed them on the outskirts of English society. Both sought acceptance from the English ruling elite whose members traditionally had acquired their money from land. Both Morris and Hunter considered the profits from land as being more noble than those from trade. Both shared a dislike and mistrust of New York's merchants, who dominated the assembly. Hunter and Morris considered merchants to be self-serving boors, inimical to Augustan tastes in manners and morals and to the attitudes of the impe-rial, landed ruling class of which Hunter was so prominent an example. It was the merchant faction in the assembly which hindered the settlement of a revenue and engineered Morris's ejection. It was this faction whose influence Hunter and Morris were determined to reduce.

Merchant greed also caused New York long and unproductive assembly sessions, or so Hunter believed, because representatives were paid 6s per day while the assembly was in session. Such payment made long sessions profitable business. Representatives' salaries for the fall session of 1710 amounted to almost half the sum the assembly voted for all government expenses for the entire year. This fee had been established by an act of the New York assembly passed during the reign of William III. Hunter believed the bill had not been confirmed in England and asked the Board of Trade to urge its disallowance.[38]

Hunter also offered the board long- and short-term solutions for the colony's and his own insolvency. His long-term solution, unique at the time, was to impose direct parliamentary rule on New York. Hunter offered the home government two possible sources of revenue: one from a tax on trade; the other from a tax on land. Hunter urged that Parliament impose either "an Impost on all goods imported and exported into and from this Province," or establish a uniform quit rent of 2s 6d per hundred acres, which would also provide "a Fund sufficient for the Government here."[39]

Such a show of authority on the part of the home government was necessary, Hunter believed, otherwise the queen would have to "rest satisfyed to have her Governour and Council here made Cyphers, Her Authority in their persons trampled under foot, and matters of Government for the future managed by the caprice of an Assembly." Such parliamentary relief could not come too quickly for Hunter, who, since his arrival in New York was without a salary. Moreover, he had personally paid for "all the absolutely necessary parts of the support of Government" out of his own pocket. By way of temporary personal relief, Hunter suggested that his arrears of salary could be paid from the government share of a prize ship laden with cocoa brought into New York Port.[40]

The assembly was, for the moment, unintimidated at the prospect of parliamentary intervention. The representatives continued in session through the month of November. Hunter, thwarted by their hostile attitude, realized that much of the problem sprang from the political situation in England. The assembly members, aware as was Hunter of the changed ministry, were also aware that the governor's threats of official intervention would probably not be carried out. In an effort at reconciliation, and also to effect the naturalization of the Palatines, Hunter suggested that the assembly offer for his approval a naturalization bill, then on the table. Such a measure was much wanted by the various European-born settlers of New York. It was also in keeping with a similar Whig measure passed in England principally to naturalize the Palatines in that country. In New York or England, the rationale of the Whig rulers was the same. The bill would expand the electorate with people who would be personally grateful to the Whigs. They would then support their patrons at the polls. The New York oligarchs may have suspected that expanding the electorate for his own benefit was Hunter's purpose in proposing that the bill be passed, or they may simply have acted out of spite. In any event, they refused to consider the bill, "despite the fact that they themselves were to be the chief gainers by it." The assembly continued in session until November 25th, when Hunter, worn out by their perversity, prorogued them until the following spring.[41]

"A freedom of Debate"

The session of the New York assembly had dragged on much longer than Hunter anticipated. Consequently, he had delayed the session of the New Jersey assembly until January of 1711. Even before the New Jersey assembly convened, however, Hunter had indications that he would face opposition in that colony. There had been controversy over whether the assembly should meet in Perth Amboy in East New Jersey, or Burlington in West New Jersey. Hunter finally insisted on Burlington because Amboy did not have enough space to house the representatives. The source of contention over assembly sites lay in the preceding century. The territory was part of Richard Nicolls's conquest, but even before Nicolls arrived in New Netherlands in August of 1664, James, duke of York had given the land which would become New Jersey to John lord Berkeley and Sir George Carteret. Nicolls, before he heard of the duke's grant, issued several patents for land in Elizabeth and Monmouth counties. Nicolls's patents, preceeding Dutch patents, and Indian purchases were all annulled by the duke's deeds of lease and release made to Berkeley and Carteret. The original owners, however, refused to get proprietary patents from Berkeley and Carteret for the price of these patents were quit rents.[42]

Berkeley kept his share of New Jersey until March 18, 1674, when he sold out to two Quakers for £1,000. Carteret, who retained his share of New Jersey, agreed to physically divide the territory with the new proprietors. There followed two separate provinces, East and West Jersey, each with its own government and with capitals at Perth Amboy and Burlington, respectively. The Quakers in West Jersey quickly subdivided their province and sold land to Quakers, Anglicans, and Scots Presbyterians. By 1687, the principal land holder in West Jersey was the Anglican, Dr. Daniel Coxe of London, physician to King Charles and Queen Anne. In 1691, Coxe sold most of his interest to the West Jersey society, a land company, and conveyed the remainder of his holdings to his son, Daniel.[43]

After Carteret's death in 1680, East Jersey was sold to William Penn and eleven other Quakers who, in turn, sold out to other proprietors, many of whom were Scots. These new proprietors included the earl of Perth, James II's lord high chancellor for Scotland. After 1685, the influx of Scots began. Soon, English proprietors vied with Scots proprietors for political control of East Jersey.[44]

New Jersey continued as two separate provinces until 1702, when some East Jersey proprietors, led by Lewis Morris, petitioned the English government to appoint one royal governor for both sections. Their request followed the failure of the proprietors to maintain order as evidenced by a riot at Monmouth County Courthhouse in Middletown, where the authority of the court was challenged and a mob seized the justices, Morris among them. In 1703, Cornbury, already governor-general of New York, was named to command the now united province of New Jersey. There would in the future be one governor, one council, and one assembly for the two New Jersey districts, but rather than choose a single capital, the seat of government alternated between Perth Amboy and Burlington.[45]

At the time of the union of the two sections, there were three separate and distinct factions in each district. In East Jersey, there were the Scots proprietary party, the English proprietary party, and the Nicolls patentee party. In West Jersey, there were the Quakers, the Anglicans, and the West Jersey Society dominated by English and a few Scots proprietors. By 1710, when Hunter arrived, natural alliances among the colony's 22,500 people had stretched across district lines to form two new parties. The East Jersey Scots proprietors, the West Jersey Society, and the West Jersey Quakers united to become the Proprietary party. They were opposed by the East Jersey English proprietors and the Nicolls patentees, who allied with the West Jersey Anglicans to form the Anti-Proprietary party. Hunter was to find the assembly in New Jersey dominated by the Proprietary party, while the council was controlled by the Anti-Proprietary party. Cornbury had allied with the Anti-Proprietors. There was no question as to which party the Scot Hunter would favor. Certainly Hunter's alignment with the Proprietary party was expected by Clarendon's protégé, Anti-Proprietary leader, councilman Peter Sonmans. On November 1, 1710, at a meeting of the freeholders of Middlesex County held to elect two representatives for the general assembly, Sonmans was heard to "speak publickly amongst All the people In the time of the Election We will not go to North Britain for Justice...."[46]

North Britain came to them, however, when, in late December, Hunter set off on yet another trip, this time to Burlington. The trip was accomplished by ferry from New York to Brooklyn, across Brooklyn by horse to the ferryman, Hanse Hendrick's house, then by ferry to Staten Island, then on horseback across the island to Colonel Farnier's house, then by ferry to Amboy. Hunter crossed Amboy, "an agreeable little place,

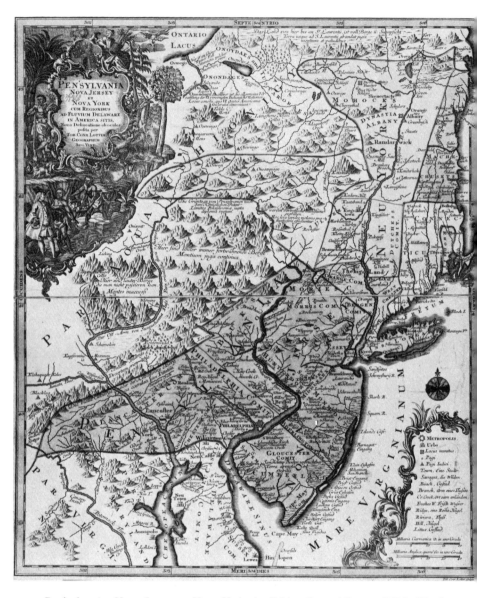

Pen'sylvania, Nova Jersey et Nova York, by Tobias Conrad Lotter, 1720, King's Topographical Collection, published by permission of the British Library. In the north of New York can be seen the territory of three of the five Iroquois nations. In western New Jersey is Hunterdon County, named for the governor-general.

surrounded on two sides by water," to the ferry across Raritan River to East New Jersey. Finally, the ride across the gently rolling Jersey terrain over the old Dutch Trail and Lower Path to Burlington took about a day and a half.[47]

Burlington faced the Delaware River. On its waterfront were "many fine *stately Brick-Houses* built, and a *commodious Dock* for *Vessels* to come in at...." The largest and most elegant house in Burlington was the lead-roofed "Great and Stately Palace of *John Tateham* Esq;..." The Society for the Propagation of the Gospel had heard of this house from its missionaries, George Keith and John Talbot. These men prompted the society to establish St. Mary's Church at Burlington in 1702, the first Anglican missionary church in the world. Talbot, perhaps ambitious for a colonial bishopric for himself, urged the society to purchase the Tateham house as a residence for an American bishop. The society instructed Hunter before he left England to look at the house with a view toward the society's purchase.[48]

The Tateham "Palace" was also the only structure in town grand enough for a governor-general's residence. So, early in November of 1710, John Barclay of Perth Amboy travelled to Burlington to have it prepared for Hunter's use. His Excellency was to have "the use of six Roomes 3 In the Lower Story & 3 above. All in pretty good repair besides a kitchen In the sellar & a Pantry with dressers and shelves which is under Lock & Key as Also a small sellar which will secure what Liquors may be putt In it...." Barclay also arranged for the delivery of wine, firewood, tables, chairs, and other necessities.[49]

Hunter convened the New Jersey assembly on January 2, 1711, shortly after he settled into the Tateham house. The legislature quickly approved measures to raise £500 for the governor's salary and to support the government for two years. Despite the ease with which the legislature approved financial support, Hunter found opposition in New Jersey from the council, "which had well nigh rendered all my endeavours for her Majesty's service there as fruitless as the humours of the Assembly have done [in New York]...." In 1709, before he left England, Hunter had requested that Thomas Gardner and Thomas Gordon be added to the council along with Lewis Morris. His purpose was to offset the influence of the pro-Clarendon, Anti-Proprietary councillors. Despite the presence of three new councillors, Hunter did not as yet have a proadministration majority.[50]

Hunter tried to control his antagonistic council with a firm hand, but this led to complaints by councillor Sonmans that the opposition was "seldome permitted a freedom of Debate but [were] interrupted by Mr

Morris[,] Gordon[,] Gardner[,] & many times by the Govr himself, who had . . . warmly declared first his own Opinion and by threatening expressions endeavour'd to Intimidate some . . . ." Sonmans, in a letter to Clarendon, further charged that Hunter treated the councillors "more like footmen & Slaves to the Assembly than a Councill."[51]

Hunter tolerated defiant pro-Clarendon councillors for the moment, but he was not as patient with those representatives who supported Clarendon. The Anti-Proprietary party had circulated a pro-Clarendon petition, which a few assemblymen had signed. The house, at Hunter's urging, quickly voted that any of its members who had signed the petition could not sit in the house until they had publicly apologized. Representatives Sandford, Mott, and Trotwell had signed, refused to apologize, and were promptly dismissed. Sandford was returned again by the voters in Bergen County, but the representatives refused to admit him. Hunter was free from assembly opposition.[52]

In retaliation for the pro-Clarendon petition, Proprietary party members prepared a representation of their own attacking the former governor-general. The statement, written by Lewis Morris and George Willocks, described the "violent and imprudent" administration of Clarendon. Morris and Willocks then charged that Clarendon's government was characterized by "Bribery, extortion and a contempt of laws, both humane and divine. . . ." About two hundred copies of the representation were printed with the assembly's approval. Hunter, however, would not permit them to be publicly circulated in New Jersey or England because Clarendon was a Tory and the Tories were in power.[53]

"No person . . . can starve in that country"

Hunter, a Whig, was right to be wary of alienating the Tory ministry in London. He had not as yet felt any diminution of support from the home government, despite the fall of prominent Whig leaders such as Sunderland, Godolphin, Somers, and Walpole. Hunter's retention of support in England may have been due to recognition of his innate ability by Tory politicians or to the fact that the severe problems he faced in New York and New Jersey made the post unattractive to Tory office seekers. It is more likely, however, that it was due to his having influential personal friends, such as the duke of Argyll and the earls of Stair, Mar, and Orkney. The intercession of these patrons kept Hunter in office, even though the Whigs and Marlborough were out of favor. Marlborough had many enemies, the duke of Argyll and the earl of Mar among them. Argyll aspired to

Marlborough's power, and Mar was resentful that he had been forced by Marlborough to back the Union of England and Scotland. Both Argyll and Mar were patrons of Hunter's. It is quite likely both had sufficient influence with Harley and the anti-Marlborough Tory ministry to prevent Hunter's recall.[54]

Help for Hunter might also have come from Jonathan Swift, who remained close to the center of Tory power. Hunter, made aware of Swift's assistance by the earl of Mar, told Addison that "your old Acquaintance the Tale of a Tub [Swift] who it seems had Power with the ruin'd ffaction was pleased to Interpose in my [Hunter's] favour. . . . "[55]

The influence of Hunter's friends kept him in office, but no one could help him with the Palatine case because it was too antagonistic to the Tory cause. The Tories were opposed to immigration and the parliamentary naturalization bill, both associated with the Whigs. Consequently, they opposed the Whig-sponsored, Palatine-staffed naval stores project in New York. The Board of Trade nonetheless kept the Palatine issue open. In January of 1711, the board invited James DuPré to report on the project. DuPré attended a meeting to pass along Hunter's request for £15,000 annually for two years. The board asked the earl of Clarendon for an opinion on the feasibility of the scheme as outlined by Hunter.[56]

Clarendon, after considering Hunter's proposal, gave a negative answer. The Tories were so strongly opposed to the Palatine immigration that it was already being whispered in London that all who supported the project were traitors to the queen. Clarendon was easily influenced by such political intrigues. He had deserted James II in 1688 at the urging of Princess Anne. Now, at the urging of Queen Anne's advisors, he was only too willing to desert Hunter.[57]

Clarendon informed the board that he considered Hunter's request for £15,000 a year unreasonable. He suggested stopping the project. The Palatines could be sent out to work, for "It is most certain that no person that has his Limbs, and will work can starve in that country. . . . " If Hunter continued to hand out government money to the Palatines, they "will be confirmed in that laziness they are already too prone to" and will expect to be supported forever. Clarendon was too much of a laughingstock in London to be taken seriously on most issues. His Palatine report, however, told the Tory ministry what it wanted to hear. Despite the board's favorable recommendation, neither in 1711 nor at any future date were there any additional funds allocated for the Palatines. Nor, except for two payments of £1,000 each, approved by the lord treasurer on August 7, 1711, would Hunter ever be reimbursed for the money he spent to subsist the Palatines for the next year and a half until he finally exhausted his credit.[58]

During the winter of 1711, Hunter, as yet unaware of Clarendon's report, continued to be optimistic about obtaining government support for the Palatine project. With the coming of spring came the time for the first step in the preparation of the pine trees. Bridger had returned to New England without being paid after the Palatines were settled in the autumn of 1710. He refused to return to New York without money. By the spring, Hunter had talked with other people knowledgeable in the production of naval stores. He now began to suspect that Bridger's methods were wrong. Therefore, when Bridger did not appear and Richard Sackett, a New York farmer, claimed some expertise in tar making, Hunter named him as the new supervisor.[59]

With Sackett in command, Hunter was sanguine about the project, at least until March of 1711 when he realized the Palatines were on the verge of rebellion. Discontent had started to ferment in the Palatine villages during the winter. In early March, Hunter sailed up the Hudson to Livingston Manor where he was the house guest of Robert and Alida Livingston. While there he visited the Palatines and explained that the nearness of the French and their Indians made the Schoharie land too dangerous for their settlement. In addition, he told them, it lacked pine trees. The Palatines seemed convinced, but when Hunter was about to return to New York, he heard they were again on the verge of mutiny. Hunter returned to the settlements and ordered each village to send deputies to him. Instead the Palatines came in a body. The governor-general ordered the contract each had signed in England read to them in high Dutch. He then demanded to know if they planned to keep to its terms. Temporarily subdued, the Palatines answered they would.[60]

The Palatines did have some just cause for complaint. Livingston liked making money. By the winter of 1710–1711, he knew the Palatine project was in danger because of lack of government backing. He therefore determined to squeeze from it every penny he could. He gave the Palatines meat that was on the verge of spoiling, in addition to skimping on the quantity and quality of food. Jean Cast told Hunter, "I never saw salted meat so poor nor packed with so much salt as this pork was. In truth, almost one eighth of it was salt."[61]

The roots of the Palatine revolt were more fundamental than poor provisions, however: the Palatines simply did not want to produce naval stores. They were vintners and farmers. They wanted to work at familiar occupations. Neither did they want to be indentured servants to the crown. Instead they wanted land of their own. Soon after Hunter left, the Palatines were again bewailing their fate to their overseers. Jean Cast, Hunter's supervisor on the site, reported they would "not listen to Tar-making."

They said, "we came to America to establish our families—to secure land for our children, on which they will be able to support themselves after we die; and that we cannot do here." The Schoharie, "the tract intended for them is, in their minds, a land of Canaan."[62]

"Noe hopes...for any remedy here"

Palatines and provincial legislatures made the spring of 1711 a particularly difficult time for Hunter. To compound his difficulties, Hunter heard from the Board of Trade that he could not collect his salary from the duties on the prize ship condemned in September of 1710. The board also informed Hunter that the New York assembly act setting the fees for attendance had indeed been confirmed in London. It was too soon to expect parliamentary action on his other proposals to alleviate the revenue situation in New York. Hunter, for the moment, had to seek salary and revenue from his province.[63]

Although he had little hope for relief from the New York legislature, Hunter opened the final session of the thirteenth assembly in April. In his opening address, the governor-general told the assembly that the control of government funds belonged to the receiver general, the appointed representative of the queen. This, he reminded the house, was "a Right which has never yet been disputed att Home, and Should I Consent to give it up a broad I should Render my Selfe unworthy not only of ye Trust Reposd in Me but of ye Society of my fellow Subjects by Incurring her [Majesty's] highest displeasure." An impasse resulted because the assembly refused to vote a revenue as long as Hunter would not yield on this issue. Without a revenue, Hunter continued to pay "all the necessary expence of the Government... particularly ffire and candle and repairs for all ye garrisons and noe hopes that I can think of for any rem[e]dy here...." The governor-general finally dissolved the assembly on April 20, 1711. He called for a new election, but had few illusions about the outcome: "I shall either have all the same members, or such others who will returne with greater fury."[64]

After the New York session ended, Hunter left almost immediately for New Jersey, where the assembly was sitting once more. By now, Hunter was determined to purge the New Jersey council, as he had the New Jersey assembly. All he needed was a reason for the removal of the councillors that would be acceptable to the Board of Trade. The council, led by Daniel Coxe, provided him with such a reason when it refused to consider bills passed by the assembly that Hunter wanted enacted. Among the rejected bills was one which would permit Quakers to serve on juries. This act was feared by Anti-Proprietary members who believed they would not get fair trials if juries were dominated by Quakers. The council's refusal of this and other legislation prompted Hunter to suspend opposition councillors. He wrote to the board to charge that Daniel Coxe, William Pinhorne, Peter Sonmans, and William Hall were fostering factionalism. Hunter recommended the removal of these men from the council or, he warned, "there are noe hopes of peace and quiet in that Province." He then suggested several candidates who would be acceptable to himself and the Proprietary party. Until Hunter received word from the board that his nominees were approved, he did not meet the New Jersey legislature except during emergencies.[65]

Hunter also sought to rid the New Jersey judiciary of troublesome Anti-Proprietary members. He told the Board of Trade that "Mr [Roger] Mompesson finding himself obnoxious to the generality of the people of that province desired to be excused serving any longer in the station of Chief Justice." In his place, Hunter appointed the former Presbyterian radical deported by order of James, duke of York, "Mr David Jamison, who acted formerly here [in New York] as Secretary in this Province with great applause, and is a Man of knowledge and Integrity." Mompesson, however, retained his post as chief justice of New York.[66]

The governor's intent was to ensure the loyalty of the government's servants by appointing men such as Jamison who were competent and devoted. To achieve that end, he effected a wholesale removal of Anti-Proprietary party sheriffs in New Jersey. This led to accusations by Sonmans that Hunter was packing political offices with his friends "Morris, Willocks, Johnstone, Gordon and that party." Nor did Hunter's purge of officers stop there. The governor-general also removed Maurice Birchfield from his profitable post as surveyor general of customs for the northern part of the English colonies in America. Birchfield's greed and shady dealings over the spoils of a condemned prize ship had offended Hunter, who was himself scrupulously honest. Birchfield was so upset with the "Treatment from Govr Hunter and his favourites that he finds himself obliged to return home by the next packet Boat and Represent things to the Board of Trade," the first of many provincials persecuted by Hunter who would go home with similar missions.[67]

"With drums beating"

As soon as Hunter had mopped up affairs in New Jersey, he found he was again needed at the Palatine settlements. The Palatines had resolved not to make pitch and tar. They wanted to go to the Schoharie immediately.

Hunter sent word to the commanding officer at Fort Albany to send sixty soldiers to meet him at Livingston Manor. When Hunter arrived at the manor, he talked to deputies sent by the Palatines. Suddenly three or four hundred Palatines appeared in front of Hunter. They claimed their intent was peaceful, but they had gathered because they feared Hunter would imprison their deputies, led by John Conrad Weiser. If this happened, the Palatines were determined to secure their release. Hunter made no move to restrain the deputies who rejoined their people. The governor-general was angry at the show of force, however. He ordered his soldiers to march after the Palatines to ensure they returned promptly to their homes.[68]

Hunter realized this was a potentially dangerous situation, but one which he knew how to handle. He had seen English troops subdue rebellious Covenanters in Scotland. He had himself disciplined un-cooperative Highlanders in Scotland and villagers in the Netherlands. A large military force was needed. Hunter sent to the Albany garrison for an additional seventy soldiers who arrived the next day. The combined force of 130 men were told to wait by the riverside until Hunter, by prearranged signal, ordered them to march "briskly to the [Livingstons'] house with drums beating." Hunter was no longer inclined to use reason and under-standing. When one of the Palatines (John Conrad Weiser) addressed him with "threatening language, the signal was made for the soldiers to march. The Governor with his own hands seized the fellow who had threatened him and some other gentlemen who were with him seized the rest." The appearance of the soldiers and the seizure of their leaders was enough to scare off most of the Palatines. They were not entirely subdued, however, because some of them defiantly fired "their pieces as they went off." The next day, Hunter sent his soldiers to disarm all the Palatines, just as Charles II had ordered his dragoons to disarm the Scots Covenanters. Hunter then revoked all Palatine military commissions, which deprived the leaders of their official powers.[69]

Hunter now put the Palatines under a stricter regime. Order was maintained by a detachment of soldiers sent from Fort Albany, who would be permanently quartered among the Palatines. The commanding officer of the detachment, Captain Henry Holland, also served on a commission whose members included Robert Livingston and Jean Cast. The commis-sion had the power to sit as a court to punish disobedience "by confine-ment or Corporal punishment, not Extending to life or mutilation, as in like cases is practiced by overseers over Servants. ... " The show of official force and the stricter regime had the desired effect. The Palatines were soon barking fifteen thousand trees a day.[70]

After quelling the Palatine uprising in late May, Hunter continued upriver to Albany to meet once more with the Iroquois and Algonkians.

Both nations had agreed to supply men to supplement a planned British land and sea expedition against Canada scheduled for that summer. Hunter met with the sachems to be sure the Indians were prepared to participate in the attack. Once this was accomplished, Hunter returned to New York City. On June 14, 1711, he concluded his first year as governor-general of New York and New Jersey by sailing down the Hudson River to his home in Fort Anne.

Hunter's first year in office had been characterized by battles with the New York and New Jersey legislatures. In addition, Hunter had also to contend with the constant cries of government creditors in New York, continually demanding payment for their just debts, which the governor-general met out of his own pocket. Hunter also had the responsibility of establishing a naval stores program and supporting its operatives — the more than two thousand Palatines who were becoming increasingly unwilling to make tar and pitch. Throughout the year, Hunter remained hopeful that the Tories would assume financial responsibility for the project. He was also aware, however, that if the Tories refused to pay the bills, he would have to decide when to stop throwing his own good money after bad. By June of 1711, Hunter had already incurred a debt of more than £4,000 over and above the £8,000 allocated by the treasury in 1709.[71]

The Palatines cared little for the governor-general's financial problems, except insofar as their awareness of the government's lack of support increased their sense of insecurity. The Palatines were penniless migrants, dependent on the government for food, clothing, lodging, and employment. By the spring of 1711, many had been in search of their land of Canaan for more than two years. The security and stability which they hoped to find in their promised land remained as elusive as it had been in 1709 when they were driven from their homes in the Palatinate.

The debt-ridden Hunter's promised land was equally elusive. Hunter had been plunged into the maelstrom of two contentious and faction-ridden colonies. The first year of Hunter's administration was a time of experimentation and testing by both governor-general and colonists. To govern effectively, Hunter had to form political alliances with key oligarchs in each colony. Hunter had taken several steps to do this during his first year. In time, these alliances would produce results, but there were no facile solutions for situations that had taken decades to develop. Hunter's problems, in June of 1711, were just beginning.

≈ 4 ≈

"Used Like a Dog"

June 1711—December 1712

The truth of the matter is this I am used like a dog after having done all that is in the power of Man to deserve a better treatment, so that I am now quite jaded.

Robert Hunter to Jonathan Swift
November 1, 1712

"A melancholly account"

OBERT HUNTER assumed the governor-generalship of New York and New Jersey with high expectations for political and financial success, but the first year of his governorship brought him a recalcitrant assembly in New York, a troublesome council in New Jersey, and a rapidly growing personal debt. Nor did conditions improve during his next eighteen months in office. Virtually the only relief to continued disappointments was provided by the arrival of his wife and children from England in the late summer of 1711. The rest was almost unrelieved frustration.

On June 14, 1711, a year to the day after he landed in America, Hunter was "a hundred miles up in Hudsons River," sailing from Albany to New York City. The governor's sloop was hailed by an upbound vessel carrying a messenger from Lieutenant General Francis Nicholson. The general, so his messenger told Hunter, had landed in Boston on June 8th with instructions to Hunter from Secretary Henry St. John relating to another attempt to conquer Canada. Lord Treasurer Robert Harley, now first earl of Oxford, was opposed to the expedition, but it had been approved by St. John while Oxford was recovering from an assassination attempt. Hunter found he had been ordered to convene a conference of colonial governors to prepare for the proposed invasion. Hunter had been put in charge of securing three months' provisions for the five-thousand-man invasion force, which would attack Montreal and Quebec by land and sea. Command of the British and New England forces, which would sail for Quebec from Boston on Admiral Hovenden Walker's fleet, was given to Hunter's friend General Jack Hill, Abigail Hill's brother. The two thousand colonial troops, which Hunter had been ordered to raise, were to proceed from Albany to Montreal under the command of Francis Nicholson.[1]

Hunter, with almost two decades of active military experience in the best regiments and under the best commanders in Europe, resented being assigned the provisioning, while command of the colonial force was given to Nicholson, "who if I be not mistaken," Hunter wrote to the earl of Stair, "had never seen troops in the field in his life...." But yet, Hunter continued, Nicholson "was sent over hither to command a land expedition here with powers inconsistent ... with those in my patent, whilst I was actually a Brigadr in ye Army and all the drudgery of Commissary of Provisions for the whole allotted to my share...."[2]

Hunter was bitterly disappointed in not being placed in command of the troops, but he fell to his onerous task as commissary with the care and determination that characterized all his public activities. When Hunter reached New York from Albany, he informed the council of the planned invasion, placed an embargo on all outgoing vessels, and instructed the bakers of New York to begin making bread for the expedition. He also ordered other foodstuffs from merchants and farmers in New York and pork from Virginia and Maryland. The governor-general then sailed for New London where, on June 21st, he opened a council of war composed of the governors of Massachusetts, Connecticut, Rhode Island, and New York. The governors ordered necessary supplies for the expedition and set quotas for the Albany army. New York was slated to provide 600 men, Connecticut 360, East Jersey 180, West Jersey 180, and Pennsylvania 240.[3]

The governors' council was still sitting in New London when, on June 24th, Admiral Walker's fleet anchored off Boston. The arrival of the fleet found the colonists unready to receive them because of the home government's poor planning and lack of foresight. The order to provision the troops had reached Hunter on June 14th, just nine days before the hungry men arrived at Boston. Obviously the soldiers, who had left England with only a three-month supply of provisions, could not re-embark for the expedition until food for the voyage had been secured. Some food, such as pork, was not available in New York and had to be ordered from Virginia and Maryland, a time-consuming task. In addition, Walker now began to fear "he would be oblidged to winter" in Canada and pressed Hunter to secure enough provisions to last the men until the coming spring. The longer it took to procure the food, the more fine summer weather was wasted, and the more hazardous would be the voyage to Quebec. Despite the short notice he had received, on June 25th Hunter was able to write to Jack Hill that some provisions were ready in New York and could be shipped to Boston as soon as he had a man-of-war to convoy the transports.[4]

After the governors' conference, Hunter returned to New York, where he convened an emergency session of the assembly on July 2nd. The assembly had been belligerent in its opposition to the English executive. They recognized, however, that French Canada threatened New York's security. They were also aware that this Anglo-American expedition was an unequalled chance to rid America of the French empire. The assemblymen quickly voted to raise £10,000 and to supply 600 men for the army. Hunter then arranged to have batteaux built to transport the colonial troops along the water route to Canada. Hunter next convened the New Jersey assembly, which he met on July 6th at Perth Amboy. The assembly voted to raise £5,000 and to supply 200 soldiers.[5]

By mid-July, New York's troops and 330 batteaux were almost ready. The Five Nations, who had promised to assist the English, were expected to arrive in Albany in late July with warriors from among their own tribes and from dependent tribes within their vast territory. The current alliance of the Iroquois with the English was of relatively short duration. In 1701, after decades of wavering between the French and the English, the Iroquois, situated to the north and west of New York's settlements, had declared their intention to maintain a policy of neutrality. In 1709, despite this settlement, the Iroquois agreed to assist the English against the French in Canada.[6]

Now that the Iroquois had allied with the English, they were anxious to eliminate the danger presented to them by the French and their Indian allies. They were, therefore, eager to join the expedition of 1711. They had been disappointed twice before by cancelled English expeditions. They therefore sent three of their sachems to Boston in July to see if there really was an English force preparing to sail and to count the men. The troops had already reboarded the transports by the time the Indians arrived, but Admiral Walker took the Indians on board and "entertained them... with Wine, Musick, and the Seamen dancing, and they appeared very much delighted therewith, and then entertained us in their Way of Dancing, which was a very different Manner to any thing ever seen in

Europe . . . ." Satisfied with the military preparations, the Indians pledged their support to Walker. They then left Boston to report on the military activities to their brethren at Albany.[7]

Soon after the fleet sailed from Boston on July 30, 1711, Nicholson and Hunter sailed up the Hudson River to Albany. They found that the colonial troops were assembled there, but that the Indians had not as yet appeared. Their absence alarmed Hunter, who needed the Indians to supplement colonial manpower. He also had to supervise their organization and see to their provisioning. Consequently, he had to remain in Albany until they arrived. The governor-general was particularly anxious to return to New York City because his wife and children were expected to arrive from England almost daily. Finally, after waiting two weeks, Hunter was delighted one morning to see 800 warriors, "a jolly crew . . . with all marks of a hearty disposition for the service," standing on a hill in front of his house. Six days later, after the Iroquois were armed, they followed the main body of colonial troops to the north. In all, more than 2,300 men marched toward Montreal to help capture Canada for Great Britain. But it was all in vain.[8]

At 10:30 on the night of August 22nd, ten vessels from Walker's fleet were wrecked on the Isle of Eggs in the St. Lawrence estuary. The foggy night was deadly to 705 men and 35 women on the sinking ships and terrified those on nearby ships: "All the night we heard nothing but ships fireing and showing lights as in the utmost distress," reported one observer. For the next two days, the *Leopard* man-of-war and some sloops "were employed in bringing off the scatter'd remains of six and twenty companys . . . which were so mangled and bruised on the rocks and naked withall, that they were not in any condition of service."[9]

Walker, an inept seaman, had long feared the treacherous St. Lawrence. More, he feared the bitter cold of a Canadian winter: he and his men would freeze or starve to death for want of provisions, he thought. Even if they survived the winter, they would be marooned in America, for Walker had been told the ice would crack the ships' hulls. All his fears seemed confirmed by the tragedy of August 22nd. On August 24th, Walker met with the captains of his men-of-war. After consulting with the pilots, the admiral and the captains reported they were "unanimously of the opinion that the River is wholly Impracticable by reason of the Ignorance of the Pylotts. . . . " The pilots did lack experience with the St. Lawrence, but Samuel Vetch, who accompanied the fleet as commander of the New England forces, was familiar with the river. He told Walker the disaster could not be attributed to "the difficulty of the navigation, but to the wrong course wee steered, which most unavoidably carry'd us upon the north shoare." Vetch urged that the expedition continue. He pointed out that twenty years earlier, Sir William Phips had navigated the river without any knowledgeable pilots and much later in the season. Walker decided to abandon the expedition. After a half-hearted attempt to capture Placentia, the fleet sailed for England on September 15th.[10]

Three days later, in New York City, Hunter received a letter from Jack Hill giving "a melancholly account of the disasters that have happend to us . . . " and reporting the decision to abandon the expedition. Hill's concern now was for the colonial forces who were marching toward Montreal, especially the Iroquois whom he realized would be disgusted with English ineptness. As the hapless Hill wrote Hunter, "What method you and Mr. Nicholson will find for informing the Indians and keeping them in the Queens interest I must leave it intirely to Your Judgment & Management."[11]

Although Hunter admitted the news "Struck me Senselesse," he nevertheless wrote immediately to Colonel Joseph Dudley, governor-general of Massachusetts, and to General Nicholson, who was camped near Wood Creek en route to Lake Champlain. He advised Nicholson to tell the Indians exactly what happened and "To send them home as soon as may be with as much Satisfaction as it is possible to contrive on soo sad an occasion." When the messenger finally overtook the hot-tempered Nicholson, he threw his wig on the ground in a raging fury, exclaiming, "Roguery! Treachery!" A few days later, the colonial troops retreated to Albany where the governor-general expected to join them shortly. Hunter informed Hill of the army's withdrawal and consoled him that "the worst of your Enemy's, If you have any[,] can never contrive to Lay any part of it [the failed expedition] at your Door. . . . " Hunter's assurances to his friend were in vain. English opinion linked Hill's name with Walker's in condemning "that ever memorable expedition to Quebec."[12]

The wreck of the fleet was not the end of the tragedy for its participants. When Walker's fleet arrived in England, the admiral and Hill went to London to explain their failure to a furious St. John. Jonathan Swift visited Hill on the morning of October 16, 1711, to hear the shocking news that "there is still more misfortune, for that ship [the *Edgar*] which was admiral of his [Walker's] fleet, is blown up in the Thames, by an accident and carelessness of some rogue, who was going, as they think, to steal some gunpowder: five hundred men are lost. . . . " The more than twelve hundred men killed in Old and New worlds as a direct result of the expedition were all from the best of Marlborough's regiments. The British army was sadly depleted by the loss. The expedition, a Tory attempt to discredit Marlborough, was an ill-planned and ill-timed venture to expand the empire by England's navy rather than by its army. Its net effect, however, was to weaken Britain's defense capabilities.[13]

Nor was this the end of the tragedy for Hunter, as he discovered in November, when a French fishing boat was sighted in New York Harbor. The *Feversham* man-of-war, acting as convoy for three transports carrying pork from Virginia and other provisions to the fleet in the St. Lawrence, had met disaster. When in New York in the summer, the *Feversham* could not sail to pick up the pork because its crew was depleted by sickness, death, and desertion. Much to Hunter's disgust, he could not impress seamen because of an assembly act which forbade this practice. On the advice of his council, however, he forcibly "borrowed" sailors from merchant ships embargoed in New York Harbor. The *Feversham*, fully manned, then left on its trip to Virginia and the St. Lawrence. On October 7th, en route to join the fleet, the *Feversham* was wrecked at night off Cape Breton. Only 2 officers and 48 sailors survived out of a crew of more than 150 men. In November, "the poor remains of H.M.S. the *Feversham's* crew," arrived in New York, another reminder to Hunter of the futility and tragedy of the 1711 expedition.[14]

The failed attack was in itself a formidable burden for all Britons, but Hunter had also to contend with the disillusioned Iroquois. Once back in Albany, the outraged sachems told Nicholson they were "now so ashamed that we must cover our Faces." Their disgust was so great that the possibility existed they might desert to the French. To prevent this disaster, Hunter hurried to Albany on October 6, 1711. The Five Nations feared reprisals from the French and their Indians in retaliation for their role in the expedition. They wanted Hunter to protect them. They also wanted the queen to have Anglican chapels constructed in their territory. The devout queen was glad to do so since the attachment of the Iroquois to the Church of England would be an additional cultural bond to hold them to British interests. Hunter promised on the queen's behalf that forts and chapels would be built. The queen sent a handsome present of communion silver for the chapel while the Society for the Propagation of the Gospel promised to send missionaries. Hunter ordered the construction of two forts at the Onondaga and Mohawk "castles" to protect them from the French. The English treasury would pick up the bill (£1,000) for the forts. Hunter also promised the Iroquois he would increase the number of soldiers stationed on the frontier in newly constructed forts. He accomplished this by retaining 150 of the Palatines raised for the colonial army in the regular companies to bring them up to strength.[15]

"Ye most selfish man alive"

The promised protection of the soldiers temporarily mollified the Iroquois, and so Hunter and Nicholson left Albany. Nicholson had observed the Palatine settlements during his New York sojourn and had criticized Hunter's management of the naval stores program to Robert Livingston. According to Jean Cast, who reported the conversation to Hunter, Livingston asked Nicholson to report on Hunter's mismanagement to English authorities. The governor-general immediately wrote to Nicholson, who was in Boston waiting transportation for England. Livingston, Hunter said, was "ye most selfish man alive but I cold never had believed that a man who lay under so many obligations to me as he dos would take it into his head to make any Representations to my prejudice without acquainting me at least, neither can I be perswaded that after ye manner wee have Liv'd togeather and ye mutual Confidence betweene us you would engage yor Selfe in anything of that nature upon ye Suggestions of such a man." Livingston, when personally upbraided by Hunter for his conduct, persuaded the governor that "Cast has misunderstood us." The governor-general believed him and let the matter drop.[16]

As for Nicholson, he and Hunter had been friendly, but something happened to change Nicholson's attitude toward Hunter between the time they parted company in Albany and the time Nicholson sailed for England in the winter of 1711–1712. While in Boston, Nicholson was visited by William Vesey, rector of New York's Trinity Church, an enemy of Hunter's and a supporter and correspondent of the earl of Clarendon. Most likely, Vesey, acting for Claredon, convinced Nicholson that Hunter was a danger to the Church of England. This religiopolitical appeal to Nicholson's Tory sympathies, just as he was going home to an England whose government was Tory, made Nicholson change his attitude toward Hunter. Nicholson urged Vesey to circulate a petition against Hunter in New York, charging that the governor-general was an enemy of the church. After the signatures were obtained, it would be sent home to England.[17]

Despite Nicholson's criticism and Clarendon's opposition, which together insured that the Palatine project would be neglected by the Tory government, it seemed to be proceeding well in September of 1711. Hunter had overcome the persistent discontent of the Palatines and one hundred thousand trees had been prepared. Hunter continued to pay the Palatines' expenses through the winter and spring of 1712. By the summer, however, he realized his credit was virtually exhausted. His first economy was to restrict beer only to those Palatines who actually worked, not to their dependents. Finally, Hunter received word from the earl of Mar "that none of my bills would be paid and then I stopt short tho' too late." On September 6, 1712, Hunter notified Cast the experiment was over, because "I have at length exhausted all the money & credit I was master of for the support of the Palatines and have, thereby, I assure you, embarrassed myself with difficulties which I know not how to surmount. . . . " Hunter instructed Cast to have the Palatines seek employment in New York or New Jersey, but they were not to settle in the Schoharie. They were to inform their supervisors of their whereabouts so they could be recalled when Hunter received government approval to continue with the project.[18]

Some Palatines sought jobs in New York City or Hackensack, some became Livingston's tenants, and "some hundred of them" in March of 1713 followed John Conrad Weiser to the Schoharie. Hunter was bitter at what he considered the ingratitude of those Palatines who left the settlements for the Schoharie. He promised "all the grants of land in my power" to those Palatines who followed his instructions, but also warned the defiant that he could "only pray God to turn away the Vengeance that menaces them and which they have richly deserved." Hunter's position was understandable, but so was that of those Palatines who could not find employment. The people, particularly the elderly, were starving to death. According to missionary John Haegar, they had to "boil grass and ye children eat the leaves of the trees. . . I have seen old men and women crie that it should have almost moved a stone. . . . "[19]

Hunter had incurred a debt to London merchants of more than £21,000 for the project. He had so overextended his finances that in 1712 he was in fear he would be jailed for debt when his governor-generalship ended: "A prisoner for life." Neither had Livingston made the profit he expected from the victualling contract. The Palatines, as might be expected, blamed both Hunter and Livingston for their misfortune, but they were wrong to do so. The fault lay with the Tory ministry in England, who, in 1712, in a final repudiation of Whig policy and the Palatine immigration, repealed the Naturalization Act.[20]

The Tories may have opposed immigration, but they were in favor of rewarding competent army officers, with the exception of the greatest soldier of all, the duke of Marlborough. The duke was hated by the queen and Oxford. Swift, who shared their dislike, reported gleefully in January of 1712 that Marlborough had been turned out of all his offices. That same month, Hunter was promoted to brigadier general, a promotion which may have been secured through the intercession of the earls of Stair and Orkney and the duke of Argyll. (Both Orkney and Argyll were also promoted early in 1712.) Hunter well realized the perils involved with colonial governorships and how quickly he could lose his post. Well aware of that, he repeatedly begged Stair to "pray take care of my rank in the army for there's my refuge at last...." " Hunter believed such a promotion was justified because like all royal governors he was actively involved in military concerns. In June of 1712, still unaware of his promotion, Hunter complained to Stair that he had "Seen Lists of Genll Officers and my name left out amongst the Brigrs, It is a piece of Justice you know was always promis'd me [by Marlborough?] and I may Expect for I have harder military Labours [here in America] then whilst I campaign'd it in Flanders [and] I have Serv'd Since the Revolution without Interruption...." "[21]

In addition to rank, Hunter was also concerned with his status and power: Hunter wanted a regiment of his own. This desire partially motivated his request to southern Secretary of State Dartmouth for more soldiers in New York's garrison. Hunter wanted either the addition of two more independent companies or an increase in his present establishment so they could be formed into a regiment. He disclaimed any personal interest in how the matter was handled, but admitted that for "disciplin['s] sake and Order I wish they may be Regimented. The Governour being Collo needs no pay, the Majors Pay is a trifle, all the other Staff we have already." The Board of Trade supported Hunter's suggestion, but no action was taken by the ministry. The pursuit of a regiment remained an elusive goal for Hunter.[22]

"Of dangerous consequence"

Whigs and Tories may have agreed on the necessity of maintaining an officer class, but there were few other points of agreement between them. Party strife prevailed in Anglo-American politics. In England, Whigs fought Tories in church and state while the ancient statist and antistatist court and country factions divided each party. The partisan picture in New York and New Jersey was reversed. There, although some of the more cosmopolitan colonial oligarchs were Whigs or Tories, the more antiquated court-country patterns were still dominant.[23]

The issues that divided court and country during Hunter's administration were well defined by the time the fourteenth assembly met on July 2, 1711. As Hunter predicted, "all the same members save one" were returned and all were as stubborn as ever. The major point of contention between governor and assembly in New York was the revenue. The split that divided the colony was between landowners and merchants. The assembly not only insisted on its sole right to frame money bills and control the disbursement of the province's funds, but also wanted to determine how the money was raised. Between 1691 and 1709, the major part of the provincial revenue (approximately 85 percent), was raised by commercial duties and excise taxes on imported goods. This placed the burden of taxation primarily on rich urban merchants who sold and used luxury items such as wines and liquors. Landowners, of course, supported this excise and opposed a land tax which would fall primarily on them. Hunter did not at first favor one form of taxation over another, but he soon allied with New York's landowning faction in supporting a tax on trade.[24]

Wealthy city merchants dominated the assembly. Their objections to the method of taxation favored by Hunter and the landowners made it impossible to establish a revenue. The merchants were led by New York County representatives, Jacobus Van Cortlandt and Stephen DeLancey. Some councilmen, such as merchant Adolph Philipse, also objected to excise taxes. Hunter, however, did not experience difficulties with the council because he controlled a majority of the members. So would he control the assembly. Gradually, a pro-Hunter court faction would dominate the assembly and usurp control from wealthy large urban merchants.[25]

This control could not be achieved quickly, however. In 1712, the governor-general was still pinched for funds because the assembly continued to refuse to vote a revenue. Defiance was so ingrained that the assembly opposed all attempts by the governor to raise funds, even when this money was raised at the expense of landowners. One such example was Hunter's effort to collect quit rents. The governor had to increase income from other sources to pay government expenses. These sources included quit rents, the profits of justice (fines and forfeitures), weighhouse duties, and admiralty court fines, confiscations, and prize shares which accounted for approximately 15 percent of the money needed for public expenses. By 1711, the revenue from quit rents had dropped to nothing. Hunter was aware there would be little chance of collecting any quit rents even through legal channels if the decisions were "left to a Jury." He, therefore, decided to establish a court of chancery to facilitate the collection of quit rents. Hunter himself would sit as the presiding judge and the inferior court personnel of two masters and two clerks were appointed by him and willing to do his bidding. The assembly opposed Hunter's attempt to collect either delinquent or current rents. Therefore, the legislators challenged the governor's right to erect such courts. They determined that such establishment "without their consent" was "against Law, without Precedent, and of dangerous consequence to the Liberty & Property of the subject. . . . " The Board of Trade backed Hunter's right to establish chancery courts with the advice and consent of his council. Hunter did so and secured from £300 to £500 a year from quit rents.[26]

In addition to raising money from quit rents as chancellor, Hunter, who was commissioned as a vice admiral, also insisted that his admiralty courts stringently enforce the Navigation Acts. Profits from fines and seizures would also increase his personal income. Admiralty court officials, appointed by the governor, received no salary except the fees from condemnations. These fees were shared with Hunter, who received one-third of the proceeds from condemned vessels and goods. The increased use of admiralty courts also offended legalist assemblymen and strengthened the convictions of Hunter's opponents. They believed the civil law admiralty court infringed on the jurisdiction of the colony's common law courts. Admiralty courts also revived sectional differences because residents of Long Island's Suffolk County and their representatives, speaker William Nicoll and Samuel Mulford, felt they had been signalled out for economic punishment by the admiralty. Eastern Long Islanders had long requested their own port, but when these requests were rejected, they persisted in illegal trading. Many were now prosecuted for Navigation Act offenses and suffered severe losses as ships and merchandise were confiscated by the admiralty court and shared by Vice Admiral Hunter.[27]

Another potential source of public income which Hunter sought to exploit at the expense of Long Islanders was the crown's right to a one-fourteenth share of the profits from whale oil and bone. Hunter based this claim on an act passed during Clarendon's administration. In 1711, Hunter sought further profit by insisting licenses be purchased for whale fishing as had been done during the administrations of Clarendon and Lovelace. These measures were opposed by Suffolk County's assemblymen, Nicoll and Mulford, because the whale fishing industry was centered near Easthampton.[28]

Another source of contention between the hungry governor-general and the aggressive assembly was the question of hiring a colonial agent. The agent's function was roughly equivalent to that of a modern-day lobbyist. The assembly passed a bill which would give their agency committee the exclusive right to appoint, instruct, and correspond with an agent. The governor-general and his council were to be completely excluded from any contact with the assembly's agent. Hunter and his council refused to give their assent to the measure. Hunter claimed that the intent of the assembly was that the queen would receive only that news from the colony which the assembly chose to pass along through the agent. This was, of course, quite impossible. The governor-general's official and unofficial correspondence with the Board of Trade and the secretary of state was given more weight by the home government than agents' reports. In addition, in this era of highly personalized politics, colonial agents were much more apt to take their orders from the governor-general than from a provincial legislative body.[29]

Agency, fishery, admiralty, chancery, all were both fiscal and prerogative issues. The assembly's attacks on the exercise of these executive authorities were, in the last analyses, not attacks on the governor-general, but on imperial government. Hunter insisted on this when he told the assembly that "however your Resentment has fallen upon the Governors, it is Government you dislike." Without denying that they opposed the imperial prerogative of the queen, the assembly reiterated that it was their "inherent right" to raise and dispose of the colony's money as they saw fit. They continued to insist that all monies be collected and disbursed by their own treasurer rather than by the crown-appointed receiver-general. The assembly also bitterly opposed the attempts of the governor's council to alter any of their money bills, even "tho' but of one word." They claimed their acceptance of amendments in the past was merely a condescension and could not be construed as a precedent. They refused to relax this view, despite the insistence of the Board of Trade that the council had every right to amend money bills.[30]

The assembly in fact insisted it was to act as "a House of Commons," a function clearly not intended by the crown. Worse, as Hunter warned Secretary St. John, should the New York council begin to act like the British House of Lords while the assembly was acting like a commons, the result would be a provincial parliament which would consider itself co-equal to "ye Great Council of ye realm," a self-sufficient legislative body with no need of the political guidance of the mother country. To accomplish this, it was first necessary for the assembly to attack the imperial sinews of the royal prerogative. Thus, New York, in Hunter's opinion, had "but one short step to make towards what I am unwilling to name."[31]

Hunter's remedy for the assembly's movement toward equality with Parliament and independence of the crown was to have the queen remind the provincials that "all such priviledges as they clayme as bodyes polliticke they hold of her speciall grace and noe longer than they shall use them for her interest and support of her government." That is, representative government in America was a privilege, not a right, conditioned on fiscal usefulness to the imperial government and subordination to the sovereign-in-parliament.[32]

The Board of Trade agreed with Hunter that the assembly had no "inherent Right" to act independently of the governor and council, particularly in the disposition of the colony's funds. The assembly, the board wrote Hunter, sits only "by virtue of a power in her Majesty's Commn to

you, without which they cou'd not be elected to serve in assembly. . . ."
The board also supported Hunter's desire to assert the imperial authority
of the crown-in-parliament in New York by requesting that the imperial
parliament tax the American province. Parliament, however, adjourned in
1711 before the revenue bill prepared by the Board of Trade could be
considered. The board informed Hunter they would again petition the
queen to command another such bill be presented for Parliament's consideration, but the bill was never passed.[33]

Despite the continued threat of parliamentary intervention, the
assembly repeatedly refused to pass a long-term revenue bill. The assembly did concede Hunter's personal income, however, on November 24,
1711, when the fourteenth assembly finally voted to give him 3,750
ounces of plate toward his current year's salary, which Hunter accepted
with alacrity. In June of 1712, Hunter was even happier because the
assembly voted him 8,025 ounces of plate to cover his back salary and the
costs of government since June of 1710. The assembly had first considered
and approved this bill in November of 1711, but had refused to accept the
council's amendments and let the measure drop. Hunter was the loser and
probably urged the council to accept the June bill without alteration. After
it was passed, Hunter, although grateful, immediately complained that the
money was barely enough to cover his back salary and did not begin to
cover such expenses as fire and candle for the garrisons, which he had met
out of his own pocket. Hunter finally despaired of receiving a long-term
revenue bill and adjourned the fourteenth assembly in December of
1712.[34]

"The late barbarous attempt"

In addition to warning the home government of incipient rebellion in the
aspirations of the New York assemblymen and acting to dismiss their New
Jersey council counterparts, Hunter had to deal with an actual uprising in
New York in the spring of 1712. New York's slave population was concentrated in New York City, where slaves constituted as much as one-third of
the urban population of approximately six thousand. The large number of
Negroes incited the fears of white New Yorkers. These fears were realized
during the night of April 6, 1712. Between midnight and one in the
morning, African-born slaves led a group of about twenty-four Negroes to
an orchard in the middle of New York. There they set fire to a building. As
whites came running to put out the blaze, they were attacked by the slaves.

Nine whites were killed and seven wounded before the "noise of the guns gave the allarm, and some escaping their shot soon published the cause of the fire...."[35]

As soon as Hunter realized he had to deal with an armed rebellion he "order'd a detachment from the fort under a proper officer to march against them, but the slaves made their retreat into the woods." The next day, Hunter called out the militia "of this town and of the county of west Chester to drive the island...." The men cordoned off the width of the island and then beat the woods. Running before the beaters, six slaves realized escape was impossible and "laid violent hands upon themselves." The others were rounded up and thrown in prison. Within two weeks of the uprising, seventy Negroes were jailed.[36]

On April 11, 1712, the first of the accused slaves was brought to trial at a Court of Quarter Sessions of the Peace convened in City Hall. Authorization for the trials came from an act passed October 30, 1708, during Clarendon's administration. If the accused were condemned, the death penalty was compulsory, but the form of execution was left to the discretion of the judges, who had vivid imaginations. The Court of Quarter Sessions sat until June 3rd, when remaining cases were turned over to the Supreme Court of New York. In both courts, the Negroes were prosecuted by attorney-general May Bickley, "a busy waspish man." Bickley called two black and seventy-six white witnesses to testify against the accused slaves. Many verdicts were passed on what seems to have been extremely weak evidence as Bickley, the jurors, and the judges responded to the hysteria that ran through the city.[37]

The condemned slaves were not just put to death, rather "the most exemplary punishment [was] inflicted that could be possibly thought of, and which only this act of assembly could Justify," as an object lesson for other slaves. The courts refused to risk Hunter's executive clemency, ordering most sentences carried out as soon as they were pronounced. Often the victims were rushed from the courthouse to the place of execution, where "some were burnt[,] other hanged, one broke on the wheele, and one hung a live in chains...." Before the terror ran its course, twenty-seven slaves were condemned, more than had been involved in the uprising, and of these, twenty were executed.[38]

As Hunter observed, New Yorkers' factionalism and pettiness extended even to their slaves. The affair soon "grew up to a party quarrel and the slave far'd just as the people stood affected to masters, more have been executed, in a cruel manner too, then were concern'd in the fact, and I'm afraid some who were no way privy to the conspiracy." One such slave was Mars, who was tried twice and each time reprieved by the Court of Quarter

Sessions. He was then tried again and finally condemned on the same evidence by the Supreme Court. Hunter claimed the slave was prosecuted because of a quarrel between attorney-general Bickley and the slave's owner, Mr. Regnier, "a gentleman of his own profession." Hunter believed the evidence against Mars "was very defective" and reprieved him and five other condemned slaves. He also suspended the sentence of a pregnant woman and on June 12th asked the Board of Trade to recommend that the reprieved slaves be pardoned. Hunter was thoroughly disgusted with Bickley's unethical prosecution. Those who offended Hunter usually did not retain their profitable posts. On June 13, 1712, Bickley resigned his office as recorder of the City of New York.[39]

Another effect of the riot was that New Yorkers turned on catechist Elias Neau and his school. Neau's students included Negroes and Indians, as well as white children. Neau, a merchant, had been appointed catechist in 1704 by the Society for the Propagation of the Gospel. Hunter was sympathetic to Neau's efforts and in January of 1711, published a broadside to encourage parents and owners to send both their children and their slaves to Neau for instruction. After the rebellion, owners were so convinced that the school had awakened discontent in their slaves that Neau was verbally abused on the streets. Neau's efforts were also opposed by Church of England priest William Vesey, minister of Trinity Church. Hunter ignored Vesey and along with Lady Hay, visiting dignitaries, and such prominent New Yorkers as Lewis Morris and Dr. John Johnston, often visited the school to encourage Neau in his efforts. Neau's role was to prepare students for conversion and baptism, but Vesey refused to admit qualified Negroes to membership in Trinity Church. Hunter, on one occasion at least, ordered the chaplain of Fort Anne, John Sharpe, to examine a female slave named June and to baptize her in the fort chapel. It was accordingly done "upon Easter Tuesday the Governour being present."[40]

Another sad result of the conspiracy was an act to suppress and punish any future uprisings. The fourteenth assembly passed this act in December of 1712. Its intent was to significantly reduce the number of freed slaves because their presence was thought to make captive slaves restless. The act demanded that owners who wanted to manumit slaves must post security of £200 to guarantee the slave's good behavior and then pay the slave an additional £20 a year for his maintenance. Hunter approved the act with reluctance and sent it to the Board of Trade, noting that even "tho' much mitigated in its severities by the Council's amendments, I am apt to believe your Lordships will still think [it] too severe, but after the late barbarous attempt of some of their slaves nothing less could please the people...." The Board of Trade refused to recommend the act. On March 15, 1716, they asked Hunter to have the act modified or they would recommend its disallowance.[41]

The board did, however, approve Hunter's request for executive clemency for the reprieved slaves and forwarded it to the queen. Clarendon, who had neither justice nor compassion, was moved by his hatred of Hunter to oppose the pardons. He was joined in his opposition by some New Yorkers, led by May Bickley, who circulated petitions against the governor's clemency in order "to confirm," as Hunter believed, "that I have neither credit nor favour at home...." They were unsuccessful in their horrid efforts. The slaves, after suffering horribly in New York's jail, were pardoned by the queen-in-council.[42]

"Fire and church"

It was relatively easy for Hunter to have the Tory government back him in a case such as that of the slaves in which the issue was an interpretation of law and in which imperial justice and mercy in racial matters could be contrasted to provincial injustice and racism. It was more difficult for Hunter to defend himself or secure assistance from England when he was exposed to vindictive but vague attacks on his character, his political acumen, and his religious convictions. Many of these attacks were promoted by the priest William Vesey, who even before Hunter's arrival, "grossly & openly abused me...." Vesey, Hunter charged, even meddled in politics and was "a constant Caballer with those who have obstructed all settlement [of] the Revenue in order to starve me out...."[43]

Vesey's meddling in New York's political affairs may have been inspired by his own insecurity. The priest had been born a Congregationalist in Braintree, Massachusetts. A convert to Anglicanism, the minister was devoted to the Tories and to the Anti-Leislerians because Governor-General Fletcher, leader of both, had appointed him rector of Trinity Church. Fletcher had also given Trinity the lease of the sixty-two-acre King's (later Queen's) Farm to the north of the city, the income of which was intended for the governor. Hunter in 1712 estimated this income at £300 a year. When the Whig Bellomont allegedly threatened the welfare of religion in New York (by invalidating Fletcher's lease of King's Farm), Vesey tried to have him recalled by circulating petitions in New York and sending malicious reports of the governor's activities back to England. Vesey's hatred was increased when his father was punished by Bellomont for Jacobitism and for slandering King William. The minister received encouragement for his attacks on Bellomont from London where, in 1700, the governor-general's Whig sponsors were out of office, replaced by a Tory ministry.[44]

Bellomont was not removed, but only because he died (in 1701) before he could be recalled. William Vesey's Toryism and high church affiliation led him next into a political alliance with the morally corrupt Clarendon, also a Tory and a high churchman. When Clarendon was recalled, he prompted Vesey to attack Hunter by convincing him that the Whig Hunter was a threat to the security of the church. After Hunter arrived, the minister revived the tactics he had used against Bellomont ten years earlier. He expected his efforts would be well received in London where there was once again a Tory ministry.[45]

Vesey found slights against himself or the Church of England everywhere and made them all causes for complaint against Hunter. One issue was the chapel in the fort, rebuilt by Fletcher for the use of his family and the garrison. The chapel had been neglected by both the Whig Bellomont and the Tory Clarendon. It was used as a storehouse, workhouse, even as a "Bear Garden," perhaps for the amusement of Clarendon. Hunter, soon after his arrival (and at the order of the queen), "repaired and beautifyed it, and caused divine service to be constantly performed in it by the Reverend Mr Sharpe, Chaplain to the fforces. ... " As Hunter explained to the society, the parish church, Trinity, built in 1697, was overcrowded. The soldiers from the garrison frequently had to stand during services and could not hear the sermon. Hunter also claimed he disliked marching the men to Trinity, thus leaving the fort undefended. To protest Hunter's diminution of his congregation, Vesey enlisted the aid of fellow ministers John Talbot of Burlington, New Jersey, and Jacob Henderson of Dover Hundred, Pennsylvania. Henderson, a "missionary with a new Light," promptly decided that Hunter's "repairing of the Chappel [was] a Schism. ... " Vesey then sent Hunter "some messages about that matter [the chapel], which for the reverence I bear his wholy [sic!] function, I choose not to repeat," Hunter told the society's secretary.[46]

Dissension between the governor and Vesey deepened with the Poyer incident, which drew other Anglican clergymen into the controversy. During Clarendon's administration, Presbyterians had installed their own minister in a parish in Jamaica, Long Island, and Clarendon had issued orders to have the minister removed. Even so, it was several years before the Presbyterian minister was ejected and an Anglican, the Reverend Urquhart, installed in his place. Following Urquhart's death, Thomas Poyer, on the recommendations of the society and the lord bishop of London, was inducted by Hunter as minister. In 1710, Poyer found that the Presbyterians had again placed their own minister, "one Mr. George Macnesh an Independent North Britain Preacher" (that is, a Scots Presbyterian), in the church and refused to admit him. Poyer complained to Hunter with a request to have the minister removed. Hunter might well have emulated Clarendon by issuing an order to remove the Presbyterian. Instead, on the advice of Chief Justice Roger Mompesson, he urged Poyer to bring suit against the congregation. Poyer was short of cash, so Hunter offered to pay the costs of the suit out of his own pocket. Hunter's motives as a former Presbyterian were suspect to Poyer, who believed Hunter to be one of the "pretended friends to the Established Church." Poyer, therefore, delayed bringing suit because he claimed he must wait for instructions from England. The real reason Poyer delayed was because he feared he would lose the case since Presbyterians would form a majority of his jurors. He realized he would be unable to appeal to the governor and council, who constituted the court of appeals, because the value of the parsonage house and the glebe was less than £50, the amount set by law for such an appeal. He also hoped Hunter would be replaced by a Tory governor, perhaps Clarendon or Nicholson, who would advance "the church" at the expense of the judicial process.[47]

By February of 1712, Hunter heard from friends in England and New York that both his would-be successors, Clarendon and Nicholson, were his declared enemies. Hunter was surprised that Clarendon, whom he had so recently help escape his creditors, should have turned on him. He was also at a loss to explain Nicholson's actions, "nothing having ever passed between us but civility & Friendship. . . ." At about the same time, Hunter also became aware that Vesey and other Anglican ministers were circulating petitions against him. The ministers, however, resolutely refused to show the petitions to Hunter or any of his friends. The governor-general wrote directly to the society to inform them of the petitions, which demanded he "answer to accusations from Persons I know not who, of crimes I know nothing of, before judges which I am not to know. . . ." Forced to guess at the contents of the petitions, Hunter surmised they concerned the Poyer incident and were prompted by those ministers who believed "all the Laws, human and divine are to be set aside when they come in competition with what they conceive to be the secular interest of the church."[48]

Nicholson tried to persuade Vesey to carry the signed petitions to London, there to "cry out fire & church." Vesey refused and Henderson went in his place. The petitions did not have the desired effect because, much to the ministers' annoyance, Hunter was not hurt by these intrigues. Instead, Hunter found a sympathetic audience in England, where the ecclesiastical hierarchy was overwhelmingly Whig and low church. While some Anglican ministers, predominantly high church and Tory, challenged the authority of the governor-general, the English hierarchy gave no countenance to such defiance. So Vesey discovered after Hunter complained of him to the bishop of London. Bishop Compton was sympathetic to his old friend, Hunter, and urged the governor "to bear with his [Vesey's] Infirmities whilst he endeavored to set him right. . . . " On being informed of the bishop's rebuke, Vesey wailed "that he was blamed by the Bishop in everything. . . . " Neither did the society, which was headed by the low church Whig, Thomas Tenison, archbishop of Canterbury, approve of Vesey's attack on the crown's prerogative power as represented in the governor-general. The society's secretary, John Chamberlayne, made a particular point of writing to Lewis Morris to congratulate him on "the noble stand you made last year [1710] in your General Assembly in Defence of the Governor, or rather of the Royal Prerogative. . . . "49

Hunter was, of course, not powerless against the ministers. Not only did he have such formidable friends in Great Britain as the bishop of London, he also had considerable power in New York and New Jersey. He did not hesitate to pursue his enemies because he was vindictive and vengeful. Hunter, emulating Bellomont, moved against Vesey by attacking his purse and that of Trinity Church. The yearly rent for Queen's Farm, sixty bushels of wheat, had been remitted by Fletcher and Clarendon, but not by Bellomont. While Hunter agreed to remit the rent for the farm, he then brought suit against Vesey and the church in his Court of Chancery for the unpaid back rents. Hunter knew the queen would halt such proceedings, but he also knew how long it was likely to take the government apparatus in Great Britain to function and calculated that withholding several years' income from Vesey would be ample reward.50

Hunter proposed a permanent solution for the indiscipline of the provincial clergy: a resident bishop of the Church of England. To this end, he advised the society in February of 1712 that he had contracted to purchase for £600 sterling the Tateham house in Burlington as a bishop's palace, subject to their approval. The society approved and on October 29, 1712, Hunter concluded the purchase. It remained to fill the house. Hunter hoped to lure his old friend, Jonathan Swift, to New Jersey. On November 1, 1712, Hunter wrote to Swift. He first apologized for having left two of Swift's letters unanswered for so long. He explained that "My unhappy Circumstances have so soured me that whatever I write must be vinegar and gall to a Man of Your mirth." Hunter went on to tell Swift that his condition in New York could be compared to that of "one of my most renowned predecessors," Sancho Panza, when he assumed the governorship of his island: *"Cuando pensé venir á este gobierno á comer caliente y á beber frio, y á recrear el cuerpo entre sábanas de holanda sobre colchones de pluma, he venido á hacer penitencia como si fuera ermitanno, y como no la hago de mi voluntad, pienso que al cabo al cabo me ha de illevar el diablo."* Hunter's expectations, like those of Sancho, had been cruelly dashed. "The truth of the matter," Hunter continued, "is this[,] I am used like a dog after having done all that is in the power of Man to deserve a better treatment, so that I am now quite jaded. . . . "

Hunter needed sympathy, but he also needed a friend nearby. After telling Swift of his troubles, he came to the point. He informed Swift he had "purchased a seat for a Bishop and by orders from the Society have given directions to prepare it for his reception. You once upon a day gave me hopes of seeing you there, I would be to me no small reliefe to have so good a friend to complain to, what it would be to you to hear me when you could not help me I know not." Hunter's desire to have the companionship of a sophisticated, intelligent, sensitive, and accomplished man such as Swift, and to obtain episcopal support for provincial government, was not to be realized. Swift badly wanted a bishopric and had the support of Oxford and St. John. The queen, however, still hated Swift. The only appointment his patrons were able to secure for Swift was that of dean of St. Patrick's in Dublin. By 1713, Swift realized he would never be approved even for a bishopric in North America. When the deanery was offered to him, he accepted it with great reluctance. The queen wanted nothing to do with Swift's advancement. She pointed out that the deanery was not a post whose disposition she controlled.[51]

Hunter, at any rate, had more immediate problems than Swift's advancement to contend with. Shortly before he wrote to Swift, a fire broke out in the Tateham house. Most of the house was saved, but it was badly in need of repair. The house, like almost everything else Hunter touched that year, had turned to ashes.[52]

Hunter also had to worry about the Tory ascendancy in London, which enabled the earl of Clarendon and Francis Nicholson to accelerate their attacks on him. Nicholson's loyalty to the Tories was rewarded on October 14, 1712, when he was commissioned to supervise the activities of English colonial governors. By the terms of his commission, the "governour of governours" was to evaluate civil and military affairs in North America. All governors were instructed to give Nicholson "access to and copies of papers required for these purposes. . . . " A few days later, Nicholson was also commissioned governor of Nova Scotia. In addition, the Society for the Propagation of the Gospel gave Nicholson a commission of "Spiritual Inspection" by which the general was to report on the conditions of the Anglican church and its ministers in America. (Hunter never forgave the society for their support of Nicholson and allowed his membership to drop.) The powers conveyed to the headstrong and unstable commander made Nicholson more unbalanced. After being named governor of governors, Nicholson's dedication to the Tories and to his assigned missions were to recognize no bounds of decency or former friendship, as Hunter would soon learn.[53]

By December of 1712, members of the country parties in both New York and New Jersey, and many high church Anglican colonial clergymen, wanted Hunter removed as governor-general. Their antagonism and backbiting not only made Hunter's life a misery but made it virtually impossible for him to conduct the business of government. On top of it all was the failure of the Palatine project and the overwhelming debt of £21,000 he had incurred. Well might Hunter complain that he had been "used like a dog." There were, however, compensations for Hunter's political and financial difficulties. For one, Hunter was strengthening his own power base in New York and New Jersey through the use of political patronage. At the same time, he was using his powers of nomination, prorogation, and dissolution to contain the influence of his country opposition. While Hunter was applying these remedies to political opposition in America, the Tory ministry in England was beginning to splinter. Even if they held on to office, the influence of the Tories was limited to the lifetime of the ailing queen. If the peaceful succession of the pro-Whig and pro-Marlborough George of Hanover were effected, the Whigs would come back into power. Hunter would then have the political influence at home to enforce his policies in New York and New Jersey.[54]

There were also financial compensations, despite the £21,000 debt. One such compensation was Hunter's army-related income. Not only did Hunter collect his own salary (half of £1 10s per day), but he also kept approximately 40 percent of the subsistence money voted by Parliament for New York's four independent companies (£7,093 3s 4d in 1713). Taking such profits was, of course, an accepted way for an army officer to supplement his income. Hunter also profitted from commissions and fees from licenses, land patents, the customs offices, and the naval offices of both New York and New Jersey. In addition, he received salaries of £500 a year from New Jersey, £1,200 a year from New York, and, until June 1, 1711, £500 a year from Virginia. Hunter also had a substantial income from his wife's estate at Croyland (£3,357 a year before taxes), and he expected to inherit the remainder of the Orby property in Lincolnshire, Surrey, and Jamaica.[55]

Despite the Palatine debt, Hunter was by no means a pauper, as evidenced by his continued purchases of land and property in New York and New Jersey during this period. One such purchase was a six-room house in Perth Amboy, situated on a knoll with a view of the harbor. The house served as a retreat for the Hunter family (which would eventually include two sons and three daughters). Watching his children grow must have been a pleasure and diversion for the governor-general who, in December of 1712, was forty-six years of age, still in good health, as active as a twenty-year old, and determined to triumph over "that eternall teazer," Francis Nicholson.

∽ 5 ∼

"Rage and Resentment"

January 1713–July 1716

... what I do is owing to perfect rage and resentment, and the mortifying sight of slavery, folly, and baseness about me, among which I am forced to live.

Jonathan Swift to Alexander Pope
June 1, 1728

"Nothin in life can ever make amends for it"

*I*T WOULD BE difficult to pinpoint which of Robert Hunter's enemies he found the most irritating. There was, first of all, Francis Nicholson, sent to America by the Tory ministry to spy on Hunter and to uncover reasons to dismiss the governor-general. There was the earl of Clarendon, vindictive and ungrateful, and, as a member of the queen's privy council, in a position to obstruct Hunter's policies. There were the colonial politicians who bitterly opposed Hunter in New York and New Jersey. And there were those provincial clergymen who were convinced that Hunter cared little for the Anglican church. Many of these people were ridiculous and unworthy opponents. Nevertheless, they hurt Hunter financially, damaged his reputation, and frustrated his ambitions. They, therefore, raised in him a "perfect rage and resentment." Hunter was intelligent enough to know how to fight them and human enough to seek revenge. But revenge was elusive as long as the Tories remained in power.

Hunter's enemies might have been successful in removing him from office but for the split in the Tory ranks which led eventually to their downfall. Divisions between the Tory leaders Harley (earl of Oxford) and St. John (viscount Bolingbroke) widened with the negotiations that led to

113

the 1713 Treaty of Utrecht. Internal dissension weakened the ministry's bargaining position with France. The result was that the peace that was finally achieved on March 31, 1713, was not particularly advantageous to Great Britain. In the Old World, most of the territory taken by Marlborough was returned to France. In the New World, Great Britain obtained only Nicholson's conquest of Nova Scotia, plus Newfoundland, and Cape Breton Island. One major trade concession was obtained by Great Britain: the South Sea Company was granted the Asiento contract which conferred to them the exclusive right to supply slaves for Central and South America for thirty years. The bulk of the commercial treaty, however, which provided a relatively free trade between Great Britain and France, was deemed outrageous by the Whigs and not the Whigs alone, for the commercial articles of the peace treaty were rejected by the House of Commons. The Whigs' opposition to the commercial treaty was strengthened by the "Whimsical" Tories who feared that Bolingbroke's pro-French attitude would threaten the Hanoverian succession. Oxford also feared Bolingbroke's Jacobitism and the distrust between the two men further splintered the Tory party. This left make-weight offices to the Whigs and preserved their colonial clients, including Robert Hunter.[1]

News of the peace arrived in New York in the summer of 1713, or at about the same time Francis Nicholson reached Boston. Nicholson had been sent as Bolingbroke's agent to prompt colonial Whig office holders into indiscreet acts that would justify their removal from office. By October of 1713, Nicholson began to badger Hunter about the condition of the regular army forces. He also told Hunter he wanted to attend the governor's next Iroquois conference. Hunter told Nicholson that the regiments were up to strength, but he was not quite sure when he would meet the Iroquois. By January of 1714, Samuel Vetch warned his father-in-law, Robert Livingston, "I doubt not but you know G:N[icholson] is no frnd to your Gover" and would make all the trouble he could, particularly in regard to the Palatines. Vetch two days later noted in another letter to Livingston that Nicholson "is a violent Enemy of Govr hunters" and would "Endeavor . . . to sift his affairs. . . . " Hunter found Nicholson more of a nuisance than a danger, but nevertheless he was an annoyance with which he had to deal.[2]

One of Nicholson's assignments was to dispose of the leftover uniforms from the 1711 Canadian expedition. Complaints over the quality of the uniforms began in England during the spring of 1711, even before the troops embarked for Boston. The coats, made either of "the best Gloucestershire cloath" or of "whole thick Kerseys," were unlined, and hence totally unsuited for North American-based soldiers. After the expedition, the coats were returned to England, where the home government wondered what to do with them. When Nicholson was assigned to investigate colonial troops, the answer seemed clear: the uniforms could be palmed off on the independent companies in New York. The redcoats travelled across the Atlantic a second time. When they, and Nicholson, arrived in Boston, the "governour of governours" began to pressure Hunter to buy them for his soldiers. The governor-general at first refused to purchase them, because he claimed the "coats are scurvy raggs without lining." Moreover, he had already purchased uniforms. Hunter feared that if he forced his soldiers to wear the unlined coats, they would desert or freeze to death during the first winter. When Nicholson complained of Hunter's adamancy to the home government, an official in the treasury department accused Hunter of disloyalty to the queen. Hunter recognized he was defeated "and tho' my cloathing was actually on ye spott, I sent for that to Boston, which Ile maintaine is ye worst and dearest that ever was given out to troops. . . ."3

No matter how groundless the charges of colonial opponents, such as Nicholson, Hunter realized they would find a Tory audience in Great Britain. He therefore consistently made use of his British friends to blunt the attacks of his enemies. When John Sharpe, minister of the fort's chapel, returned to England in the late winter of 1713, Hunter sent in his care a letter to Jonathan Swift. In a brief paragraph, Hunter managed to sum up his unhappy situation in New York:

Quonorough Quaneough Dvradadega Generoghqua aguegon tehitche nágarcé, Or least you should not have your Iróquoise dictionary at hand, Brother I honor you and all your tribe tho' that is to be taken cum grano salis for one of them [Vesey] has done me much harm. God reward him &c. For that and what besides you want to know that relates to me I referr you to the bearer Mr Sharp our Chaplain[,] a very worthy Ingenious conscientious Clergy man[.] I wrote to you sometime agoe by a merchant ship and therein gave you some hints of my sufferings which are not diminish'd since that time. In hopes of a better settlement I wish'd for your company[,] untill that comes I can contribute to nothing but your spleen. Here is the finest air to live upon in the Universe and if our trees and birds could speake and our assembly men be silent the finest conversation too . . . You must understand, according to the customs of our Countrey the Sachems are of the poorest of the people . . . In a word, and to be serious at last, I have spent these years of life in such torment and vexation that nothin in life can ever make amends for it.4

Sharpe asked Swift to use his influence "amongst some leading men in the Society for the propagation of the Gospel in Foreign Parts who have been much imposed on by the clamourous memorials of some indiscreet Missionaries abroad." Sharpe added that Hunter had "the Just Esteem of two thirds of the Clergy in his Governments and the greatest part of the Layety. . . . "[5]

The hopes of Hunter's clerical enemies for securing his removal increased on the night of February 9, 1714, when vandals broke into Trinity Church and defiled sacred vestments and prayer books with human excrement. Trinity's minister, William Vesey, was scandalized to find "That Vestment, so Reverenc'd by the Antient and Modern World, beskirted and Bedaub'd with what I must not name!" He believed that the outrage had been prompted by the governor-general, even though Hunter was in Burlington at the time the garments and books were desecrated. During Hunter's absence, Vesey demanded the council investigate the incident. Several witnesses were called, but none of the deponents had any personal knowledge of the act. Robert and Anne Drummond, however, swore that Vesey had "proposed to send word to my Lady Hay [Hunter's wife], that his Excellency our Governour had to doe with Lievt Riggs wife and that it might have occasioned my Lady to loose her child. . . ."[6]

The council made no progress in its investigation. Vesey asked that the governor be informed and that his attention be called to "some Busey mockers & scoffers of Religion, who Ridicule both sacred things & Orders by their profane Lampoons thereby vilifying the Ministers of Christ, & Exposing them & their Holy Function to Reproach & Contempt. . . . " This was a direct thrust at the governor-general and his circle, who prided themselves on their worldly wit. Neither did they hesitate to show the scorn they felt for rough, unpolished, and rather stupid provincials such as Vesey. Hunter, for instance, wrote that Vesey would be "a Notable Fellow, if he had but a Competent Doze of Brains; but These are so shallow that a Louse may suck 'em up without surfeiting, which renders that noble Portion of *Malice*, with which he is Liberally endow'd of little use to the Public."[7]

The council informed Hunter of the desecration and forwarded to him an account of the hearing. Hunter was furious, both with Vesey's accusations of adultery and with his references to "scoffers of Religion." Nevertheless, the governor-general had to respond. On March 3rd, almost a month after the crime, he offered a reward of £55 for information leading to the arrest and conviction of those guilty of the desecration. In the proclamation, Hunter maliciously called attention to the "avowed enemies of religion in general, or to the civil and religious constitution of England in particular, *or such as for filthy lucre, or worse purposes, may have in appearance conformed to, or complied with either, but by their unchristian and lewd conversation, and their disloyal and seditious conduct, sufficiently manifest their aversion to both* . . . . "[8]

Hunter's reference to the "enemies of religion" and of "the civil and religious constitution" was an attack on the high Tory colonial ministers and their followers. The duty of Anglican clerics was to uphold their church's injunctions to passive obedience and constituted authority. Rather than supporting the crown-appointed governor-general, the colonial clerics instead continually sought to undermine Hunter's authority. Hunter's reference to those who "for filthy Lucre" conformed to the Church of England was aimed at the convert, Vesey, born a Congregationalist. Vesey and his followers immediately recognized the affront. They wrote to tell General Nicholson of Hunter's latest outrageous attack. "The Proclamation," they claimed, "throws the guilt of this unpardonable outrage on the very persons who have complained of it, and who are sincerely in the interest of the Church, and reflects in such an unchristian manner on Mr. Vesey, by pretending that he conformed to the church for filthy lucre . . . ." Vesey's friends were also offended by Hunter's tardiness in issuing the proclamation and, however shallow their intellects, they also sensed an absence of indignation on the governor-general's part. Moreover, Hunter failed to personally commiserate with Vesey, "notwithstanding the unexampled affront to religion . . . ."[9]

"REVENUE and SLAVERY"

Tory churchmen and generals were bad enough, but Hunter had also to contend with the New York assembly, which would do nothing "effectually for support of her Majesty's Government. . . . " Hunter had dissolved the fourteenth assembly in March of 1713, when he ordered new elections held. In an effort to weaken the power of New York City merchants, Hunter created a new assembly seat in Dutchess County. He then tried to persuade Robert Livingston to run for that seat. Livingston refused because he feared his potential opponent, Leonard Lewis, had too strong a following. Livingston did, however, have plans to run for the assembly, but he sought a more secure route. In 1713, he petitioned the governor and council for a new patent for Livingston Manor which would bring with it an assembly seat. Livingston would have no competition for this seat. Indeed, he could expect every vote cast by the tenants of his manor. Hunter did not have any strong reason to oblige Livingston as far as the patent was concerned. The petition was temporarily tabled.[10]

Despite Livingston's abstention during the 1713 campaign, other men committed to Hunter did run. The governor attempted to persuade voters to support his candidates with the publication of an anonymous pamphlet, "To All Whom These Presents May Concern." In the pamphlet, Hunter defended the prerogative right of the governor-general to impose indirect taxes on trade. He also pilloried "A few Whimsical, Factious and Angry Men," who had influenced voters by leading them to believe that "REVENUE and SLAVERY are Synonimous Terms. . . . " Hunter's efforts were partially rewarded because six new members were returned by the voters, most of whom were Leislerians who supported the governor-general and his policies.[11]

The first session of the fifteenth assembly met in the spring of 1713. The assembly, which now had a Leislerian majority, showed signs of conciliation with the executive. They quickly resolved to impose a customs duty for the support of government, a blow to New York City merchants. The assembly was perhaps spurred by Hunter's threat "of a speedy dissolution" if they failed to act, as well as by his promise "of a general alteration in the Commissrs of peace and militia. . . . " Hunter's continued threat of parliamentary intervention may also have moved the assembly. At least the governor-general noted they feared "the promised remedy at home. . . . " The amount allowed by the assembly for government expenses was only £2,800, but they agreed to place it "in her Majesty's receiver's hands," instead of insisting, as they had in the past, that their own treasurer retain control of the funds. This concession on the part of the assembly was the first significant indication that they might prove amenable to imperialist reason. Hunter reported this £2,800 covered "barely the salary appointed me by her majesty, [but] not all I have expended firing and candle for the Garrisons and not one farthing for all my contingent expences of Government."[12]

The spirit of legislative concession was still active at the third session of the fifteenth assembly which began in the spring of 1714. The Leislerian representatives wanted to pay members of their party money owed them by the government, in some cases since 1687. An assembly committee, chaired by Hunter's friend Lewis Morris sat for two months to consider methods of paying the debts to the Leislerians and others of the colony's clamourous creditors. The assembly finally authorized payment of "sundry sums of money to several persons" from an issue of £27,680 in provincial bills of credit. This paper was to be financed by an impost on wine and European-made goods, tonnage duties, and an import duty on slaves. The raising of government revenue by excise duties was another major victory for Hunter, Morris, and the landowners and another blow to the predominantly Anti-Leislerian urban merchants whose goods were being taxed to pay off the debts of their political and economic enemies. Hunter made a concession to achieve the debt bill. The assembly reclaimed control of the largest share of the purse with its demand that the impost be collected and disbursed by its treasurer. Still, it allowed the less lucrative tonnage duties and duties on slaves to be collected and disbursed by Her Majesty's receiver-general, councillor Thomas Byerley.[13]

Hunter was included in the list of persons who were to be reimbursed by the province of New York. The governor-general claimed the amount owed to him in 1714 was £5,000, "which arrises from my arrears of Salary, rebuilding and repairing the Forts and Magazines and other public services." Hunter's salary had been brought up to date in 1713. He could only have been owed one year's salary, or £1,200 in 1714. Hunter, therefore, was given £4,297 for military maintenance and "other public services." It seems unlikely that a governor as hard-pressed for funds as Hunter had been from 1710 to 1714 would have incurred an additional debt of £4,000. The assembly act was probably a generous gift meant to appease the governor-general for past slights. Livingston was also delighted with the award to Hunter, because the governor still owed him £1,967 for Palatine-related expenses. Livingston promptly asked Hunter for the money, but neither Hunter nor any other claimants could collect until the bill had been approved by the queen-in-council. As Hunter wrote, "If these bills miscarry, I shall be in a more deplorable condition than the worst of my enemies could wish me."[14]

Some of Hunter's colonial enemies on the assembly bitterly opposed the 1714 debt act. Among them was Suffolk County representative Samuel Mulford, who was determined to obstruct "any support of Government" in New York. During the assembly session of 1714, Mulford, angry at Hunter's determination to collect admiralty fees, whale fees, and quit rents, charged that the governor controlled all branches of government in New York, including the assembly, appointed whomever he pleased to office, and decided what they would be paid. When Mulford later published his speech, Hunter decided Mulford had attacked his personal integrity and insisted the council and assembly expel him from his assembly seat. After they did so, Hunter justified his action to the Board of Trade by claiming Mulford was expelled not for delivering the speech, but for having it published. The governor-general then brought charges against Mulford, whom he termed "a mutineer," for "false scandalous and malicious libel unjustly reflecting on the Govr and Government of this Province (as that Assembly which expelled him termed it) with an intent to raise Sedition amongst the people. . . . " Mulford appeared in court four times with no decision being reached. Finally, at an assembly session in 1716, that body presented an address to Hunter on Mulford's behalf, asking the governor-general to forgive the representative. Hunter demanded that, as the price of pardon, Mulford admit his speech was "scandalous libel." Mulford refused and fled the province for London to avoid further prosecution. Once in London, he personally laid his complaints against Hunter before the Board of Trade and the privy council.[15]

The driving force in the New York assembly that was able to push the 1714 debt bill past Mulford's opposition was Lewis Morris. Hunter rewarded Morris for his efforts in March of 1715, when New York's chief justice, Roger Mompesson, died. Hunter immediately appointed Morris, "a sencible honest man," in Mompesson's place. The Board of Trade approved of Hunter's choice, in spite of merchant opposition to the appointment in London. They urged Secretary of State Stanhope to confirm such gubernatorial patronage. They believed that "if this method were observed it would be an encouragement to gentlemen to exert themselves for the publick good, and would strengthen the Governors in the execution of the trust reposed in them. . . . "[16]

By 1714, most New York politicians, with Morris's leadership, were showing signs of cooperation with the governor-general. Hunter had also found similar indications of compliance in New Jersey. The governor met the New Jersey assembly on December 7, 1713, after he learned his recommendations regarding council changes were approved by the queen. During this session, which was held in Burlington, thirty-eight bills were passed, including a bill long wanted by Hunter which would permit Quakers, "that People being by farr the most numerous and wealthy in the Western Division," to serve on juries. This bill was passed despite the opposition of Daniel Coxe, who, on being ousted from the council, ran for the assembly and was elected representative from Gloucester County "by those who are link't to him by land purchases. . . . " Coxe's opposition aside, a spirit of conciliation prevailed through this session. Before Hunter adjourned the assembly on March 17, 1714, they voted measures to pay the colony's debts and establish a revenue for two years. Hunter believed the failure of the legislature to settle a revenue for a longer period was due to rumors being circulated by Coxe that Hunter was to be replaced. On learning of Coxe's activities, Hunter ordered George Clarke to try to obtain copies of the seditious correspondence, "that I may trounce Coxe." Hunter was unable to obtain sufficient evidence to subdue Coxe during this session, but the incident strengthened his determination to suppress the Anti-Proprietary party.[17]

Despite the Tory dominance, which had seriously hampered Hunter's first few years in office, the governor-general, in the summer of 1714, had achieved provincial political victories in New York and New Jersey. Yet his recall by the Tory ministry in England was still a very real possibility. Nicholson waited in Boston, while Clarendon lobbied in London, each hoping that he had been named to replace Hunter. Many prominent Whigs had fallen at home, including Cadogan, who had been deprived of all his posts. Hunter, like Cadogan, had friends who were close to the ministry, but he well realized such friendships were not sufficient to keep him in office if Bolingbroke purged colonial office-holders.[18]

Hunter would have welcomed a recall. As he acknowledged in letters to the earls of Stair and Montrose, "I remaine here [in New York] loaded with many Thousands of pounds of publick debts all contracted by the Queens order and for her Service." Personal responsibilities added pressure to Hunter's precarious financial situation. As he told his correspondents, "my Family Increases in proportion that my means decrease." He feared he could not support his "family of bratts who are In Election to Starve with me." Hunter was also faced with "A nasty people" in New York, who were indifferent to their own welfare and ungrateful for Hunter's efforts to protect them. The governor triumphantly admitted, however, that despite these problems he still had "as much health and Mirth as Ever," as well as "the Constitution of a horse, that will not breake under all these pressures."[19]

"I am as able to carry a muskett as I was ten yeares ago"

Unbeknownst to Hunter, pressure from the home government eased in the summer of 1714, just after the queen demanded the resignation of the moderate Oxford as lord high treasurer. Oxford's resignation left Bolingbroke in command for the moment, but Bolingbroke never had a chance to alter the ministry, much less the provincial executive. On August 1, 1714, Queen Anne died. Moments before her death, the queen thwarted the extremism of the high Tory, Bolingbroke, by placing the treasurer's staff of office in the hands of the political moderate, Charles Talbot, duke of Shrewsbury, who thereupon became in effect the "prime minister." Because the queen had no living children, Parliament had passed an Act of Settlement in 1701, giving the crown to George of

Hanover on the queen's death. As soon as Anne died, Shrewsbury put into execution the Regency Act of 1706, which provided for a caretaker government by committee until the arrival of King George.

The king's dislike of the Tories and his indignation at the Peace of Utrecht were well known in England. By the time the monarch arrived in September of 1714, the Whigs were firmly in control. Bolingbroke, perhaps motivated by Marlborough's malicious suggestion he would be executed, ran away to join the Stuart heir, James Edward, in Paris. George I formed his cabinet from such Junto Whigs as Somers, Halifax, Orford, Stanhope, Walpole, and Townshend. Marlborough, who had been in self-imposed exile during the last few years of the queen's reign, was reinstated as captain general. The earl of Stair, perhaps Hunter's closest friend among the British aristocracy, was re-elected a representative peer for Scotland, named a member of the king's privy council, and was appointed minister plenipotentiary at Paris. Joseph Addison, another of Hunter's close friends, was appointed secretary to the lords justices.[20]

The welcome news of George's accession did not reach Hunter in New York until October 4, 1714. He immediately grasped the consequences the Whig ascendancy would have on the Anglo-American empire in general and on his administrations in New York and New Jersey in particular. Even more important, Hunter, who had been an active participant in the Glorious Revolution which substituted legislative selection for hereditary succession to the throne, saw a final vindication of his actions and principles. The accession of the Hanoverian was conclusive proof of the sovereignty of Parliament. It had selected a Protestant prince to rule Great Britain over the heads of more than fifty people with more direct hereditary claims to the throne.[21]

The jubilant Hunter was galvanized into action when news of George I's accession reached New York. He quickly wrote a letter to Stair, meant for public circulation, in which he detailed the resistance he had encountered in New York and the enormous debts he had incurred in subsisting the Palatines. He also asked Stair to remember him to their commander-in-chief, the duke of Marlborough, with the somewhat wistful hope that the duke "has not forgott me; I have beene his faithful servant in all stations of life, and you see I have ye honour to be his fellow sufferer. Pray assure him of my lasting gratitude and tell him, if you please, that I am as able to carry a muskett as I was ten yeares ago."[22]

Hunter needed support from his friends in the peerage if he was to retain his office in New York. To provide for the smooth transition of governmental authority, all royally appointed colonial officials were continued in office for six months after the death of the queen. After the six months, however, all officials, including governors-general, had to be recommissioned by the new sovereign. The ministry was preoccupied by internal problems immediately after the death of the queen. It was not until January 25, 1715, almost six months to the day from Queen Anne's demise, that Secretary of State Stanhope ordered the Board of Trade to prepare drafts for the commissions and instructions of Robert Hunter as governor-general of New York and New Jersey.[23]

Hunter's recommissioning was strenuously opposed in London by the father and brother of Daniel Coxe. The Coxes were aided and abetted by another ousted New Jersey councilman, Peter Sonmans, and the rector of New York's Trinity Church, William Vesey, who, without a word to another person, had run "away for England...." Sonmans and Vesey were in London to complain about Hunter to various governmental agencies. The Coxes lodged complaints with the now-predominantly Whig Board of Trade concerning Hunter's activities in New Jersey. The board informed Hunter of the Coxes' charges, but recommissioned the governor on June 17, 1715, even before Hunter's replies reached London.[24]

Hunter was outraged by the Coxes' activities and those of Clarendon, who opposed the 1714 debt bill. Clarendon objected to the bill because he claimed he was still owed money from his term as governor-general of New York. Yet he was not included in the list of persons drawn up by the assembly to whom payment would be made. As Hunter noted, "of all men, that Noble Lord ought to have been, most silent in this case," because it was to Clarendon's misappropriation of public funds "that we owe a great share of these publick debts" that plagued the province. In retaliation for Clarendon's latest thrust, Hunter delivered his coup de grace—he sent home the 1711 address written by Lewis Morris, passed by the New Jersey assembly, and suppressed by Hunter during the Tory administration, in which the assembly claimed that Clarendon had "treated her majesty's subjects here not as freemen who were to be governed by laws, but as slaves, of whose persons and estates he had the sole power of disposing." In addition to the New Jersey address, Hunter also sent the board a copy of an address prepared by the New York legislature in which that body denied Clarendon was owed money by the colony. The earl was unsuccessful in his protests against the revenue bill, which was approved by the king-in-council in the summer of 1715.[25]

Francis Nicholson found himself as ignored by the Whig government as was Clarendon. He went home in March of 1715 without having executed either of his two "Strange Commissions," one as governor of governors and the other of spiritual inspection. The nearest Nicholson ever came to Hunter and New York was Boston, where he waited in the expectation he would be named governor-general in Hunter's place. Having despaired of that after the queen's death, Nicholson sailed for England. Hunter had no fear of further interference from Nicholson for he knew that terrible-tempered Tory would not find favor with the Whig ministry: they "have no manner of occasion for madmen," Hunter smugly surmised.[26]

"This hitherto unsettled and ungovernable Province"

In the spring of 1715, with Nicholson gone and Whig support assured in England, Hunter converted a successful gubernatorial career to a triumphant one. On May 3, 1715, he convened the first session of the sixteenth assembly. To strengthen the legislative power of Hudson River Valley landowners against New York City merchants, Hunter created yet another assembly seat in Dutchess County. The Dutchess County representative elected in 1715 was one of six new members chosen that year, most of whom were sympathetic to Hunter. The driving force of the assembly was Chief Justice Lewis Morris, who, with Hunter's blessing and encouragement, maneuvered another and still more favorable financial settlement through the assembly by the skillful use of compromise. Hunter wanted to be reimbursed for his personal expenditures on government and, in addition, wanted a guaranteed support for government for an extended period of time. The assembly wanted a naturalization bill, a colonial agent, and control of the colony's money.[27]

Hunter granted the naturalization bill, but it was not a major concession. Hunter himself proposed that the assembly consider a similar bill in 1710. As a Whig, the governor-general was in favor of naturalizing Protestant foreigners. At that time, the assembly, in a particularly obstinate mood, had refused to consider the measure. The bill passed by the sixteenth assembly naturalized all persons of foreign birth who had held lands and were living in New York in 1683, thus confirming the land titles of their heirs in the present generation. In addition, all Protestants of foreign birth living in New York in 1715, including the Palatine refugees, were also naturalized.[28]

The governor and the assembly compromised the agency issue. The Assembly had long insisted they alone be permitted to hire and control a London-based lobbyist. In 1715, the governor agreed an agent should be hired. The agent, however, was to be appointed by and would receive his instructions from the governor, council, and the assembly, not from the assembly alone. John Champante, who had served the colony of New York as agent since Bellomont's administration, was rehired as colonial agent at an annual salary of five hundred ounces of silver plate. Champante died the next year and was succeeded by Hunter's and Addison's friend, the poet Ambrose Philips. The governor-general had not yielded much power over the agency issue since the choice and control of the agent was still largely in the hands of the executive.[29]

The major concession made by the governor-general to secure the settlement of 1715 was his agreement that the disbursement of colonial money would be by the assembly's treasurer rather than the receiver general. Hunter claimed that this arrangement was made by the council and Receiver General Thomas Byerley, but in this surrender of the crown's prerogative, the council and Byerley had acted with Hunter's full approval. Hunter realized the significance of this concession and apologized to the Board of Trade: "if I have done amiss, I am sorry for't, but what was there left for me to do, I have been struggling hard for bread itself for five years to no effect, and for four of them unpitty'd, I hope I have now laid a foundation for a lasting settlement on this hitherto unsettled and ungovernable Province...."[30]

The centerpiece of this "lasting settlement," received in return for these three concessions—naturalization, agency, and treasury—was a bill "for settling a Revenue for the support of his Majesty's Government for five years." By the terms of the bill, expenses would be met by "the striking of mony bills to the value of £6,000 for the present uses mention'd in the bill, and these bills being lodged in the Treasurer's hand (no Act could lodge them otherwise) to be sunk yearly at the rate of £1200 pr Annum...." Thus, Hunter's legislature was financing government operations in New York with the issue and investment of paper money, much as the Whig government and the Bank of England had financed the War of the Spanish Succession at home.[31]

Hunter, by securing a five-year revenue, had implemented a major legislative victory, but he had paid a price because the royal prerogative had been diminished. In the future, all ordinary government expenses were paid out by the assembly's treasurer on warrants issued by the governor and council. The crown's receiver general collected only quit rents. It is doubtful, however, if any lesser trade would have worked in New York. And Hunter had to find a New York solution because even after the Whigs took power, the new ministry was too preoccupied with problems brought by the succession to deal effectively with colonial concerns.[32]

By June of 1715, Hunter, in New York, had the promise of an adequate revenue and through his powers of patronage and appointment had filled key posts in the province with men personally loyal to him. There was, however, still opposition in the assembly, particularly among New York County's four troublesome merchant representatives, Jacobus Van Cortlandt, Stephen DeLancey, Samuel Bayard, and John Reade, who had all opposed the revenue bill. In August of 1715, Hunter dissolved the sixteenth assembly. In the election held in the spring of 1716, all four incumbent New York County representatives were defeated. They were replaced by new men loyal to Hunter: David Provoost, John Jansen, Jacobus Kipp, and Garret Van Horne.[33]

Hunter assured further legislative support for his programs by creating two additional assembly seats in the Hudson River Valley: one in rapidly growing Orange County, the other in Livingston Manor. In 1715, Hunter still owed Livingston money for unpaid Palatine bills. Instead of paying Livingston, Hunter approved his request for a new patent for 160,000 acres, as well as his manorial rights. The tenants elected Livingston as representative. He and Orange County's new representative, Peter Haring, were firm supporters of Hunter.[34]

With the 1716 election, the assembly majority changed from mercantile to landowner. Merchants and other outsiders did not become politically inactive, however. As Hunter usurped their power bases in the province, they looked for alternative ways to attack the governor-general. It was difficult to mount opposition attacks within the colony, because Hunter now controlled the legislature, the judiciary, and the militia. Hunter could be attacked, but it was necessary to travel personally to England, there to lodge complaints with a civil or religious agency of the empire: the Board of Trade or the privy council, the Society for the Propagation of the Gospel or the bishop of London. Hunter realized complaints would be filed against him, but he had the support of government leaders and had little to fear. Indeed, Hunter would have been a relatively happy man had it not been for the persistent Palatine debt.[35]

"Were I but free of debt"

The Palatine issue was far from resolved during this period. In addition to the Palatines who remained on the Hudson, there were about forty families in the wilderness of the Schoharie. This tract had reverted to the crown, and it was within Hunter's power to dispose of it. In the spring of 1714, Hunter issued a patent for six hundred acres to Adam Vrooman. In the summer of 1714, the governor-general issued additional patents for ten thousand acres to Myndert Schuyler, John Schuyler, Peter Van Brough, Robert Livingston, Jr., and Henry Wileman. The patentees sent the sheriff of Albany to tell the Palatine squatters to leave or pay rent, but he was chased away by the Palatines.[36]

In the spring of 1715, John Conrad Weiser led some Palatines on a rampage against Adam Vrooman. The Palatines tore down a stone house and fences belonging to Vrooman and beat up his son. Weiser had also led the 1711 rebellion which Hunter quelled with troops and had then defied the governor-general during the winter of 1712–1713 by leading the Palatines to the Schoharie. In June of 1715, Hunter, enraged by Weiser's latest act of disobedience, ordered his arrest. Weiser fled to Boston, where Hunter sent orders to have him apprehended and returned for trial "for a terror to the rest." Weiser escaped, however, and finally made his way to England, where he hoped to file charges of mismanagement against Hunter. Weiser arrived in England after a harrowing ocean voyage during the course of which he was captured by pirates. All his money having been stolen by the pirates, he soon contracted debts in London. Thrown into debtors prison, Weiser remained there until word of his plight reached his family and friends in the Schoharie. Weiser was released from prison after money was raised by the Palatines in New York and sent to London. He promptly petitioned the Board of Trade for a hearing to present his charges against the governor-general.[37]

Weiser's fate in debtors prison was also one feared by Hunter, who cowed merchants "upwards [of] £20,000" for subsisting the Palatines. The governor-general feared he would be seized when his "Government . . . [no longer] protects me from arrests." As Hunter admitted to Stair, he stood "bound for a great part" of the money spent on the Palatines, but had no way to pay the debt. He begged Stair's assistance in gaining approval from the king-in-council to use New York's quit rents to pay his expenses. A similar request to Queen Anne had been denied, despite the fact that Hunter had an "order for subsisting that People under Her late Majesties hand and seale." The debt was a constant source of anxiety to Hunter. As he told Stair, "Were I but free of debt I would still dance after a drumm, follow another man's plow, or teach other men's children for bread to my own; but whilst that remains over my head," he concluded, "I can dream of nothing but starveing in a gaol and seeing my innocent infants perish for want before my eyes. . . . "[38]

"Palpable Lyes Contradiction and Absurdity"

Hunter's concentration on Palatine debts and New York politics in the spring and summer of 1715 had caused him to delay calling the New Jersey assembly, which did not meet until the spring of 1716. The delay gave Daniel Coxe, the displaced councilman, an opportunity to stir up trouble for Hunter in West Jersey by circulating the inevitable petitions against the governor-general. Hunter, aware of the petitions, remained confident that he could handle the situation, "there being no real ground for their uneasiness, unless it be in their nature, for they are all from New England who have signed it. . . . "[39]

Displaced New Englanders in New Jersey were being stirred up by the Anglican Daniel Coxe, who dispensed rum to the electorate with great liberality. Swilling the New Jersey planters and tenants with bumbo led Coxe again to be elected representative from Gloucester in the spring of 1716. His support came from unthinking people of the "middling sort," who, according to Hunter, were swayed to Coxe by "palpable Lyes Contradiction and Absurdity backed with a Large dram botle [which] have more force upon the minds of the lower Rank of men in these parts than Self-Evident truths and their own Interest it Self." The Anti-Proprietary party, with a majority in the assembly, elected Coxe as speaker. Hunter had called the seventh assembly to meet at Perth Amboy. Quibbling immediately began over Hunter's choice. The Anti-Proprietary party based its objections to Amboy on an as yet unconfirmed 1709 act (passed after Lovelace's death while Richard Ingoldsby was lieutenant governor). This act provided that the assembly meet only at Burlington. Hunter's legal foundation was a confirmed act of 1708 which provided for alternating meetings at Amboy and Burlington. In addition, Hunter defended his right to choose assembly sites as part of the prerogative power of the crown he represented. On April 28, 1716, after days of bickering, Hunter prorogued the assembly for a month.[40]

When the assembly met again, Coxe and his faction sought to stop its proceedings by absenting themselves. Hunter promptly sent out warrants for their arrest on the charge that they were obstructing the business of His Majesty's government. Enough members were intimidated into attendance by Hunter's show of authority to form a quorum. Hunter then called the assembly's attention to those representatives who "by their wilful absenting themselves" had halted the business of government. He ordered the assembly "to take the usual Methods to oblige your fellow Members to pay their attendance[.]" The now-obedient assembly ordered one absent member arrested and expelled seven others, including speaker Coxe. They were charged with a conspiracy to "hinder the General Assembly of this Province from Sitting and acting as a General Assembly." Coxe and his followers were also accused of an attempt to "foment sedition & disturbance amongst His Majesties Leidge People. . . . [and] are suspected to be Persons Disaffected to His Majesties Person & Government, and to be confederating and conspiring against the same."[41]

Conspiracy, sedition, and treason were weighty charges and convinced the remaining representatives that Hunter was determined to triumph. They, therefore, were quite willing to comply with Hunter's wishes. Consequently, on May 21st, the assembly elected John Kinsey as speaker, a choice Hunter could "heartily approve." When elections were ordered to fill the seats of the expelled members, several of them were returned again. Hunter prohibited them for taking their seats on the grounds that they were "Enemys to his Ma'tys Government and the Peace of the Countrey. . . . " Alternate members were chosen by the electorate, giving Hunter an agreeable assembly which he kept in existence for the remainder of his tenure as governor-general.[42]

Hunter also rid himself of the presence of Daniel Coxe, who lost voter support when his defiance of Hunter "Opened the Eyes of ye whole Country." Hunter, determined to prosecute Coxe for ignoring his warrants, insisted he be arrested. Coxe "and his pitiful Crew," with Hunter's agents on their tails, had no place to hide in New Jersey. They fled to Bristol, Pennsylvania, leaving behind family, friends, and property. Hunter now expected that Coxe, Talbot, and their faction would go to London to complain of him and his administration. The governor-general was so certain of his support from the Whig ministry, however, that he gleefully anticipated that his enemies would have to "apply to the house of Commons since they cannot prevaile with the King, the Minsrs, or the Lords ha ha ha."[43]

Hunter used Coxe's flight from New Jersey to obtain better control of that province's militia. He now appointed competent friends as militia officers in place of Coxe and his associates. He justified the purge of the militia by accusing Coxe and company of fomenting and abetting Jacobites in France and Scotland! The Jacobite effort to place the Old Pretender, James Edward Stuart, on the British throne began in the fall of 1715, led by Hunter's former patron, the earl of Mar. Mar, on September 6th, raised the royal Stuart standard at Braemar. The rebel force of about twelve thousand men might have succeeded but for the death of Louis XIV in September of 1715, which prevented any significant French aid for the Jacobites. George I took immediate steps to suppress the rebels that same month when he dispatched the duke of Argyll to Scotland with an army of four thousand men. Although Argyll kept the rebels from Edinburgh, he took little direct offensive action, or so charged Cadogan, who did not believe Argyll was aggressive enough. Cadogan, who became nominal commander-in-chief after Marlborough's first stroke in November of 1715, raised six thousand Dutch auxiliaries and proceeded to Scotland. In January of 1716, Argyll and Cadogan, who despised each other, finally forced Mar to retreat northward with the Pretender, who had joined Mar at

Perth. The Pretender, Mar, and some other leaders embarked at Montrose for France, their troops quickly dispersed, and the rebellion was over.[44] News of the uprising and its suppression had been received in America by the spring of 1716, when the New Jersey assembly met. Hunter said that Coxe and his faction were all Jacobites who were ready to use their commands in the New Jersey militia to swing that colony to James's cause. "Indeed," Hunter charged, "their whole conduct was but an echo to that on the other side, if there should be any doubt of this, Mr. Smith the Secretary of the Jerseys may be interrogated upon oath in what manner and in what terms Mr. Cox told him, long before the Pretender's landing, that he was at the head of 50,000 men in Scotland. . . . " The commitment of many English high Tories to a legitimate succession left them open to charges of Jacobitism. The danger of Jacobitism in New Jersey was probably not real, but it was a handy club for Hunter to swing at the heads of political and clerical enemies. It was also one Hunter still wanted. While he was victorious over his secular opponents in both governments, his skirmishes with the Anglican clergy continued unchecked.[45]

"They'l destroy all Government and good Manners"

Hunter's English support from the ecclesiastical hierarchy had weakened on July 7, 1713, with the death at Fulham of Henry Compton, bishop of London, aged eighty-one. On August 8, 1713, Compton was succeeded by John Robinson. For unknown reasons, the new bishop disliked Hunter. Robinson had served on Marlborough's staff as a political envoy and as an interpreter, so it is likely that Robinson and Hunter met during the War of the Spanish Succession. Robinson's dislike of Hunter was so intense that the bishop immediately, deliberately, appointed the governor's archenemy, Vesey, as commissary, or so Hunter believed. This post conferred on Vesey the nominal leadership of New York's Anglican clergy. Hunter recognized the appointment as a personal affront and acknowledged that he knew "the Bishops Spleen and the Cause of it but was In hopes it was Long ago forgott." Hunter feared the bishop would also promote other of his clerical enemies such as John Talbot of Burlington. Hunter's only consolation was that "tho' I know no good they have ever done I know no great hurt they can do at present. . . . "[46]

With the secular Whigs in power after 1714, Hunter felt free to take his somewhat petty revenge on Commissary Vesey, who was then in England. The commissary had been temporarily prevented by illness from returning to his colonial post. His salary as minister of Trinity Church was paid by taxes imposed on the people of the city, most of whom were not Anglicans. When Vesey failed to return as expected, the city vestry, elected by the people of the city and led by Hunter's Scottish friend Mayor John Johnston, consulted their pocketbooks and eagerly fell in with Hunter's desire to hurt the minister. They voted not to pay Vesey his salary for the time he was absent. Vesey complained to the bishop of London and on August 19, 1715, orders were issued by the king to Hunter to pay Vesey his salary. The city vestry, which received the order from Vesey's hand in November of 1715, ignored it. The king was supreme in London, but Hunter was supreme in New York.[47]

Hunter also sought to destroy the influence of colonial clerics with their superiors in London. On April 9, 1715, he wrote the board that "if the Society take not more care for the future than has been taken hitherto in the choice of their Missionaries, instead of establishing Religion, they'l destroy all Government and good Manners." The board agreed with Hunter and asked the bishop of London to send only men of unblemished character as missionaries to America, not such men as Hunter described and the bishop had promoted.[48]

Vesey cared little about the board's opinion as long as he had the bishop's approval. Hunter reported that Vesey, puffed up with his promotion, had "Enter'd New York in Triumph like his friend Sacheverel," who had been prosecuted by the Junto Whigs in 1710 only to emerge a national hero. Vesey "immediately on his arrival assur'd every body that I had neither Intrest nor Friends at home," Hunter reported. The continuing enmity of the clergy, now backed by the bishop of London, moved Hunter to increasingly vicious counterattacks. In November of 1715, perhaps confused by the recorded conviction of Vesey's father for Jacobite activities (or perhaps with deliberate malice), Hunter told the Board of Trade that Vesey himself "stands on record in the Council books at New York for base and Indecent Language of his Sovereign King William. . . . " In a letter written a few days later, Hunter charged that ministers Vesey and Talbot were both Jacobites who had allied with Clarendon and Nicholson to destroy him. To prove his charges of conspiracy, Hunter forwarded to the board copies of several of the clergymen's seditious letters, intercepted by his agents.[49]

Vesey and Talbot continued to plague Hunter throughout 1715. The governor-general had ejected Talbot as minister of St. Mary's Church in Burlington. The bishop of London, however, sent Talbot a letter instructing him to resume his pulpit. When Hunter was in Burlington in October of 1715, Talbot, on a Sunday morning, triumphantly walked to the Tateham house where Hunter was staying, waving the bishop's letter in his hand. Talbot then proceeded to the church, where he demanded the warden admit him so he could conduct services. Hunter refused to attend the church while Talbot officiated. Instead he "went away to the Sweedish Church which he understands as much as I do Arabic," Talbot told the bishop.[50]

The ministers continued their opposition to Hunter until the spring of 1716. Then the Board of Trade brought pressure on the bishop of London to halt the clergy's harrassment. On March 22nd, the board informed Hunter they had spoken to the proper authorities about Vesey and Talbot and promised that their action would make the governor-general "easy in that Matter." They were correct, because both Vesey and Talbot soon established a truce with Hunter. The governor noticed that "the Comissary [Vesey] here is the humblest Clergy man And warmest Whig all of a Suddain...." Vesey's new "humble" behavior continued. He soon came to Hunter "to acknowledge his errors and promise very warmly a more commendable conduct for the future...." In return for Vesey's promises of future compliance, Hunter promised to do all he could to get the city vestry to pay him his salary. They did so in August of 1716.[51]

Talbot also tried to cooperate with the governor-general. In February of 1717, he informed Hunter of a plan contrived by the Anti-Proprietary party to burn down the Quaker meetinghouse and several houses belonging to Quakers. In addition, Talbot assured Hunter that he had never done any "harm in your Province but have prevented a great Deal that would have been done by others...."[52]

"I would hang them if I cou'd"

With the submission of the clergy, Hunter's triumph was virtually complete. It had been achieved through Hunter's acumen in colonial politics, much reinforced by the ascendancy of his Whig patrons in England. Hunter also contributed to his revenge in New York by making laughingstocks of some of his more irritating enemies. Among these were Vesey, Nicholson, and Clarendon. While Hunter hated Vesey, he realized the minister was merely the tool of Nicholson and Clarendon. Hunter had a keen eye to recognize and a sharp pen to caricature the ludicrous aspects of these men.

Clarendon, grandson of Charles II's lord high chancellor, had neither the mentality nor the temperament to live up to the reputation of his pious, accomplished grandfather. After debt drove him to seek a colonial governorship in New York, his behavior grew scandalous. His indecent dress, his excessive drinking, his mounting debts, and his misappropriation of public funds ultimately caused Clarendon to be recalled to England in disgrace, despite his kinship to Queen Anne and much to the amusement of the provincials who despised him.[53]

Nicholson also provided occasions for colonial mirth. As lieutenant governor of New York in 1689, Nicholson had abandoned his post when confronted with Leisler's rebels. Later, as governor of Virginia, he initiated a ludicrous courtship of the rich, beautiful, and young heiress Lucy Burwell. Nicholson, a rather unkempt and untidy man, more than a generation older than Lucy, fell deeply in love with a girl who did not return his affection. Nicholson was undeterred by Lucy's coolness and took to chasing rival suitors from her door, whip in hand. He threatened that if she married another, he would "cut the throats of the bridegroom[,] the clergyman, and the justice of the peace giving the license." The colonists and Hunter were also amused by Nicholson's military pretension, which contrasted so sharply with his lack of military experience which was exposed by the failure of three Canadian expeditions he commanded. Soon after the Hanoverian succession in 1714, Hunter picked up his pen to prick his enemies.[54]

Hunter's satirical weapon was one that had been employed with skill by several of his correspondents, including Ambrose Philips, Jonathan Swift, Richard Steele, and Joseph Addison. Swift and Steele, for instance, had been engaged in a bitter satirical paper war since the spring of 1713, a war which caused Swift to direct his venom toward Hunter. The origin of the quarrel between Swift and Steele lay in Steele's belief that Swift had attacked him in print. Swift denied the charge but a pamphlet battle ensued. Finally, in January of 1714, Swift published a satirical poem, "The First Ode of the Second Book of Horace." In the poem, Swift urged Steele to give up politics and return to his playwrighting career. Swift apparently felt playwrighting might be more financially profitable for the perpetually indebted Steele:

> Methinks I see thee, spruce and fine,
> With Coat embroider'd richly shine,
> And dazzle all the *Idol-Faces*
> As thro' the HALL thy Worship paces:
> (Tho' this I speak but at a venture,
> Supposing thou hast *Tick* with Hunter)[55]

This passage was a nasty attack on Steele's insolvency. It was also a snide reference to Robert Hunter's £21,000 debt for expenses he had incurred in subsisting the Palatines. (In eighteenth-century usage, "tick" meant "credit.") Swift's motives in calling attention to Hunter's misfortune may not have been entirely malicious, however. Certainly Hunter did not regard Swift as an enemy and in a 1714 letter spoke warmly of Swift. In addition to making his point against Steele by calling attention to a cause célèbre, Swift may well have believed that putting Hunter's name in the poem was a way of assuring that Hunter would be remembered through the ages. Swift himself had once asked Ambrose Philips, "When you write any more Poetry do me honor, mention me in it: tis the Common Request of Tully and Pliny to the great Authors of their Age; and I will contrive it so, that Pr[ince]. Posterity shall know I was favored by the Men of Witt in my Time." Hunter, however, may well have preferred assistance to eternal fame.[56]

Revenge was not the sole motivation of eighteenth-century satirists. All found satire an effective weapon with which to discipline those who misused power. As Swift noted:

Wicked Ministers of State
I can easier scorn than hate:
And I find it answers right:
Scorn torments them more than Spight.

Satire was also a way to prompt people to moral behavior, "for, as / It is well observ'd by HORACE, / Ridicule has greater Pow'r / To reform the World, than Sour." Swift and other Augustan writers used their satire both to get even with opponents for past slights and to reform the manners and attitudes of others. This had been Swift's motivation when he wrote *A Tale of a Tub*, in which he unleashed his outrage at corruption in the Anglican Church. In this and later satirical works, Swift employed the type of satire used by Juvenal, which seeks to punish opponents. As Swift admitted to Alexander Pope, his intent was "to vex the world rather than divert it." Addison, on the other hand, used satire in the more polite and gentler Horatian manner. Addison taunted his opponents, but always behaved as "a gentleman, in whom the quickest sense of the ridiculous is constantly tempered by good-nature and good breeding."[57]

Addison's use of satire is perhaps best seen in his *Spectator* essays. The *Spectator* rose from the ashes of the *Tatler* in March of 1711. Steele was again publisher of the news-sheet, but the principal contributor was Joseph Addison. To make specific educational points, Addison created a spokesmen, Sir Roger de Coverley, who introduced himself to readers in the very first issue. De Coverley was gracious, charming, kind, cultured, shy, and intelligent, much like Addison himself. Unlike Addison, however, Sir Roger was heir to an ancient estate. His (fictional) hereditary landed wealth gave de Coverley the social prestige necessary to become an arbiter of taste. Also, unlike Addison, Sir Roger was merely "a Spectator of mankind," rather than an active participant in current affairs. De Coverley was indeed a paragon of virtue, as Steele pointed out in the second issue of the *Spectator*: "His tenants grow rich, his servants look satisfied, all the young women profess to love him, and the young men are glad of his company." With such a likeable, distinguished personage as its spokesman, the *Spectator* was ready to guide Britain's new rich to the paths of cultured enlightenment.[58]

Much to Addison's and Steele's delight, the *Spectator* was enormously successful in setting standards of behavior. Not only did the paper establish the moral tone for society, it also told the boorish, uncouth urban merchants and their country cousins, the unsophisticated rural squires, how to behave, what to like, what to see at the theater, what poems, or books, or pamphlets to read, how to dispense charity, how to treat servants, and how to dress. The authors were aware of their influence. Addison, who estimated the readership of the *Spectator* at sixty thousand in London and Westminster alone, expressed the wish that his readers "will take care to distinguish themselves from the thoughtless Herd of their ignorant and unattentive Brethren."[59]

The influence of Addison's and Steele's satire did not stop at Britain's shores, but spread throughout the empire. Addison gave "the law in taste here, took it up, and sent it about the kingdom in his polite and popular essays." The *Spectator* was as eagerly devoured in Edinburgh, Dublin, New York, or Philadelphia, and their cultural hinterlands, as it was in London and Westminster. The Augustans set the standards of taste and elegance, manners and morals, and the provincials did their best to emulate them. The shared culture that resulted was a cohesive ingredient in bringing together the threads of empire.[60]

With such examples before him (and undoubtedly Hunter subscribed to the *Spectator*), Hunter knew how to punish and educate his New York and New Jersey enemies. To revenge himself on the colonial rustics who had annoyed and obstructed him, Hunter wrote a vicious play, *Androboros*. He promptly had the play published in New York. In Hunter's play, the duplicity, the religious fanaticism, and the misplaced passion of his enemies, were turned against them. The play was probably acted by the governor-general's friends and read by many who did not see it performed.[61]

Hunter's *Androboros* was the first play printed in America. *Androboros* may even have been the first play written in America. Whether it was also publicly performed has been questioned because "the plot turns on so filthy an incident" as the defilement of the vestments in Trinity Church. However, neither the filthy subject matter nor the bawdy language would have offended eighteenth-century Britons of any rank or of either sex. If the play was not performed, it was from a lack of skilled actors to fill the roles and not from any false (Victorian) sense of delicacy. The play was, and is, determinedly, delightedly, vulgar.[62]

Hunter had a wide range of characters in his play, including "Tom o'Bedlam." The character had originated with the paupers and vagabonds in England who, with torn clothes and bloodied faces, terrorized villagers with pranks and tricks until they were given food or money. "Tom" eventually became part of English folklore and, by the late sixteenth and early seventeenth centuries, the character had come to signify a visitor from hell (or Bedlam) who had temporarily come to earth to assist humans with specific problems. The character became such an accepted and even admired folk figure that it was the subject of one of the most popular ballads of the seventeenth century, undoubtedly still sung in Hunter's time. Hunter viewed his own situation with Nicholson, the legislatures, and the clergy, as desperate (and ludicrous) enough to warrant the intercession of Tom. In the play, Tom could say and do the outrageous things that a staid governor-general was prevented from doing even in stage life because of his rank. Tom was also a protector and an avenger, and it was through Tom's intervention that the "Keeper," the governor-general in the play (and the custodian of that Bedlam, New York) was saved from murder and his enemies killed in his stead. Both Tom the prankster and Tom the avenger sprang from the very depths of Hunter's being. Like the Tom of the ballad, Hunter's alter ego came,

> From forth my sad and darksome cell,
> And from the deep abyss of hell
> Poor Tom is come to view the world again
> To see if he can ease distempered brain
> Fear and despair possess his soul
> Hark how the angry furies howl.[63]

The "angry furies" had reason to howl after they became aware of Hunter's dissection of them in *Androboros*. Hunter used both the Juvenalian and Horatian modes of satire, as evidenced by his treatment of the eighteen characters in the play. These characters are recognizably patterned, either on Hunter and his friends, or on Hunter's enemies. Hunter took for himself and his friends the roles of rational, polite, resigned, and detached Augustan gentlemen. Their personalities are much akin to that of Addison, or to Addison's spokesman, Sir Roger. Like Sir Roger, Hunter and his friends in the play teach manners and morals through polite example. Hunter's bitter and vicious characterizations of his enemies, however, are in the Horatian/Swiftian manner. Although less polite than Addison's satire, such vicious caricature permits Hunter to show his opponents as the uncouth boors he thought them to be. The governor-general himself ensured the identity of his characters would not be lost when he wrote real names against the cast of characters on a printed copy of the play which survives to the present day.[64]

The antihero of the play's title role was Francis Nicholson, "Old Nick-nack," according to Tom, "who had paganiz'ed himself with that Name ['Androboros"], which interpreted, signifies a Man-Eater. He is now very far gone indeed. He talks of nothing but Battles and Seiges, tho' he never saw one, and Conquests over Nations and alliances with Princes who never had a being...."[65]

In addition to Nicholson, Hunter's targets were: the "Speaker," William Nicoll, Anti-Leislerian and speaker of the New York assembly; "Babilard," Samuel Bayard, Anti-Leislerian merchant, landowner, and assemblyman; "Coxcomb," Daniel Coxe, New Jersey councilman and assemblyman; "Fizle," minister William Vesey; "Flip," Adolph Philipse, the New York merchant and councilman who opposed Hunter's revenue plan; and "Lord Oinobaros," that is "the sot," the earl of Clarendon.

These villains were defeated by the "Keeper," Hunter himself, and his friends and allies: the "Deputy," George Clarke, secretary and auditor of the province of New York; "Aesop," David Jamison, chief justice of New Jersey, recorder of the city of New York, and attorney general of New York; "Solemn," Lewis Morris, assemblyman, councilman, and chief justice, who helped Hunter write the play; and, of course, the governor-general's court jester and alter ego, "Tom o'Bedlam."[66]

The first act of the play is set in New York, "Moropolis," or "the city of fools." It begins with a "Senate" meeting in which Tom assumes the role of clerk in order to caricature the Keeper's legislative opponents. Both the characters and situations satirize the actions and words of actual New York and New Jersey legislative meetings. The Speaker (Nicoll), who defied the crown by insisting on the assembly's right to control the revenue, here announces "That Laws and Liberty were things Incompatible." Babilard (Bayard), the greedy and troublesome son of the former owner of the Schoharie tract, is made to declare that the Senate "has an Inherent and Undoubted Right to the undoubted Property of those we Represent," while

Coxcomb (Coxe), the opinionated and egotistical politician, insists "That no Body be allow'd to speak but himself because for want of the Attentive Faculty, he is like to have no share in the Hearing, and so ought to have compensation in Speaking." Mulligrub (Mulford), stupid and verbose, gives several pompous addresses and finally exhorts the senate (in the style of Puritan republicanism typical of Long Island's New Englanders) to "be Valiant Therefore and Vindicate our Rights There-from, Our Birth-Right Parliamentary Rights, settled upon us by the Ten Commandments."[67]

The Senate meets with "Expectation of some mighty Deliverance" from the rule of their Keeper, the governor-general. This is to be brought to them by Androboros. While waiting for Androboros, the senate declares its intent not to be "bound by any Laws, Rules or Customs, any Law, Rule or Custom to the Contrary Notwithstanding." Solemn (Morris) objects to the Senate's anarchistic statement and recites the legalist and royalist metes and bounds of colonial assemblies which were called into being only to serve a specified purpose and did not have an inherent right to exist. Neither, Solemn charges, did the representatives serve their constituencies. The members of the Senate are offended, and the Speaker tells Solemn that "for *Reasons* best known to our selves, you are Expell'd." So the New York assembly had expelled Morris in 1710.[68]

Tom, the clerk, is then sent by the Senate to conduct Androboros, Fizle (Vesey), and Flip (Philipse) to the Senate chamber. Androboros congratulates the Senate for having expelled Solemn, "that wandring Plague, that Kibes in the Heels and Piles in the posteriors of Mankind," from the house. The general then utters his personal defiance against the sun king, Louis XIV: he swears "not to pare these Nails, wash this blew Visage, or put off this speckled *Shirt* Until I have made that Haughty Monarch Confess himself, in all his Projects for Universal Dominion, my Inferior; and My Delamya [Lucy Burwell], fairer then the fairest Princess of his Blood or Empire." The senate immediately resolves that Androboros has conducted himself with "Courage, Conduct and Prudence" on this Canadian expedition. It has not even begun. After Androboros finally departs for his expedition, the Keeper, disgusted with the actions of the Senate as reported to him by Tom, dissolves them with the command, "To Your Kennels, ye Hounds." Babilard, Fizle, Flip, and Coxcomb now realize the governor-general has too much control over their activities in the senate, where "You see he can Dissolve our Senate with a Crack of his Whip, so there is nothing to be done that way. Let us incorporate ourselves into a Consistory; That I believe He dare not touch, without being Reputed an Enemy to the Consistory. . . . "[69]

Fizle then convenes that Tory, clerical institution, the consistory of "New Bedlam," with Tom, the Keeper's spy, as clerk. The members promptly decide they want the Keeper recalled from his government so that Lord Oinobaros (Clarendon), can be reinstalled. Aesop (David Jamison) warns them that they "would repent the Change," for "a man who could never yet Govern himself, will make but a sorry Governour for others." Yet the conspirators persist, for they have been assured by Oinobaros that "secret Representations and Remonstrances" against the Keeper would ruin him and secure Oinobaros's return.[70]

This method is deemed too slow by Coxcomb, however, who wants to get rid of the Keeper immediately. Coxcomb insists the conspirators "must Accuse him [the Keeper] of something more Flagrant; Trifles won't do." Fizle agrees and decides to defile clerical vestments. The conspirators will then charge that these vestments, which belong "to the Chief of our Number. . . . [were] Inhumanely Tore and Bedaub'd with *Odour*" by the Keeper "or some of his People." After Fizle returns with the soiled garments, the consistory agrees to report the Keeper's alleged sacrilege to Oinobaros. After Fizle completes the address to Oinobaros which details the Keeper's actions, Tom is directed by Fizle to read the address aloud. He does so, but he persistently makes errors which maliciously show the true intent and character of the consistory members. Substitutions such as "That so we may give a *Loose to Our Knavery,*" are made for Fizle's staid, "Get Loose from our Slavery.[71]

After the address to Oinobaros is finally completed, Androboros, who has quickly returned from his "expeditious Expedition," sends a messenger to inform the consistory that the conquest of Canada is not needed. Instead, the Tory peace has magically turned the French from being "our Reputed Enemies" into "our good and faithful Friends and Allies. . . . " The French, Androboros further reports, even made trade concessions to the English "generously resigning and yeilding to us that [trade] of the two Poles, reserving to themselves only what may lie between e'em."[72]

The Keeper recognizes that the pro-French, pro-Tory ministry has sent Androboros to America "Cloathe'd . . . with Sham-Powers meerly to get rid of his Noise and Trouble; and must fall to my share, I'll humour him to keep him quiet." But he also realizes it would be impossible to keep Androboros quiet as long as he is alive, so he eagerly falls in with Tom's suggestion to "Persuade him [Androboros] that he is dead. . . . " Androboros, treated as a corpse by the Keeper's friends, not only believes himself dead, he even resolves to remain dead when he hears Tom describe the reaction of the fair Delamya on hearing the news of Androboros's death. "She's Inconsolable, ready to burst her sides," is Tom's paradoxical remark: "Yes, Sir, Excess of Joy makes some People Weep; Excess of Grief makes her [laugh] Inordinately...."[73]

The deception continues until Tom overhears Fizle and Flip plotting to kill the Keeper by placing his chair over an unbolted hatch. This would enable Androboros to succeed to the Keeper's post. Tom promptly tells Solemn, who determines that Androboros should be brought back to life long enough to be punished for the duplicity of his friends and his own arrogance and stupidity. Androboros meets his end when he rushes to assume the Keeper's office by the symbolic act of occupying the Keeper's vacant chair. Fizle and Flip try to restrain Androboros, and all three men fall to their deaths.[74]

Thus, Hunter, through satire, murdered three of his most annoying enemies:

> Like the everlaughing Sage
> In a Jest I spend my Rage
> (Tho' it must be understood,
> I would hang them if I cou'd.)[75]

The writing of the play was cathartic to Hunter. At one stroke he ridiculed Clarendon, Nicholson, Vesey, and Coxe, as well as the high church Tories and the Tory ministry. Even more important, the play won Hunter popular support. The opposition "were so humorously exposed that the laugh was turned upon them in all companies and from this laughing humour the people began to be in a good humour with their Governour and to despise the idol of the clergy."[76]

By July of 1716, Robert Hunter had won the support of the majority of the politically active colonists in New York and New Jersey. The tide had clearly turned in Hunter's favor. In England, the Whigs were in power, led by Hunter's old army superiors and political patrons. In America, the governor-general had secured a five-year revenue from a formerly defiant assembly in New York and had quieted party strife in New Jersey. Hunter, Lady Hay, and their five children spent the summer of 1716 at their six-room house in Perth Amboy. There, the governor-general looked forward with equanimity, after six difficult years in America, to a relatively trouble-free, perhaps even a happy, administration.

6

"God Did Never Intend Life for a Blessing"

August 1716–July 1719

*I hate Life, when I think it exposed to such Accidents, and to see so
many thousand wretches burthening the Earth, while such as her dye,
makes me think God did never intend Life for a Blessing.*
> Jonathan Swift, *Journal to Stella*,
> January 3, 1713 (On death of
> Lady Ashburnham.)

"The most afflicted Man alive"

*I*N AUGUST OF 1716, Robert Hunter was only two months short of his
fiftieth birthday. His wife, Elizabeth Orby, Lady Hay, was thirty years
old. Aside from her age, virtually nothing is known of Lady Hay, except
that she was born into a military family and herself married two soldiers,
first John lord Hay and then Robert Hunter. Her personality and her
appearance are both mysteries, although a portrait of her was known to
exist until 1937. Virtually the only trace left of her existence in America
was a gift she made to the Reverend Alexander Innes, once chaplain of
New York's fort, of a handkerchief "formerly belonging to King Charles the
First," the royal martyr whom her grandfather had served.[1]

Lady Hay died on August 9, 1716, at Perth Amboy, New Jersey. Her
death was reported in the *Boston News-Letter* by the New York correspondent: "On Thursday at Amboy dyed the Right Hon. my Lady Hay, much
Lamented by all that knew her, being a Lady of rare Endowments and
Vertues, one of the best of Wives, and a most Excellent Mother, and has
left His Excellency Brigadeer Hunter our Governour the most afflicted
Man alive. She was Interr'd here in the Chappel in Fort George." In
keeping with her life, the cause of Elizabeth's death is also a mystery. It

141

may be that she died from smallpox, which swept through New Jersey during 1716 and 1717. It is also possible she died in childbirth. Only two facts emerge with any certainty from her death: Hunter was devastated and at fifty, an advanced age for the time, he was left with the responsibility of raising five infants. Hunter's children, Charles, Thomas, Henrietta, Katharine, and Charlotte, the oldest of whom could not have been more than eight or nine in 1716, helped fill the void left by the death of his wife. Hunter never remarried, but for the remainder of his life he was rarely without the companionship of at least one of his children.[2]

The governor fell ill immediately after his wife's death. Hunter wrote home to request a leave of absence from his post to attend to the details of his wife's estate and to recover his health. The request was granted on October 10, 1716, when Hunter was given permission to return to England for eight months. Before he left, however, the provinces' affairs also had to be settled. Hunter took steps to do so immediately following his wife's death when he convened the second session of New York's seventeenth assembly in August of 1716. With a pro-Hunter, landowner majority, contention was reduced. The session was uneventful with routine legislation passed for New York's defence and expenses.[3]

On November 27, 1716, Hunter met the New Jersey assembly at Chesterfield, because "the small pox are raging at" Burlington. Hunter asked for and received a three-year revenue bill. He also extended an olive branch to past enemies when he pardoned all the "rebellious" assemblymen who had absented themselves from the 1716 session. As Hunter anticipated, without the presence of "that Boutefeu" Coxe, he "had a very happy Session of Assembly." Hunter planned to meet the New Jersey assembly again in the spring of 1718. He realized he could not take advantage of his leave of absence before then because he wanted "to perfect what is so happily begun."[4]

In other words, Hunter wanted to be certain that his Anti-Proprietary opposition remained subdued and that he collected some of the rewards of his command of the legislature. When Hunter next met the New Jersey assembly in April of 1718, it was "their busy Seed time, so Hunter adjourned them to the following year. Hunter met the New Jersey assembly for the last time in the spring of 1719, at which time that body passed routine acts for the administration of the province.[5]

As Hunter explained to the Board of Trade, his intent was to leave "the government" of both colonies "on such a foot that anyone could govern them." He had insured that the legislatures in both New York and New Jersey would remain compliant by nominating friends and allies to their councils and by proroguing the congenial assemblies elected in 1716 in both provinces, thus keeping them in existence for the remainder of his tenure as governor-general. In New York, Hunter's opposition after 1716 came not from the assembly, but from merchants who opposed his tax policies.[6]

The primary source of contention was the debt bill of 1717. This bill called for another issue of paper money to the amount of £32,000, raised by an excise on retailing and a duty on imported liquors. Of this sum, £12,000 was to pay the province's creditors, while the rest was loaned out at 5 percent interest. Among the allottments was one for 2,525½ ounces of plate for His Excellency, "for Incidents and sundry Extraordinary disbursem'ts for the Public Service of this Colony, for which no Provision has been made." The assembly, according to Cadwallader Colden, "calculated to half a penny weight in the allowance to the Governor to shew how careful they had been not to allow him a half penny weight too much." Robert Livingston also made up for any past losses for his services to the province. He, along with several other "of the leading men in the Council and Assembly . . . had considerable payments made them generally for services don without mentioning any particular service. Mr. Livingston had 3,710 ounces of plate. I believe," Colden commented, that Livingston "never was exceeded in soliciting for himself, by any man."[7]

The additional tax burden brought by the debt bill of 1717 angered many New York merchants. On November 29, 1717, the grand jury of New York, composed primarily of merchants, sent a protest to the governor-general asking him to veto the bill. Hunter ordered the sergeant-at-arms to bring the jurors before the assembly for contempt of the two houses. When the jurors explained that they did not intend their actions to be contemptuous, Hunter dropped the charges. This was merely the beginning of the battle. After Hunter approved the measure and forwarded the bill to London for royal confirmation, complaints from New York merchants began in earnest. Hunter and Chief Justice Lewis Morris sought to counter New York-based opponents of the bill by declaring that all who opposed the measure would be prosecuted for sedition. New York merchants persisted, however, and were soon joined in their protests by London merchants, led by Charles Lodwick and John Lloyd, who placed petitions against the bill "on the tables of most Coffeehouses in the City [of London]." Lodwick and Lloyd then sent the signed documents to the Board of Trade with their request that the board not recommend royal confirmation because the bill was "prejudicial. . . to the trade and credit of the province." They also questioned the legality of the measure since the creditors named in it had not been included in earlier and presumably all-inclusive bills.[8]

Despite merchant opposition, the assembly's passage of the 1717 bill made it obvious that Hunter's court party controlled that body. After a frustrated William Nicoll, using the excuse of ill health, resigned as speaker of the house, the assembly promptly elected Robert Livingston to replace him. Livingston now worked energetically with Hunter and Morris to secure the confirmation of the debt bill in London. In return for Livingston's active support of the bill, Hunter instructed Ambrose Philips to urge the Board of Trade to recommend the confirmation of a 1709 repeal of the old Leislerian bill to confiscate Livingston's estate. The repeal stood and Livingston kept his land. Hunter also benefitted in this game of favors when, in September of 1718, Livingston gave Hunter a release for all Palatine-related debts.[9]

"A gentleman of as refined a taste"

Hunter's legislative concerns diverted his mind from his bereavement, as did the presence of his children. No matter how many nurses, attendants, and teachers the "motherlesse infants" may have had, there must have been many problems that could only be handled by a parent. In addition, Hunter had to provide for the children's future. In 1718, he drew a will to dispose of his New York property and to appoint guardians for his children. The governor-general was also concerned with his sons' employment. He seemed determined to have Charles and Thomas follow him in his military profession. In 1718, both boys were commissioned as captains of two companies of cadets in New York.[10]

Hunter also eased his loneliness by the friendships he formed among a colonial circle of literary and scientific savants. Hunter, "a gentleman of as refined a taste as any we have known or perhaps heard of in America," was interested in art, music, literature, science, and mathematics. During the years Hunter was in New York, he did all within his power to foster these disciplines among intelligent colonists. Hunter's protégé, noted scientist Cadwallader Colden, wrote Hunter "was fond of men of learning and encouraged them whenever he had opportunity. In short he was a gentleman of extraordinary abilities both natural and acquired and had every qualification requisite in a Governor."[11]

A majority of the colonial elite who formed Hunter's coterie were Scots-born, as was Hunter himself. Most were of obscure origin and would have remained unknown if they had stayed in Great Britain. Perhaps the sole exception to this last statement was James Alexander, the Jacobite rebel. Alexander was heir to the earldom of Stirling and a descendant of Sir William Alexander, the original proprietor of Nova Scotia. He was also the father of the patriot general William Alexander, soi dissant earl of Stirling, who would fight in the American Revolution.[12]

James Alexander, whose grandfather had owned land in New York before its conquest in 1664, was sent to Hunter by the duke of Argyll, whose family were traditional patrons of the Alexanders. There were more than eight hundred Jacobites sent to America after the 1715 uprising, but most were transported as indentured servants to southern plantations or the sugar islands, there to work in the blazing sun. Alexander instead arrived in New York with a personal letter of recommendation from Secretary Stanhope to Hunter. Stanhope, after informing Hunter that the proprietors of New Jersey had "constituted James Alexander to be Receiver General and Collector of all their quitt-rents," asked the governor-general to "give him all the protection and countenance in your power...." A short time later, the West Jersey proprietors also appointed Alexander as surveyor-general.[13]

Hunter needed little urging from Stanhope to favor Alexander, whose family he had known in Scotland. The young man soon became one of Hunter's closest and most trusted friends. In 1718, as tokens of the governor-general's favor, Alexander was named recorder of Perth Amboy and deputy secretary of New York. In 1719, he was named one of the commissioners to establish a boundary between New York and New Jersey. This was just the beginning of Alexander's provincial career. He was later a member of both the New York and New Jersey councils and attorney general of New Jersey.[14]

Another of Hunter's Scots protégés was David Jamison, whom Hunter nominated to the New York and New Jersey councils in 1715. On receiving Hunter's nomination, the Board of Trade wrote to ask Hunter if this was the same Jamison about whom the earl of Bellomont had complained. Hunter replied that this was indeed the same man, but insisted Jamison's character was above reproach. Indeed, he believed Jamison was "ye greatest man I ever knew, and I think of umblemished life and conversation of any of his rank in these parts...." The board accepted Hunter's recommendation of former "Sweet Singer" Jamison, who eventually served on the councils of both New York and New Jersey.[15]

Alexander and Jamison shared Hunter's interest in the arts and sciences. All three men participated in literary discussions and scientific experiments with other prominent colonials, including James Logan of

Philadelphia, whose father had been an impoverished Quaker minister in Scotland. During the Restoration, the Logan family had fled to Ireland from Scotland to avoid religious persecution, only to meet political discrimination in Ireland from Anglo-Irish and religious persecution from Irish Catholics. James Logan was born in Ireland in 1674, his childhood a nightmare of terror, as Catholics plundered his family's house and burnt their fields. As Logan later recalled, "In the days which should have been my gayest, I knew nothing out of school but terror and horror."[16]

Logan's refuge from terror was in learning, and he was instructed by his schoolmaster father. In time, the son outstripped the father in intellectual prowess. Logan soon acquired a substantial library of his own, one he was forced to sell in 1697 to invest in an unsuccessful venture in trade. The young man was almost without any prospect of achieving financial success when in 1699 Pennsylvania's Quaker proprietor, William Penn, asked him to be his secretary. Logan agreed and set sail with Penn for America. Soon after their arrival in America, Penn named Logan commissioner of property and receiver general of Pennsylvania. In 1702, Penn added Logan to his council. Logan's successful career in Pennsylvania as politician, judge, landowner, and Indian trader, lasted until his death in 1751.[17]

Logan apparently took the first step in initiating a friendship with Governor-General Hunter. On September 20, 1712, Logan wrote to Hunter that he had heard from friends in England that Hunter was "not only famed for his great Abilities & exact Justice," but that he also gave himself to the pursuit of knowledge. Hearing this, Logan said, "raised a zeal in me to pay my respects personally" to Hunter. The governor responded quickly and positively to Logan's offer of an intellectual friendship.[18]

A close friend to both Hunter and Logan was yet another Scot, Cadwallader Colden, born in 1688. Colden had studied medicine at the University of Edinburgh and in London. He settled in Philadelphia in 1710 to practice medicine and engage in trade. Colden formed a firm friendship with Logan. Then, his bright and inquiring mind brought him to Hunter's attention. The governor-general was so intrigued with Colden that, much to the lonely Logan's dismay, Hunter persuaded Colden to move to New York with the promise that he would appoint him surveyor general of that province. Colden was convinced. On May 15, 1718, Hunter had him commissioned master of the weighhouse of New York Port. This was followed in 1719 with a commission to be ranger of Ulster County. After Hunter's return to England, he secured for Colden the promised post of surveyor general. These were merely the first steps in

Colden's official New York career which culminated in 1761, when he became lieutenant governor of the province, a post he held until his death in September of 1776. In return for Hunter's patronage, Colden provided the world with a vivid description of Hunter's personality and military and gubernatorial careers, thus ensuring Hunter's place in history.[19]

Although Hunter, Logan, Colden, and their circle were all consummate politicians, the true basis of their friendship was their interest in literature and science. Their literary intake was impressive and varied. In 1717, Logan and Hunter worked on an Italian translation of Addison's recently published and well-received poem, "Cato." Logan and Hunter also debated the relative merits of poetry by Ambrose Philips, John Gay, and other contemporary Augustan poets. In addition, Hunter, at least, wrote poetry in Latin. When Hunter sent Logan a copy of his latest Latin ode in 1716, Logan translated it into Greek, although with many misgivings that he was not skillful enough to effect an adequate translation. Nevertheless, Logan persisted. Finally, with much trepidation, he sent the translation to Hunter for his comments. Much to Logan's surprise, Hunter admired the work, although Logan continued to insist. "that there is nothing to recommend it but the Original. . . . "[20]

Besides language and literature, this colonial intelligentsia was much given to scientific experiments with pendulums and reflections on Newton's theory of gravitation. On clear nights in 1718, Hunter, Governor William Keith of Pennsylvania, and other members of this colonial elite used a quadrant to observe and measure the declination of celestial bodies. Each would carefully note his observations and then report the results to the others for comparison.[21]

Hunter, Logan, and Colden were representatives of an era when many politicians were actively involved in scientific explorations. During this period, men of affairs formed the majority of the members of the Royal Society. Most statesmen were keenly interested in scientific advances. Laymen were able to contribute to scientific knowledge because the stage of learning was still at such a level that a physician, such as Colden, could understand and apply Newton's theories. The involvement of men of affairs in science began to lessen in England following the rise to power of Robert Walpole when "political stability" was achieved. The political atmosphere during the Walpole era discouraged intellectual curiosity or indeed any action that might rock the governmental boat of office. In 1718, however, the climate still fostered scientific speculation. Hunter and his fellow colonial amateur scientists gave full rein to their Renaissance minds.[22]

"That unhappy difference at Court"

Hunter and his coterie were, of course, professional politicians and as such keenly interested in and able to evaluate political news from Great Britain. In the spring of 1717, they were disturbed to hear that Stanhope, Townshend, and Sunderland had changed offices. Logan received the news first from "a young Scotsman lately arrived from Lisbon." He assumed that all the changes had been promotions, or "a kicking them upstairs as some call it, that is that they left their former places for better."[23]

Logan's surmise was partially true, but the changes in the ministry were potentially threatening for Whig officeholders because they were indicative of a split in the Whig ranks. Two factions vied for power; the first allied with Marlborough and the second with Argyll. In 1716, the Marlborough faction, which included Sunderland, Stanhope, and Cadogan, succeeded in displacing the Argyll faction, which included Townshend and Walpole. Sunderland was named northern secretary in Townshend's place. He promptly brought in his old protégé, and Hunter's friend, Joseph Addison, as southern secretary with dominion over the colonies. Stanhope became first minister when he became first lord of the treasury. Cadogan, who had led the British forces which subdued the Scottish Jacobites, was acting commander-in-chief under Marlborough, who had been incapacitated by a second stroke.[24]

Despite Addison's ascendancy, Argyll's loss of power was a blow for Hunter, who counted on the Scottish duke's favor. Hunter was deeply disturbed by the changes as shown by his comment to Board of Trade Secretary William Popple that "That unhappy difference at Court sits heavier upon me than my private concerns can ever do [.] I pray God put an end to't tho' I cannot yet pray he may forgive those who have occasion'd it. . . . "[25]

Hunter believed he experienced a decline in support from the home government, first apparent when Daniel Coxe and Samuel Mulford reached England. Samuel Bustall, whom Hunter described as "a very mean wretch, but chief instrument of Mr. Cox's," had travelled to London

John Campbell, second duke of Argyll, 1740, by Thomas Bardwell, National Portrait Gallery, London. Described by Swift as an "ambitious, covetous, cunning Scot, who has no principle but his own interest and greatness," Argyll was, in fact, interested in helping fellow Scots such as Hunter.

with Daniel Coxe. Shortly after his arrival in London, Bustall wrote to his wife in New Jersey to inform her and their friends that the lord high chancellor, Thomas Parker, first earl of Macclesfield, and Lord Townshend were both sympathetic to their complaints against Hunter. Bustall claimed that Hunter now had few supporters for "My Lord Summers is dead and the Duke of Argile is out of every thing and by the King was banished ye Cort so that Coll. Hunter had not one friend att Cort...." The letter was seized by Hunter's friends in New Jersey and sent by the governor-general to Ambrose Philips, his London agent. Philips presented the letter to the Board of Trade with the notation that "Mr Ld. Chancellour says that all that relates to him is pure fiction," an indication that despite Hunter's fears, he continued to enjoy government support.[26]

Hunter's agents also seized a later letter written by Bustall. In this letter, Bustall told his wife that John Robinson, bishop of London, was planning to attend a hearing at which charges against Hunter were to be considered, presumably to testify against the governor-general. Bustall again gloated that "Coll. Hunters interest is intirely sunck at Court since ye King's displeasure with the Duke of Argyle.... My Lord Cadogan can't heare him named with any tollerable patience." Bustall further compared Hunter's rule of New York and New Jersey with Daniel Parke's misrule of the Leeward Islands. He observed that "Even Parliament men [Whigs] wonder how a Province of freeborn Englishmen cold beare to be kept under soe much tyrany and oppression without serveing him even as the people of Antigua served Generall Parkes. ... " Hunter immediately seized on the reference to Parke, Marlborough's former aide-de-camp who had been murdered in 1710 by the islanders of Antigua, as being an assassination threat. He reported the matter to the Board of Trade to further discredit his colonial enemies in London.[27]

Hunter may not ever have been in danger of being assassinated (the informant was obviously stupid as well as indiscreet, and Hunter was usually surrounded by two companies of armed soldiers). He was, however, annoyed with reports that his enemies had gained ground in England. Daniel Coxe, who wrote a letter to friends in New Jersey which was also intercepted by Hunter's agents, reported that his petition was read to the king "in Council, and contrary to the expectation of Coll. Hunter's friends referred to a Committee of H.M. Council for heareing appeals from the Plantations...." Coxe was delighted with the disposition of his petition to the privy council because he had feared it would be referred to the Board of Trade which was full of Hunter's supporters.[28]

More irritation came from Samuel Mulford, who in 1717 sent back to Long Island several petitions against Hunter which his agents circulated for signatures. Hunter learned of the petitions in November. At his urging, the New York council launched an investigation only to find that the signatures were obtained by threats or deception. Many people, the council reported, had been told they were merely signing a petition in support of duty-free whale fishing. Hunter's people now circulated a pro-Hunter petition among the same people who had signed Mulford's petition. By the use of threats and intimidation, Hunter's agents were able to obtain the signatures of virtually the same signers on their petition for Hunter as on Mulford's petition against him. These signators included at least three relatives of Samuel Mulford—Isaac Mulford, Thomas Mulford, and John Mulford.[29]

"The place of Treaty"

Mulford had also caused problems with the Iroquois, as Hunter learned when he met with the sachems of the Five Nations in June of 1717. The Iroquois sachems told Hunter they had heard of an agreement between the French and the English to exterminate all the Indians in North America to make room for Europeans. Hunter reassured them that this was not the intent of the English. The source of the Indians' fear was Samuel Mulford, who had long advocated a policy of native extermination. When Hunter returned to New York City, he asked the assembly to make a formal declaration to repudiate Mulford's genocidal plans and to affirm the colony's friendly attitude toward the Iroquois. The assembly did so in a resolution that declared it had never been New York's policy to reduce "the Indians by force . . . ."[30]

The main purpose of Hunter's June 1717 meeting with the Iroquois sachems was to discuss the problems caused by Indian wars in the south. These had begun in 1711, when the Tuscarora, an Iroquoian people whose territory was in North Carolina, attacked Swiss and Palatine settlers. The Tuscarora were badly beaten by white and red forces. Finally, Governor-General Alexander Spotswood of Virginia negotiated a treaty with the Tuscarora. Spotswood also extended an offer to the Tuscarora to settle on a six-mile-square reservation in Virginia. Some Tuscarora agreed to become tributaries of Virginia, but about five hundred families moved north to ask the Five Nations for shelter. The sachems of the Five (soon to be Six) Nations agreed to accept the Tuscarora as associates of the league peoples and part of the Oneidas' land was assigned to them. By September of 1714, when Hunter met the sachems in Albany, many Tuscarora had already migrated to New York. The Iroquois promised their good behavior and in return asked Hunter to "look upon the Tuscarores . . . as our Children who shall obey our command & live peaceably and orderly[.]"[31]

With the Tuscarora defeated, the English in the south could push westward until their settlements threatened other Indian tribes. In 1715, the Yamasee, Coweta, Talapoosa, Abihka, Alabama, Choctaw, Catawba, and Sara, feeling the pressure of English expansion, attacked some towns in South Carolina. In August of 1715, Hunter, in response to pleas from South Carolina Governor Charles Craven, urged the Iroquois to either negotiate a peace treaty with the troublesome Indians or to "Interpose with your Power to put an end to this warr." The Iroquois hated the Carolina Indians, or "the Flatheads," who only a few years earlier had helped destroy the Tuscarora. The Iroquois warned Hunter that negotiation with the Flatheads was futile and they could only be defeated by force. Hunter agreed to supply the Iroquois warriors with arms and ammunition to achieve this end.[32]

By October of 1715, the Iroquois raiding parties were on their way south. Hunter believed they would speedily "put an end to the Carolina War by putting an end to the enemies of that Colony." It turned out their intercession was not needed. Spotswood, who continued in his self-appointed role as peacemaker, effected a treaty with some of the warring tribes, including the Catawba, who agreed to give Spotswood hostages as a token of their good faith. An Iroquois raiding party, perhaps ignorant of the peace treaty, attacked the Catawba hostages and killed five, wounded two, and took two prisoners. Spotswood, angry at this breach of good faith, requested Hunter to convey his displeasure to the Iroquois sachems. He also insisted that Iroquois raiding parties stay out of Virginia. Hunter reported Spotswood's messages to the sachems in June of 1717, along with Spotswood's request that the sachems meet him in Virginia. The Iroquois, unimpressed with Spotswood's anger, claimed their warriors had not known of the treaty. They then refused to meet Spotswood anywhere but in "Albany [which] is and hath always been the place of Treaty, neither are the Brethren of Virginia[,] Maryland[,] and New England ignorant thereof. . . . "[33]

Spotswood was understandably indignant when Hunter told him that the Iroquois insisted he or his deputies travel to Albany. In October of 1717, he and Pennsylvania Governor Keith came to New York to see Hunter. Once they arrived at Fort George, Spotswood repeated to Hunter his sense of outrage that he, a royal governor-general, should have to travel to Albany to meet the Iroquois sachems because they refused to come to him. Hunter, who was equally concerned with protocol under other circumstances, told Spotswood "it was silly to insist on punctilios" when dealing with the Iroquois. Spotswood apparently agreed, for he indicated his willingness to travel immediately to Albany to meet the sachems. Hunter, however, informed him it was too late in the season for such a trip. Hunter promised that at his next conference with the Iroquois he himself would repeat Spotswood's message to the sachems to keep their raiding parties out of Virginia.[34]

Hunter was more inclined to humor the Iroquois than was Spotswood. Virginia's Indians had been subdued in the seventeenth century. The few and scattered remnants of tribes that remained were confined to reservations. In addition, Virginia was somewhat protected by its mountains from Indian raids. Colonists in New York (or New Amsterdam), on the other hand, had prospered and grown because of their alliance with the Iroquois, whose territory abutted colonial settlements. Since the first Dutch settlement, Europeans and Iroquois had enjoyed a symbiotic relationship, with the Dutch exchanging weapons and household goods for peltry. The firearms enabled the Iroquois to devastate rival nations so they could control the fur trade. When the Dutch were supplanted by the English, the Iroquois continued the trading arrangement. White traders did take advantage of the Indians, but Hunter sought to protect the Iroquois by establishing government-controlled trading posts at Albany. At these posts, Indians were able to sell furs and buy goods at a comparatively low mark up of 200 percent as compared to the outrageously exorbitant profits of 1000 percent or more common among individual traders.[35]

In return for protection and trade, the Iroquois helped to keep the French and unfriendly Indian tribes away from English communities. This mutually beneficial relationship was neatly summed up by the Iroquois sachem Dekanissore, on June 15, 1717: "Since ye very first beginning that Christians began to settle at N. York we have liv'd always in amity & in peace because we have always been one heart one mind & one blood intirely united, & no man ever hated his own flesh. We very early entred into a Covenant with one another, which has been kept inviolable by both sides to this day & hope shall ever continue, and had had a continuall trade & commerce together. . . . "[36]

Hunter, aware of how much New York depended upon the Iroquois, realized that offending or alienating them would endanger New York and all continental English colonies. The Iroquois could not prevent French incursions along the Mississippi, but they did keep the French away from English settlements. Hunter also capitalized upon the belligerency of the Iroquois by urging them to fight and subdue other Indian tribes. This extended their own territory and New York's sphere of influence.[37]

"Weary of this life"

When Hunter was not preoccupied with Indian affairs, his attention was taken by his enemies in London. His interests in London, however, were protected by such friends as Secretary of State Joseph Addison. In August of 1717, Addison showed the king a letter from Hunter complaining of malicious reports being sent to England against him. Addison was pleased to report to the Board of Trade that George I had indicated he was "very well satisfyed with the Conduct of Governor Hunter, which you will please to signify in such a manner, as you shall think the most likely to silence such reports, and defeat such practices for the future. . . . " The board promptly wrote to notify Hunter of the king's support in the hope that it would silence Hunter's enemies. It did not silence them, but it may have influenced the attorney general of England, who, on February 18, 1718, reported to the board that Hunter's enemies had not submitted proof of their charges against Hunter so he could not advise any proceedings against him.[38]

During 1718, the board also continued to consider New York's 1717 debt bill as well as the petitions against it circulated by London and New York merchants. On August 20, 1718, the board's attorney, Richard West, reported that in his "opinion that the merchants of London are not proper to object to what debts ought to be allow'd or disallow'd, that being a thing which is absolutely in the power of the General Assembly. . . . " West acknowledged that the merchants could object to the bill on the basis that it might hurt Great Britain's trade, but "it does not clearly appear to me, that ye merchants can be any lossers in consequence of these bills. . . . " The board endorsed its attorney's opinion and forwarded the New York bill to the king-in-council. It was confirmed on May 19, 1720, a victory for New York's governor-general and the colony's landowning faction.[39]

Hunter believed complaints by provincials, whether from organized merchant groups or from individuals such as Coxe or Mulford, were given more attention in London than they deserved. He constantly expressed his astonishment that these colonial "Criminals" and "common disturbers of the publick peace" should even be allowed the courtesy of a hearing in London. He expected the home government to back him and ignore these complaints because his arbitrary methods had produced satisfactory results. As he pointed out, if the board would but "look back into the affairs of this Province. . . & compare the former confusion with the present happy tranquility," they would be inclined to "make some allowance for failures of small consequence. . . . " Hunter was certain that the intent of his opponents was to annoy him until he resigned in frustration, much as the

Tories had forced Marlborough to resign: "For who would for anything this world can give be ty'd down to the perpetual drudgery of answering such stuff."[40]

His enemies' complaints forced Hunter to make a long-delayed decision to return home. Hunter had received permission to leave his post in 1716, shortly after his wife's death. Yet he remained in America, partially from political considerations because he wanted to be sure the colonies were under control. Hunter may also have postponed his return because of a liaison he formed with a New York seamstress, Betty Holland, whose mother was a much-respected nurse in New York City. At some time after the death of Lady Hay, Hunter's mistress gave birth to a female child who was christened Elizabeth Hunter. His romantic attachment for a woman of modest family whom he could never marry may well have led Hunter to tarry (and dally) in New York.[41]

In the spring of 1719, however, Hunter, "weary of this life" in America, at last decided to go to England. In addition to feeling the need to defend himself against Coxe's and Mulford's accusations in person, and in so doing assess the changed English political situation, Hunter was also motivated by personal considerations. He wanted to secure his wife's estate for their children and to re-establish his own contacts with friends and family in Great Britain.[42]

Hunter was also prompted by illness to return home. In the autumn of 1718, the governor-general, who had formerly gloried in his good health, began to suffer from rheumatoid arthritis, "the Scottish disease." Hunter's condition crippled him during the winter of 1718–1719. He walked with a limp when not confined to bed, a sad blow for a man of formerly "uncommon strength and activity." James Logan extended his sympathies to Hunter and also noted he had personally found rest and warmth to be the best remedies for his own less serious condition. Rest and warmth were not, however, the suggested medical treatment of the day. In a letter to the physician Colden, Logan, who was bothered by rheumatoid back pains, reported that he had tried "cold Baths a dozen mornings, but to very little purpose." If Colden or other physicians prescribed so for Hunter, it is not surprising that the governor-general's condition persisted into the warm weather of the spring of 1719. At that time Hunter complained "I live in Such Torture with a violent pain in my hipp or Bautick. . . . " He had little faith in colonial medicine and had "try'd all remedys Christian and Pagan, Palenieal Chymical and Whimsical to no purpose[.] Aix La Chapelle is all my present Comfort." Finally, when in June of 1719, the *Pearle* man-of-war sailed into the harbor, Hunter prepared to sail for England.[43]

"Vile affections"

On June 24, 1719, at a joint session of both houses of the New York legislature, Hunter addressed that body for the last time. Hunter told the legislature that because of "my late uncertain state of health, the care of my little family, and my private affairs on the other side," he had at last decided to leave. He told them, however, that he went "with a firm resolution to return to you again," but promised that if this were not possible, he would "be watchful and industrious to promote the interest and welfare of this country, of which I... account myself a countryman." Hunter reported he was pleased with the "present quiet and flourishing state of the people here," which was in direct contrast to "that in which I found them at my arrival." He rejoiced that "the very name of party or faction seems to be forgot" in New York.[44]

Like most politically aware Britons of his day, Hunter clung to the belief that factionalism was merely a temporary aberration which would be eliminated when political stability was achieved. He was mistaken, for throughout the colonial era in New York there would always be a court and a country party, or the "ins" and the "outs." Hunter had not eliminated dissension in New York, he had merely quelled his opposition by buying them off, by forcing them to flee, or by bullying them into silence and inactivity. He had further assured his political success and effectiveness by creating and maintaining a court party of intelligent, competent, and conscientious men whom he nominated for the council, encouraged to run for the assembly, and appointed to fill key posts in the judiciary and militia. Thus, in both New York and New Jersey, the government was run by men, who while by no means blind to the profits of office, shared Hunter's commitment to the furtherance of the interests of the British Empire. On the eve of his departure, Hunter's methods had proved so successful that he could truthfully say "that all is well in both Provinces, and a perfect harmony reigning among all parties...."[45]

Hunter, however, had not only relied on force and patronage to achieve political stability in his governments. He was also quite willing to use compromise and conciliation because he was politically astute enough to realize that the complete subjugation and degradation of his enemies would hinder his ability to govern. Hence, while he controlled the anti-imperialism of merchants, he still afforded merchants a platform within government from which they could state their grievances. This helped to prevent the formation of a politically effective opposition. In New York, one example of Hunter's concessions to his enemies was his retention of merchant Adolph Philipse, the "Flip" of *Androboros,* on the New York council, where he was more or less under the governor-general's control. The solutions to New York's and New Jersey's problems were, however, Hunter's and would endure only as long as he was actually present and in control of the provinces. Under less able administrators, New York and New Jersey would again become ungovernable, faction-ridden colonies.

Dissension would return in the future, but in 1719 when Hunter announced his intention to leave, the New York assembly, packed with the governor-general's allies, was a relatively harmonious and cooperative body. The day after Hunter's address, the assembly replied to Hunter. The speech, written by Lewis Morris and Robert Livingston, fulfilled the 1709 prediction of Richard Steele who had said that when Hunter returned to England "from his government, there will be a monument with these words: 'Here the people wept, and took leave of Eboracensis, the first governour our mother Felicia sent who, during his command here, believed himself her subject.'" On June 25, 1719, the New York assembly addressed Eboracensis:

> When we reflect upon your past conduct, your just, mild and tender administration, it heightens the concern we have for your departure, and makes our grief such as words cannot truly express.
>
> You have governed well and wisely, like a prudent magistrate, like an affectionate parent, and wherever you go, and to whatever station the divine Providence shall please to assign you, our sincere desires and prayers for the happiness of you and yours, shall always attend you.
>
> We have seen many Governors, and may see more; and as none of those who had the honor to serve in your station were ever so justly fixed in the affections of the Government, so those to come will acquire no mean reputation, when it can be truly said of them, their conduct had been like yours.
>
> We thankfully accept the honor you do us in calling yourself our countryman; give us leave then, to desire you will not forget this is your country, and (if you can) make haste to return to it.
>
> But if the service of our sovereign will not admit of what we earnestly desire, and his command deny us that happiness, permit us to address you as our friend, and give us your assistance when we are oppressed with an administration the reverse of yours.[46]

The exchange between governor and legislature was graceful and mutually complimentary. Hunter, for his part, seemed to exhibit in the speech a genuine affection for the assemblymen. But whether this affection was sincere or not is another matter because Hunter was as much of a social snob as any of his peers. As Cadwallader Colden pointed out to his son in 1759, "Assemblies in North America consist generally of a low rank of people who have no generous principles. But it was much worse at that time [1719]. Several of the Assembly were Dutch boors, grossly ignorant and rude, who could neither write or read nor speak English." Colden also remembered that a few days before Hunter delivered his address to the assembly, he privately told Colden his real opinion of his office and the people he governed: "People think it a fine thing to be a governor. A governor by _____ a Tom Turdman's is a better office than to rake in the dunghill of these people's vile affections."[47]

Some colonists in turn spoke with candor about the governor-general. One of these was Samuel Smith, the colonial historian who was born in 1720 and published his history of New Jersey in 1765. Hunter, he said, "had a ready art of procuring money, few loved it more; this foible 'tis said drew him into schemes, gaming, and considerable losses; tho' not in all respects accomplished: His addres here was engaging and successful, he assented to most of the laws the people wanted, and fill'd the offices with men of character." Smith was right about Hunter's attitude toward money, but since no other reference survives about Hunter's "gaming," it does not appear likely that the governor-general was addicted to gambling. Smith was also correct in claiming that Hunter had suffered losses, for he was still owed £21,000 by the government for his Palatine expenses. Since one of the reasons Hunter had undertaken the Palatine project was for the profit he hoped to make on their subsistence, Smith's charge that he suffered losses through greed was correct.[48]

Hunter did not fare too badly with other income, however. According to Captain John Riggs of the New York garrison, Hunter had an estimated yearly income of more than £9,000. Riggs believed that in less than seven years of office, the governor-general had earned more than £40,000 "and when recalled may, if he pleses, purchis ye north of Scotland. . . ." Riggs may have been accurate, but his claim is suspect because he was a jealous subordinate. In addition (if Vesey's accusations were true), Riggs may have been a jealous husband as well.[49]

Hunter made some money in the colonies through land investments, although his holdings were modest indeed when compared to those of Alexander Spotswood. At the time Hunter left America, he owned several lots and houses in Amboy, three houses in New York, five hundred acres on the Raritan River, and held an uncertain title to Burlington Island. The net worth of this property was estimated as being between £3,000 and £3,100. Much of Hunter's land was leased, and payments from various mortgages and bonds were made to Hunter for the rest of his life through his personal New York agents, Abraham De Peyster and James Alexander. As Hunter prepared to leave, he may well have reflected that, except for the Palatine fiasco, he had not done too badly financially as governor-general of New York and New Jersey.[50]

After a farewell visit from William Keith, Hunter oversaw the loading of his provisions, personal belongings, and furniture on board ship. James Logan wrote to express his dismay that Hunter was leaving and asked that Hunter write to him from London, "tho' I can Scarce expect to be remembered at Such a distance & in Such company." On July 13, 1719, exactly nine years and one month after the first ship of the Wonder Fleet arrived in New York Harbor, Hunter turned the government of New York over to Peter Schuyler and that of New Jersey over to Lewis Morris, both men presidents of the councils. A last good-bye was said to Betty Holland, who remained in New York with her daughter, both destined never to see lover and father again. Hunter, with his five children by Lady Hay, boarded His Majesty's ship *Pearle* and sailed home for England.

ⒸⒺ⒧ *7* ⒮⒨

"The Giddy Turns of State"

July 1719– January 1728

But God has, wisely, hid from human sight
The dark Decrees of future fate,
And sown their seeds in depth of night;
He laughs at all the giddy turns of state,
When mortals search too soon, and fear too late.
                    John Dryden,
                    "Horace, The Twenty-Ninth Ode"

"The season of buss'nsse"

H.M.S. *Pearle,* which carried Governor-General Robert Hunter from New York to England, arrived at Plymouth on September 24, 1719, and was temporarily halted there by contrary winds. The more than two months on board ship had been a period of almost unremitting pain and discomfort for Hunter. The dampness of the ship had aggravated his arthritic condition so that "Untill we came within 100 leagues of land I could not stir off my bed . . . I intend for the bath as speedily as may be. . . . " He assured Board of Trade Secretary William Popple, however, that he expected "to return to to[w]n in full vigour by the season of buss'nsse. . . . "[1]

The "town" was, of course, London, with a population of more than half a million. Hunter's first sight of the city, after an absence of more than nine years, was from the crowded waterway of the Thames. As seen from the river, the public and private buildings were tightly packed and graced by the spires of church steeples, many designed by Sir Christopher Wren. Towering above the buildings and dominating the cityscape was Wren's masterpiece, "St. Paul's; a building exceeding beautiful and magnificent. . . . "[2]

London, in 1719, was the political, legal, financial, social, and artistic center of the empire, crowded with government buildings, private homes, business centers, and markets (fourteen meat, three fish, two herb, one cherry and apple, two corn, four meal, six hay, one leather, two hide and skin, two coal, one bay, one broadcloth, and a "Bubble market" in Exchange Alley for speculation). There were in all 21 public gaols and 119 spunging houses (or debtors prisons), 3 pest houses, and various other "tolerated prisons." The London to which Hunter returned was a city of striking contrasts, whose elegance and horror, sophistication and sordidness, loveliness and squalor, were captured on canvas with unexcelled accuracy and vividness by the artists Canaletto for beauty and Hogarth for horror.[3]

Despite the arthritic pain he suffered, Hunter must have gloried in the fact that he was at last home from the provinces, among cultivated friends in elegant surroundings. He was again able to savor the literary and musical delights of the city and to have his portrait painted by Sir Godfrey Kneller, the most fashionable portrait artist in England. In the portrait, which still survives, Hunter is shown in a dragoon officer's dress uniform, wearing a red coat lined with leopard skin, the fur worn to indicate service overseas. Hunter is wearing a cuirass, while his left hand rests on a helmet, with a gold fringed sash knotted about his waist. A battle scene from the War of the Spanish Succession is depicted in the background of the portrait, showing an otherwise unknown incident in Hunter's military career. The red-coated dragoon, presumably Hunter, is seen mounted, discharging a pistol held with both hands over his rearing horse's head. The shot from the pistol hits a blue-coated mounted Frenchman with upraised sword who is knocked backward from his horse. It is not surprising that Hunter should have chosen to immortalize a wartime scene in his portrait. He was, after all, the ideal courtier, who remembered to his dying day that "the first and true profession of the courtier must be that of arms...."[4]

A courtier also needed to maintain his contacts with the centers of power. Consequently, Hunter on his return assessed the intrigues that continued to shake the Whig ministry. As had been usual throughout Hunter's life, England's political situation in 1719 was unsettled. Shortly before Hunter sailed for England, his patron, Argyll, had made peace with the Sunderland faction, but to do so he had to abandon Prince George, who had broken with his father, the king, as well as Townshend and Walpole. Argyll was then, in February of 1719, named steward of the household by the king. Much to Argyll's dismay, however, Walpole and Townshend began to negotiate with Sunderland and Stanhope to arrange a reconciliation between the king and the prince. Whatever hopes Hunter may have had of using Argyll's influence were dashed on April 23, 1720, when the reconciliation was finally effected. The prince, who resented Argyll's defection, had him dismissed from office. Sunderland and Stanhope remained dominant at court, but after the reconciliation between the king and the prince, the opposition was also back in power. Walpole was named paymaster general of the forces and Townshend president of the council.[5]

Hunter did not despair at Argyll's fall, however, because other patrons, such as the earl of Stair, were still in favor. Hunter also enjoyed the support of Stanhope and in December of 1719, asked Stair to recommend him again to Stanhope's attention. Hunter also dealt with the immediate problems connected with his return, chiefly his poor health. He was finally compelled to resort to "a most violent medicine," which he believed had been of some benefit, although he remained preoccupied by "intolerable paine." Hunter's condition apparently had eased by December of 1719, when he told Stair that "I am now free from pain and only want Strength which comes apace. . . . "[6]

In addition to almost constant pain, Hunter was further distressed on his return by the loss of many of his papers. The governor-general had brought back his personal furniture, including his writing desk. Many of his papers suffered irreparable damage because "of ye unhappy accident which befell to my scritoire coming up ye River being stav'd by ye anchor on ye bow of a ship and thrown into the River where it remaind an houre before they could recover it."[7]

Hunter was also upset by reports he received from Secretary of New York George Clarke and some New York councillors that president of the council, Peter Schuyler, temporarily in command of New York's government, had tried "to break into the measures, that the Govr had with much labour settled for the peace of that Country. . . ." Schuyler had already made changes "in the Magistracy," and Hunter believed his intent was the "dissolution of this present Assembly[,] the most dutifull to their Sovereign and ye most attentive to the true Intrests of the Colony that ye Province could ever boast of[.]" The Board of Trade shared Hunter's concern about Schuyler's meddling. They quickly complained to Secretary of State James Craggs who told Schuyler that he was not to "make any other alterations than such as shall be thought by the Council to be absolutely necessary, and particularly, that you do not presume to dissolve the present Assembly."[8]

Although Hunter throughout the winter of 1719–1720 remained actively concerned with the problems of New York and New Jersey, he had no intention of returning to his post. But, as Governor William Keith of

Pennsylvania realized, "he will have a great stroke in nameing his successor. . . ." Hunter's choice was William Burnet, comptroller of the customs, son of the Scot bishop and historian Gilbert Burnet. Both the father and the son were old friends of Hunter's. William Burnet and Hunter agreed to exchange offices. On April 19, 1720, Burnet was officially appointed governor-general of New York and New Jersey. Once Burnet arrived in New York, he kept Hunter's assembly in existence and in other ways continued Hunter's policies. Burnet also continued in office the men who had proven personally loyal to Hunter, including Lewis Morris, Cadwallader Colden, David Jamison, and James Alexander.[9]

Hunter took Burnet's office in the customs because it was potentially an excellent source of income, although the official salary was modest. It had been set at £1,000 in 1685 when there were only forty-nine outports. The number of outports had grown to seventy-two by 1718, when Burnet petitioned the Board of Customs Commissioners for an additional £200 a year. Burnet at that time noted that from 1685 to 1718, the amount of paper work done by his department had doubled. The Board agreed to give Burnet the additional money. Although Hunter's salary was only £1,200 a year, as was usual in government posts, this was probably only the tip of the iceberg. Posts in customs were much sought after for the extra, unreported income they brought.[10]

The offices of the customs department, a subdepartment of the treasury, were in the Customs House. The original Customs House, built in 1671 to Sir Christopher Wren's design, had burnt down in 1715 to be rebuilt in 1718 by Thomas Ripley. By the time Hunter took office in 1720, the Customs House was considered one of the showplaces of London. In 1725, Defoe commented on "the stateliness of the building" and noted that the steady increase of business had already necessitated its further enlargement. Within these elegant environs, Hunter served Sunderland until the latter's resignation as first lord of the treasury in April of 1721. Hunter then reported to Sunderland's successor, Robert Walpole. Some of Hunter's other associates in the treasury and customs were the playwright William Congreve, an old friend, and the merchant William Sloper, Senior, another old friend who also acted as Robert Walpole's financial broker. Sloper had long traded to New York. During Hunter's administration, the governor had held Sloper's power of attorney.[11]

Hunter's knowledge of colonial affairs must have served him well in his new customs post, where colonial affairs were handled by the board of customs commissioners, part of whose function it was to enforce the Navigation Acts and to oversee the appointment and promotion of regional customs officers. The board consisted of fourteen commissioners, five of whom were in Scotland, seven in London, and two in the English outports. Hunter's duties as comptroller were established as far back as the reign of Edward I. The comptroller kept checks on the collectors, kept records of all transactions, and examined and signed all accounts and dispatches.[12]

In 1720, much of the custom department's time was taken in enforcing a quarantine on vessels from the Mediterranean, which had been imposed by the treasury department. There had been an outbreak of plague on the continent, and the ministry was determined to prevent its spread to Great Britain. Vessels from Mediterranean ports and from the British islands of Mann and Guernsey were quarantined for forty days. After that time, the cargo was to be opened and aired for a week. In the London area, the ships with their exotic cargoes of raisins, wine, whisks, wormseeds, boxwood, cream of tartar, coffee, marble, fustic, straw, tombstones, human hair, and kidskins, were kept at anchor in the Stangate Creek on the south shore of the Medway River before comptroller Hunter's agents could collect the government's duties.[13]

In addition to securing a new post, one of Hunter's primary concerns on his return home was the squelching of his provincial opponents who remained in London. Soon after his arrival, Hunter turned his attention to Daniel Coxe and Samuel Mulford, both of whom had appeals pending before the privy council's Appeals Court. Hunter had feared the council would condemn him unheard, but such was not the case. The Appeals Court (and for that matter the entire privy council) was solidly on Hunter's side. Colonial complainants such as Coxe and Mulford were given attention, placated, and heard if they were in London. The privy council, however, refused to consider the case against Hunter, much less reach a decision, until he was actually there to defend himself. Between 1715 and 1719, Mulford's and Coxe's appeals were each brought before the council on at least seven different occasions. Each time the petitioners were put off with excuses. Mulford, Coxe, and their witnesses were forced to remain in London, both because they could expect no peace if they returned to Hunter's jurisdiction and because their appeals would be ignored if they were not actually present. London was an expensive city in which to live, and their resources dwindled rapidly. When Hunter finally returned to London, Mulford and Coxe dropped their petitions. An attack on a governor-general was an attack on the royal prerogative. Coxe and Mulford realized they could not hope to receive a favorable decision with Hunter present to defend himself before a court predisposed in his favor.[14]

Hunter also dealt expeditiously with John Conrad Weiser and his petition to the Board of Trade. Weiser charged that Hunter refused to settle the Palatines on "the land Call'd *Schorie* which the Indians had given to the late Queen Anne for their [the Palatines] use . . . . " and instead insisted they settle along the Hudson River. When the Palatines persisted in their demands to move to the frontier, Hunter, "in a passion stamped upon the ground and said, here is your land (meaning the almost baren Rocks,) where you must live and die." Weiser also recalled that after the 1712 abandonment of the Palatines by Hunter, some fifty families decided to move to the Schoharie. They remained there despite the demands of the legal owners, newly patented by Hunter, to move out or pay rent. The Palatines refused to become tenants because they claimed the rents demanded were "extravagant." Weiser reported that in June of 1717, Hunter told the Palatines they must either move or become tenants. Until they agreed to accept tenancy, they were not to plant any crops in the Schoharie tract. During the winter of 1717–1718, the Palatines sent three emissaries to New York City to ask the governor-general's permission to plant crops during the coming spring, but Hunter again refused. Two of those Palatines who defied the governor's orders against planting were jailed and, according to Weiser, were still in prison in Albany.[15]

Hunter was angered by the charges. Many of the statements of the petition were marked "not true" or "utterly false," probably by Hunter himself. Hunter pointed out to the board that the great majority of the Palatines were still living on the fertile Hudson River land where he had settled them. As for the Palatines in the Schoharie, Hunter, moved by "compassion to the Innocent Women and children," had interceded with the new owners of the tract and finally "prevailed with the proprietors of these lands to make them an offer of the Lands free from all rent or acknowledgement for ten years and ever after at a very moderate Quit Rent." Hunter pointed out that most of the Palatines in the Schoharie were willing to accept these terms, but were prevented from doing so "for fear of the rest. . . . " As to what was to be done with the Schoharie Palatines, Hunter proposed that they be resettled on a fifty-mile tract of land formerly granted to the Reverend Dellius but "resumed by act of Assembly" during Bellomont's administration.[16]

The Board of Trade, after considering Weiser's petition and Hunter's replies, decided the Palatines had not presented any evidence of their various charges against Hunter. The board consequently issued an order to Governor-General Burnet to settle the Schoharie Palatines on land of his own choosing with the further observation that the Palatines had behaved undutifully both to Hunter and the king. The Palatines had the last word, however, in their long, bitter, and unnecessary struggle with Hunter. In 1722, Hunter asked George Clarke to have the Palatines sign a statement certifying that he had subsisted them. Hunter needed the affidavit to obtain reimbursement of the money owed him by the government. The majority of the Schoharie Palatines refused to sign. Clarke reported to auditor general Horatio Walpole that "the greatest part of them [the Palatines] have purchased in pensilvania and are determined to go thither, thus the Brigadeer is baulked. ... " Clarke's rueful prediction proved correct. Hunter himself acknowledged, "I have been undone by Serving that poor people. ... " Although Hunter continued to file applications for reimbursement for the rest of his life, he did not collect the £21,000. A defeat in the colonial backwoods in 1722 was a sad end to an undertaking that had disappointed all concerned.[17]

In addition to Palatine-related problems, Hunter was also called to Board of Trade meetings to comment upon other colonial concerns, particularly regarding the Albany-Montreal trade in duffles and strouds and its ramifications on Indian relations. Hunter estimated the trade in English-made goods was worth about £10,000 to £12,000 a year. Burnet, who had been ordered to suppress the Canadian trade, had the support of New York's landowning faction, headed by Lewis Morris. The landowners believed the Canadians' contact with the Iroquois interfered with English hegemony. The trade was favored, however, by New York and English merchants, who wanted the profits and cared little who maintained hegemony over the Indians or their territory. In New York, Burnet, as imperial minded as Hunter, followed his predecessor's example and allied with the landowning faction. Shortly after his arrival, Burnet approved a bill passed by the assembly which made the Albany-Montreal trade illegal.[18]

Hunter did his best to see this bill was enforced by urging the Board of Trade to authorize the construction of a fort on the New York side of the Great Lakes. A fort, built behind the Seneca nation near Niagara, was, Hunter believed, "the only way to secure & Maintain our claim" against the French. Burnet agreed that the English should extend their territorial control of North America, especially because this would divert the fur trade between western Indians and Canadians to New York. In 1725, Burnet, acting on Hunter's suggestion, established a trading post at Oswego. Two years later, Burnet had a fort constructed there, an act resented by Canadians and Indians alike. Despite the presence of the fort and colonial legislation, Burnet's efforts to suppress the Indian-Canadian trade and the Albany-Montreal trade were largely unsuccessful.[19]

The Board of Trade continued to ask Hunter's advice about colonial concerns throughout his residency in England. In 1726, Hunter attended a board meeting along with several other of his fellow past and present governors-general: Francis Nicholson (South Carolina, 1720–1728);

Alexander Spotswood (Virginia, 1709–1722); Samuel Shute (Massachusetts, 1716–1723); and Richard Phillips (Nova Scotia, 1717–1729). The generals discussed a proposal by Galfridus Gray for the construction of a colonial road. The frontier road, according to Gray, was to be 1,050 miles in length and would extend "from the head of the Bay de Chaloner, which Runes up about 90 miles into Nova Scotia out of St. Laurance River From then to the westernmost Bounds of South Carolina...." It was to be defended by men housed in one thousand newly built blockhouses. Gray anticipated that "Such a Line will be a Barrier, Boundary & Communication And also will be of Servis for Intelligence & Trade." An additional benefit was that government-controlled trading posts, such as that Hunter established in Albany, would also be set up along the road.[20]

The road and the controlled, continent-wide rather than colony-wide, Indian trade, were exciting ideas in themselves. What must have been equally interesting was the sight of five governors-general in various stages of enmity, rivalry, and friendship, all seated at the same table. Unfortunately, only the official minutes of the meeting survive, so whatever backslapping, gladhanding, or snide remarks were exchanged are forever lost. Gray's proposal had obvious merit, but the governors agreed the cost of the road would be too high. They also feared that colonial legislatures would never be coerced into financing such an ambitious program. Gray naturally took exception to the decision, but the governors were undoubtedly correct in their assumption that colonial assemblies would neither provide money for such a project nor cooperate with other colonies to build it.[21]

"The reigning Amusement of the town"

During this eight-year English hiatus in Hunter's American commands, he continued to acquire land and culture. One of his first acts on returning to Britain was to extend his real estate holdings by buying land in Scotland, or perhaps he merely purchased manorial rights there. At least Cadwallader Colden's father, Alexander, informed his son on October 3, 1721, that Hunter "hath bought the Lordship of Melross from my Lord Haddingtoun." Cadwallader Colden was much on Hunter's mind after he returned to England. In 1720, Hunter wrote to Colden to ask that he extend his speculations on "Natural Philosophy or any thing Else wtout reserve for they give pleasure to others as well as my Self and let me know what progress you make in ye Natural History of ye Country...."[22]

While encouraging diligence in his colonial protégé, Hunter did not neglect his own role as patron of the arts, although some adaptation was needed on his part. Tastes in London had changed during Hunter's nine-year absence. The fascination with poetry, which had been the most prized means of expression for London wits in the first decade of the century had declined. By the 1720s, the cognoscenti had further developed their interest in the opera and its practitioners. In 1723, John Gay wrote to Swift in Ireland that:

> As for the reigning Amusement of the town, tis entirely Musick, real fiddles, Bass Viols and Haut Boys not poetical Harps, Lyres, and reeds, Theres nobody allow'd to say I Sing but an Eunuch or an Italian Woman. Every body is grown now as great a judge of musick as they were in your time of Poetry, and folks that could not distinguish one tune from another now daily dispute about the different Styles of Hendel, Bononcini, and Attilio. People have now forgot Homer, and Virgil & Caesar, or at least they have lost their ranks, for in London and Westminster in all polite conversation's, [the sopranist] Senesino is daily voted to be the greatest man that ever liv'd.[23]

Hunter was quick to grasp the changing current. By 1722, he was "one of the Directors of the Opera" at the Haymarket Theater. The Haymarket, used principally for plays after its 1705 opening, had been converted for operatic performances in 1720. Handel was musical director and composed several operas for the company, most of them performed between 1721 and 1728. The literary elite, who had previously concentrated on poetry, were now collaborating with musicians on operas. Alexander Pope, for instance, had joined with the duke of Buckingham in writing a musical version of *Julius Caesar*. After the duke's death, the duchess of Buckingham wanted to stage a performance of the new opera at the Drury Lane Theater and enlisted Pope's assistance in hiring singers to fill the roles. Pope, on learning that Hunter was a director of the London Opera Company, asked if he "wou'd permit them [the singers] to perform" at Drury Lane. Hunter replied through Lord Percival that the "chief Singers engaged, wou'd not be permitted to perform at Drury Lane," but offered the services of the Haymarket's musicians when they were not playing for the London Opera. Hunter also suggested that Pope contact singer Maria Gallia, lately returned from Italy, who "sings to his judgment extreamly well" and was not under contract to the Haymarket. The duke's opera was finally performed on January 10, 1723, at Buckingham House by Mrs. Robinson, Mrs. Barbier, and Mrs. Clark, under the direction of Signor Bononcini.[24]

Much as Hunter enjoyed the sophisticated delights of London, he did not spend all his time there. The bulk of his English estates, inherited from his wife's family, the Orbys, was in Lincolnshire. Hunter had held the 6,599-acre estate of Croyland since his marriage to Elizabeth Orby Hay. After the 1724 death of his father-in-law, Sir Thomas Orby, the 1,506-acre estate of Burton Pedwardine also came into Hunter's possession. Hunter was needed in Lincolnshire to supervise the affairs of the hundreds of tenants on both estates. He managed the estates with his usual efficiency, and in 1723 ordered a survey of the tenants. The results of the survey was an increase in the rents, which had remained unchanged since the civil wars.[25]

Even in the flat fenland of Lincolnshire, Hunter was not lacking in intellectual companionship. There were many other educated minds in the county who wanted to further their interests in science, literature, and antiquities. On March 9, 1726, Hunter joined the Gentleman's Literary Society at Spalding, undoubtedly aware that the society had been started at the behest of his friends Steele and Addison, the latter now dead. Hunter apparently passed on his values and interest in literature and science to his son Thomas, who joined the society on October 10, 1734. Hunter also used his time in Lincolnshire to expand his knowledge of foreign languages. James Logan noted that he had heard from Andrew Hamilton, Pennsylvania attorney general (in England from 1724 to 1726 as agent for the Pennsylvania proprietors), that Hunter had "two Arabians at thy house [at Croyland] for some time . . . instructing thee . . . in their language." Logan asked Hunter if this were true, since he too had studied Arabic and needed clarification from Hunter of "a point or two Concerning their Pronunciation."[26]

"The composition of real happiness"

Despite Hunter's pleasurable activities in the arts and sciences, the time he spent in England must have been emotionally wearing, partially because of the continued political upheaval. Some of the chaos had been caused by the South Sea Bubble. The South Sea Company, a finance company, had been established in 1711 by Harley as a counter-balance to the Whig-dominated Bank of England. The company had a monopoly of the trade to the south seas and control of the Asiento contract which supplied slaves to the Spanish mainland and island colonies. The company claimed that the profits from this trade were small. Consequently, the directors decided to take over a large portion of the national debt at a fixed rate of interest to earn larger profits. It then planned to use its credit to finance capital expansion. The South Sea Company had a working capital of more than £40 million, bright prospects guaranteed by the Asiento contract, and, in addition, offered speculators stock at bargain rates. Investors clamored for the opportunity to invest, and the price of all stocks soared, as Britons gave way to investment mania.[27]

Stock speculation continued until August of 1720, when the price of stocks began to decline. The lucky investors had sold out before August, but many of those who did not sell in time lost large fortunes. Although many personal fortunes were destroyed, Great Britain's basic economy was sound, and the country withstood the debacle, as did Stanhope and Sunderland who continued in power. Sunderland was forced to resign as first lord of the treasury on April 3, 1721 (his post went to Walpole), but still retained supreme power because of his posts as groom of the stole and first gentleman of the bedchamber, which kept him close to the king.[28]

The South Sea Bubble had been of definite advantage to Walpole, since it elevated him to high office. But it had by no means eliminated his competition. Sunderland and Stanhope remained in power. Walpole's dominance was achieved not so much by his political acumen, as by the hand of fate, which removed by death his rivals for power. The first to die was Stanhope on February 5, 1721. His place as northern secretary was taken by Walpole's brother-in-law, Townshend. Sunderland remained supreme even after Stanhope's death, however, and appointed his friend and protégé, Carteret, who was also a close friend of Cadogan's, as southern secretary. Sunderland might well have retained complete control of government but for his unexpected death on April 19, 1722. Except for Carteret and Cadogan, the path was clear for the Walpole-Townshend faction of the Whigs.[29]

Walpole seemed temporarily blocked following the death of the duke of Marlborough in June of 1722, because Cadogan was given most of the duke's military offices. Walpole and Townshend now feared that Cadogan and Carteret would try to destroy them. Walpole and Townshend, therefore, decided to act first. In 1724, Carteret was discharged by the king from his office as secretary of state and put into semipolitical

Robert Walpole, first earl of Orford and Mortimer, 1710–1715, by Sir Godfrey Kneller. National Portrait Gallery, London. One of a series of more than five hundred portraits done by Kneller of members of the Kit Cat Club, this portrait shows Walpole before his dramatic rise to power as Britain's minister of the treasury.

retirement as lord lieutenant of Ireland. He was replaced as secretary by Walpole's choice, the competent, but scarcely brilliant Thomas Pelham-Holles, duke of Newcastle. Cadogan fell only a year later, and his post as chief of staff was given to the duke of Argyll, a change which Hunter must have applauded. Walpole disliked Argyll almost as much as he did Cadogan, but he needed Scottish parliamentary support, and Scottish patronage was under the control of Argyll and his brother, the earl of Islay. Through the combined influence of the brothers over Scottish elections, Walpole received a proadministration majority in the forty-five representatives elected in Scotland. In 1726, fate again took a hand in determining Walpole's future. Cadogan, around whom an opposition party might have formed, died suddenly on July 17th. Walpole was now supreme, and his supremacy continued even after the death of George I on June 11, 1727. Walpole quickly ingratiated himself with the new king, George II, and continued to expand his power base.[30]

Now that Walpole was "prime minister," he was free to implement his policies of commercial imperialism. His goal was to extend the British Empire by trade, not by armed conquest. To accomplish this, Walpole had to maintain a peaceful environment in which trade could flourish and Britain prosper. Moreover, continued peace meant that the size of the army and the navy could be reduced and taxes lowered. Walpole's goals were noble (if unrealistic), but he sought to achieve them by corrupt methods.[31]

Walpole needed strong parliamentary backing to implement his plans for economic prosperity. Consequently, he packed Parliament with his own men whose elections he ensured by bribery, patronage, and personal influence. This was not an unusual practice in eighteenth-century Britain. Indeed, Hunter had used somewhat similar methods in governing New York and New Jersey. The major differences were that Hunter did not resort to bribery and his appointees were competent men. Walpole instead based his nominations almost solely on the loyalty of the candidate to him. Government posts were given as rewards or favors with little consideration for the ability of the man to fill the office. Walpole also ensured his own continuation in office by nominating men such as Newcastle for ministerial posts. Such men were loyal, but not overly intelligent. Hence, they were not threats to Walpole's political power.[32]

Many of the men nominated by Walpole were from the mercantile and professional classes. The rise to power of these groups caused England's poor to feel alienated from the center of government. The natural patrons of the poor were members of the traditional (and largely Tory) ruling elite, who were now out of power. The predominantly Whig merchants, doctors, lawyers, and goldsmiths who constituted the new ruling elite were primarily interested in increasing their own wealth and maintaining their own security, with no sense of responsibility for the poor. One result of the alienation experienced by the masses was a rising crime wave. Thefts, robbery, murder, drunkenness, and mayhem accelerated during the Walpolian era, despite the enactment of increasingly severe penalties for crimes, particularly those against property.[33]

Ministerial corruption, inept government officials, rising crime, and what was seen as a general disintegration of society offended many Tories, who yearned for the values of a bygone (and overly glorified) era. The Tories took out their frustration on Walpole, who became the symbol for dishonesty and corruption. Jonathan Swift is said to have used *Gulliver's Travels*, published in 1727, as a means by which to excoriate the prime minister. In the first book of the *Travels*, the character of Flimnap is presumably patterned after Walpole. The wily and slippery "Flimnap, the treasurer, is allowed to cup a Caper on the strait Rope, at least an Inch higher than any other Lord in the whole Empire." Walpole was further attacked in the fourth book of the *Travels*, where Swift declares that "a *First* or *Chief Minister of State* . . . was a Creature wholly exempt from Joy and Grief, Love and Hatred, Pity and Anger. . . That he never tells a Truth, but with an Intent that you should take it for a *Lye;* not a *Lye* but with a Design that you should take it for a Truth. . . . "[34]

A Tory backlash against foreign influences, seen as destroying traditional English values and hastening the era of capitalism, also developed during the Walpole era. One example of such influence was the Bank of England, inspired by the Dutch Bank of Amsterdam. The Bank of England, which supplied the money for the War of the Spanish Succession, also brought England a national debt, paper currency, and credit, all abhorred by the Tories as symbols of capitalism and their own decline. Many Tories now saw most things foreign as threatening, including the Italian opera performed at the Haymarket. The result was that in 1728, John Gay produced *The Beggar's Opera*, with a British story line and more than sixty "old English and Scotch Tunes. . . . " The opera was more than an example of British chauvinism, but was also "a Satyr on the Inconsistencies and unnatural Conduct of the *Italian Operas,* which tho' they charm the Eye with gay Dresses, and fine Scenes, and delight the Ear with Sound, have nothing in them either to reform the Manners, or improve the Mind. . . . " The London wits, particularly Tories, were still intent on reforming society and were determined "to expose Malice, Avarice, Brutality, and Hypocrisy" within the Walpole ministry. In *The Beggar's Opera*, Gay emphasized Walpole's greed and corruption by patterning his main characters, Peachum and Macheath, on two notorious real-life criminals,

Jonathan Wild and John Sheppard. London audiences were quick to grasp the similarities in the behavior of Peachum and Macheath with that of Walpole and his ministers and quicker still to laugh at the officials. Gay was encouraged in his efforts by Alexander Pope and Jonathan Swift, but not by Robert Hunter. Despite overt examples of corruption, Hunter remained committed to Whig principles. Neither could he risk alienating Walpole or his ministers because he was dependent on the ministry for future employment.[35]

Hunter used his contacts among the Whigs when he tired of his post among the bureaucrats of the customs office. His future was settled on July 4, 1726, when Henry Bentinck, duke of Portland, governor-general of Jamaica, died on the island. Portland's death left available the highly lucrative post which Hunter had coveted since 1709. Walpole controlled all patronage and undoubtedly, either directly or indirectly, recommended Hunter for the Jamaica post. On February 14, 1727, Robert Hunter, sixty-one years of age, was officially named governor-general of Jamaica.[36]

Hunter may have taken the Jamaica governorship because of his concern for his health. Jamaica's warm, moist climate would be soothing for his rheumatism, but few Britons would have gone to Jamaica for their health alone. There is certainly truth in Edward Long's pithy comment that "it is well understood that our governors have not gone thither merely for the sake of taking the air. ... " Long also observed that "They who in general visit this island do [so] ... for the purpose ... of accumulating money. ... " Hunter may well have taken the post to make money, but his reasons were monetary only in part. James Logan was among those of Hunter's friends who realized that Hunter was seeking more than financial rewards: "What advantages may accrue from thence in point of Interest to thy family, may be every Man's thought, but as for me, I am much more concern'd that it may equally answer in those momentous points that enter into the composition of real happiness." Real happiness for Hunter came with activity. Much more than money, Hunter wanted to be in command. Once savored, the independence, responsibility, and authority inherent in a governorship were addictive, as the duke warned Sancho Panza in *Don Quixote*, that favorite book of Augustan gentlemen. When Sancho told the duke he was prompted to take the governorship of the island "because I wish to see what it's like to be a governor," the duke answered: "Once you try it, Sancho, ... you will be eating your hands off for it, so sweet a thing it is to give orders and be obeyed."[37]

In February of 1727, Hunter's right "to be obeyed" was reconfirmed when he was commissioned as captain of one of the two independent companies stationed at Jamaica, one at Port Royal, the other at Spanish

Town. On March 1, 1727, he was promoted to major general, one of only fourteen major generals in the British army at that time. Hunter's commission and instructions as governor-general were then drafted by the Board of Trade. As in New York, Hunter was told to obtain a permanent revenue from the Jamaica assembly. In November of 1727, with commission and completed instructions in hand, Hunter prepared to leave Great Britain once more.[38]

The new governor-general of New York, Colonel John Montgomery of the Third Scots Foot Guards, was also scheduled to leave for his governorship at about the same time as Hunter was to depart. Montgomery was to replace Burnet, who was transferred to the governorship of Massachusetts. Burnet's New York administration had not been a success because he had alienated New York and English merchants with his heavy-handed efforts to suppress the Albany-Montreal fur trade. He had also, contrary to Hunter's advice, expelled the merchant, Adolph Philipse, from the council. Hunter, who also despised Philipse, had nevertheless warned Burnet to keep him on the council as he had done. Once Philipse was out of office, and out of the governor-general's control, he became a focus for the merchants whose opposition finally caused Burnet to lose control of the colony. Burnet's efforts to govern were further hampered by the desire of the Walpole ministry to appease mercantile interests. Complaints from English and American merchants finally led the ministry to repudiate Burnet's policies by ordering the repeal of all assembly acts passed in New York during Burnet's administration which hindered the fur trade.[39]

When Hunter reached Jamaica, he would himself feel the negative effects of the commercial imperialism of the Walpole era. In the autumn of 1727, however, Hunter's immediate concern was to go to his new post. His daughter Katharine, known as "Kitty" to the family, was married just a few days before Hunter sailed. She brought her husband, William Sloper, Junior, a generous dowry of £6,000. Hunter decided to take both his sons with him to Jamaica, but "left all ye Girls with good Mrs Sloper. . . . " Just before his departure, Hunter asked Montgomery to carry with him to New York a letter for James Alexander. In the letter, Hunter inquired whether "Mr Burnet is to part with the house at Amboy which I Sold Him[. If so,] I should be contented to have it again at the price he pay'd unless he has added and Improv'd. . . . " Hunter also asked Alexander to send to him in Jamaica bacon, hams, pickled pork, hard cider, and "flower. . . of ye finer Sort, they [his sons] Complain of this tho' it makes ye bread I like. . . . "[40]

Some time during the first week in December of 1727, Hunter sailed from England on H.M.S. *Lark*. On January 29, 1728, Hunter, his sons, and "divers other Gentlemen," arrived at Kingston. Hunter reported to the Board of Trade that he had had "a very agreeable passage of eight weeks." In Jamaica, Hunter had his commission published. He then took the oaths of office on the island which was to be his home for the rest of his life.[41]

CℛↃ *8* ↄℛↃ

"A Never-Ceasing Wheel"

January 1728– September 1730

. . . everything moves in a circle, that is to say, around and around:
spring follows summer, summer the harvest season, harvest autumn,
autumn winter, and winter spring, and thus does time continue to turn
like a never-ceasing wheel. Human life alone hastens onward to its
end, swifter than time's self and without hope of renewal, unless it be in
that other life that has no bounds.

Miguel de Cervantes
Don Quixote

"Jamaica, one of the richest jewels"

Ↄ OBERT HUNTER'S new home was "Jamaica, one of the richest
jewels in the crown of Great-Britain. . . discovered by Christopher
Columbus in 1493." The 4,411 square miles of the island contain mountains, plains, valleys, and 100 rivers, none deep enough for navigation. It
lies south of Cuba, north of what was then the Spanish South American
mainland, and to the west of Hispaniola, (now Haiti and the Dominican
Republic). The original inhabitants were the Arawak Indians, most of
whom were exterminated by the Spaniards. Spain held the island until
1655, when it was taken by a combined naval and military expedition sent
out by Oliver Cromwell under the command of Admiral William Penn and
General Robert Venables. The leaders of the expedition had been ordered
by Cromwell to seize Hispaniola. After a bumbling and undisciplined
attempt on that island, Penn and Venables turned their attention to
Jamaica and managed to take possession of the sparsely populated and
poorly defended island in 1655, after the Spanish and their slaves retreated to the mountains.[1]

The English made the ancient town of St. Jago de la Vega, or
"Spanish Town," their capital of Jamaica. The town was "situated in a

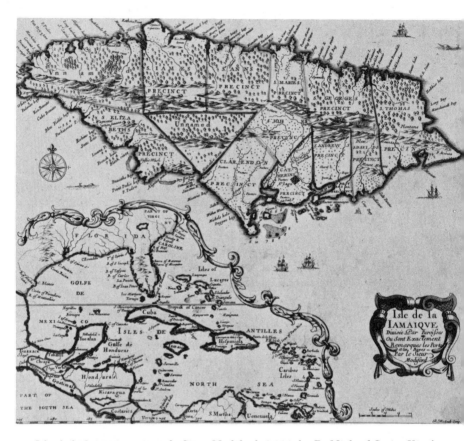

Isle de la Iamaiqve . . . par le Sieur Modiford, 1666, by R. Michael Scrip, King's Topographical Collection, published by permission of the British Library. This map, drawn the year of Hunter's birth, shows the strategic importance of Jamaica in the middle of the Spanish Main.

delightful plain, on the banks of the Rio Cobre" on the south side of the island. In 1728, the population of St. Jago numbered about four thousand people "of all colours and denominations." The town's white population, like all of Jamaica, was predominantly English, Scottish, Irish, and Jewish. It had a rather sleepy atmosphere unless the assembly was in session. The town came alive again at Christmas because that was when the "Slaves by Custom are Indulg'd their diversions." St. Jago reflected the military character of the English postconquest government and was under military rule.[2]

Hunter and his sons lived in the King's House at St. Jago. King's House was an old Spanish building made of stone which had "lately [been] rebuilt by his grace the Duke of Portland . . . a little court adjoins to the main dwelling house, where are several handsome apartments . . . it has a curious garden towards the west, which is generally kept in excellent repair." The governor's house in Spanish Town was ten miles from the sea and Jamaica's notorious port, Port Royal. That town, "the Sodom and Gomorrah of the Indies," was perched on the end of a peninsula in Kingston Parish. It had been the buccaneering center of the Caribbean until 1692, when it was partially destroyed by an earthquake and tidal wave.[3]

After the disasters, Jamaicans despaired of reconstructing a major commercial port city on what was left of Port Royal. Instead, a sizeable town was laid out directly across Kingston Bay from Port Royal. As Hunter noted in 1730, "Kingston arose out of the ruins of Port Royal and is at present the most considerable place of trade and merchandize. It is very regularly built and has a great many good houses and fine habitations in it. . . . "[4]

Upon Hunter's official arrival in Kingston, he was entertained by the chief magistrates and residents, who gave him "a subscription purse." After the welcoming revelries were completed, Hunter had an opportunity to inspect his surroundings and to be impressed by the island's unsurpassed natural beauty. Although Hunter was widely travelled and had served in North America, this was his first introduction to a tropical island. The varied animal life and the lush vegetation were exotic fare for a man raised in the cold, cropped, treeless, blandness of the Scottish Lowlands. In Jamaica, "mountains of an immense height seem to crush those below them; and these are adorned with a foliage as thick as vivid, and no less vivid than continual. . . . " The variety of the native fruits alone delighted the governor-general, who confirmed that Jamaica's climate and soil were conducive to a varied agriculture. As Hunter noted, "The Natural soil is very fertile and produced sugar, molosses, rum, indigo, cotton, ginger, piemento or all spice, fustick, ebony, lignum vitae, mohogony and other valuable timber, and of late coffee, and if the island were improved, there is land uncultivated sufficient to make sugar to serve all Europe."[5]

Sugar was the single most important and profitable staple crop in Jamaica, and sugar worth £300,000 sterling was exported in 1730. It was not indigenous to the West Indies, but had been introduced by the Dutch and the Sephardic Jews who brought cane cuttings and slaves to work the fields, along with a knowledge of cane culture, processing, and marketing from Brazil to Barbados and thence to Jamaica and other British islands.[6]

The introduction of sugar cultivation in the 1670s led to a disproportionate ratio of blacks to whites on Jamaica. Sugar required a sizeable
investment in land, equipment, and labor force. The small farmers, who in
the first two decades of English settlement had produced the food needed
to sustain the island's population, did not have the funds to convert to
sugar cultivation. Many farmers turned to buccaneering and many more
migrated to other West Indian islands or to the North American mainland.
The remaining plantation owners, who had previously used both white and
black laborers, now turned to black slaves. The Jamaica legislature
unsuccessfully tried to discourage the exclusive use of black slaves by the
annual passage of "Deficiency Acts" which required planters import at
least one white servant for every ten black slaves. Planters preferred
slaves to servants because slaves not only worked for life, but cost less to
feed and clothe than white servants. In addition, it would have been
impossible to find in Great Britain the large number of servants needed to
work the sugar fields.[7]

Another reason for the disproportionate number of blacks to whites
was that many planters looked for the slightest excuse to return to England. The exodus of whites, whether planters to England, farmers to North
America, or either to other islands, had an unfortunate economic effect on
Jamaica's trade. With the small farmer gone, virtually all produce, as well
as meat, invariably salted, had to be dearly purchased from the mainland
of North America. The mainlanders, while eager to sell their goods to
Jamaicans, were not eager to buy Jamaican sugar. They preferred instead
to take specie for the goods they sold in Jamaica to the French West Indies
to buy cheaper sugar. The French were able to undersell the English
because fewer French planters were nonresidents. Present planters produced sugar with less waste and more efficiency. To compete with the
French, British sugar growers had to increase production and lower
prices. Planters' profits continued to drop, however, despite increased
sugar consumption in Europe and North America during the early
eighteenth century because supply steadily outgrew demand.[8]

Concern about their economic survival increased the apprehension
of the 3,655 free whites who constituted Jamaica's miniscule ruling elite.
A more basic fear among the gentry and the almost four thousand white
indentured servants on the island was the disproportionate number of
black to white. There were more than 75,000 Negroes on Jamaica, of
whom 74,525 were enslaved. White Jamaicans lived in constant fear of a
slave uprising, and these fears were exacerbated by the presence of some
thousand rebel Negroes in the mountains.[9]

Another source of apprehension among blacks and whites was disease. Many Jamaicans suffered and died, particularly during the "seasoning" period, or the first year after their arrival, from malaria, yellow fever, dysentery, dropsy, leprosy, yaws, hookworm, elephantiasis, the "dry gripes" (which may have been a form of lead poisoning), and the more usual European diseases of smallpox, typhoid, and typhus. Proportionately more whites than blacks died during the "seasoning" period, a fact which as late as 1800 caused black Jamaicans to gloat in the hearing of white newcomers in song:

> New-come buckra,
> he get sick,
> He tak fever,
> He be die;
> He be die.

This island, whose natural beauty clothed an unnatural terror, whose tropical atmosphere and lazy charm alternately attracted and repelled, whose extremes of upper class dissipation and lower class degradation corrupted the newcomer, was to be Robert Hunter's home for the rest of his life.[10]

"Take post in the several passes in the mountains"

Even before he left England, Robert Hunter had decided to encourage the settlement of Jamaica's northeastern Portland Parish, as had his predecessor, the duke of Portland. Settlement lagged because the north side's heavy rainfall both increased the humidity so that the heat was unbearable and brought a large malaria carrying mosquito population. Settlers were also discouraged because the Spanish aimed their attacks on this sparsely settled and poorly defended area. The Spaniards wanted Jamaica back and claimed it was not included in the 1670 Treaty of Madrid, which guaranteed English ownership of land they at that time held in the New World. The last attempt of the Spaniards to retake Jamaica had been in 1726, when they launched an attack on the north shore and destroyed several plantations there.[11]

North side settlement also lagged because of the nearness of the rebel Negroes, whose largest settlement at Nanny Town was only twelve miles away from Portland's chief town, Titchfield, at Port Antonio. These "slaves in rebellion" made frequent raids on frontier plantations near Titchfield for food, supplies, and slaves.[12]

The mountain communities of rebel Negroes originated in the Spanish era when runaway slaves and some "marooned" buccaneers roamed the almost impenetrable mountains and woods of Jamaica. The fugitives lived on vegetables, fruits, wild hogs, and stray cattle. The ranks of these "Maroons" was increased following the English conquest when the Spaniards abandoned their slaves. These former slaves concentrated in the windward, or northeastern, section of the island. In the 1690s, another settlement of slaves runaway from the English also grew in the leeward interior. During Hunter's administration, however, the windward rebels, who resented English incursion into their territory, presented the greatest threat to white settlement. These rebels "often came down and continued some time near Several Plantations, which obliged the Proprietors to abandon them, so that almost all St. Georges, and part of St James, St Anns and St Marys were deserted, and the Roads in many places, were so infested that it was very unsafe Travelling."[13]

Hunter, soon after his arrival, sent out military expeditions to attack the Maroons in their mountain strongholds. He realized, however, that merely sending troops against the rebels would not defeat them. The type of guerilla warfare the government forces experienced in Jamaica, allegedly unknown to British soldiers until the Seven Years War, was, in fact, an old story to soldiers such as Hunter. In Jamaica, Hunter faced a dangerous enemy, holed up in impregnable mountain strongholds. They emerged periodically to raid low-lying settlements and to attack travellers on the island's roads. When troops were sent against them, the rebels clearly had the advantage. Troops marched many weary miles over dangerous terrain while the enemy waited. The rebels invariably chose the moment to attack. Naturally this moment was to their advantage, usually when the government forces were exposed to their fire in a dangerous pass. It was the Highland wars all over again.[14]

Hunter's plan to reduce the rebels was also familiar and had been employed in Scotland by the Romans, Cromwell, and William III: the construction of a large citadel or fort in the wilderness. The rebels could then be "pacified" by the harrassment from nearby regular troops. Hunter planned the first of these major forts at Titchfield. Even before he left England, he contacted army engineer Colonel Christian Lilly, to ask him to design and supervise the construction of such a fort. Lilly agreed to follow Hunter to Jamaica as soon as his commission as engineer was prepared and approved by the home government. His commissions were ready in early 1729. After having collected guns, ordnance stores, and a portrait of George II (all ordered by Hunter prior to his own departure), Lilly sailed for his new post.[15]

Lilly arrived in Jamaica in the late spring of 1729. Much to Hunter's annoyance, he found that Lilly had come without his engineering tools. Hunter, who apparently was an amateur engineer, supplied Lilly with tools from his own collection and then hurried the forgetful colonel to Port Antonio. As was true of Governor-General Hunter, Jamaica was to be Lilly's final home. Unlike Hunter, who enjoyed comparatively good health for the first several years of his stay in Jamaica, Lilly fell ill soon after his arrival. The engineer remained ill throughout the autumn and winter of 1729–1730. Hunter was sympathetic at first, but Lilly's illness meant that construction work on the fort stopped. Even more serious was the fact that Lilly used his illness as an excuse to postpone preparation of cost estimates for the fort. Hunter needed the estimates to present to the Jamaica assembly so they would vote funds to complete the project. Lilly continued to procrastinate, despite a personal visit to Port Antonio by the governor-general during January of 1730. Hunter sailed with Admiral Charles Stewart and remained on board Stewart's ship throughout his visit. The lack of building activity at Titchfield was a source of disappointment to both Hunter and Stewart. The admiral was anxious that Port Antonio be developed as a naval center so the Royal Navy would have a base on the north side. At the request of the admiralty, Lynch's Island in Port Antonio harbor was vested in the crown. Stewart promptly ordered the construction of barracks, warehouses, and a hospital there.[16]

Once the harbor and plantations were protected, it was expected that both north side shipping and planting would increase dramatically. The possibility of large profits helped to overcome the reluctance of many Jamaicans to settle on the north shore. Hunter himself sought to encourage settlement there by taking out some patents for land in Portland Parish. He soon began cultivation of sugar on a plantation named "Hunterston," after his family's estate in Ayrshire. Hunter sent slaves to work the plantation. He, however, recognized that the safety of the area was of primary importance. Consequently, he instructed Major Jasper Ashworth, senior commanding officer of the regular troops stationed at Port Antonio, to use his slaves in the construction of the Titchfield fort.[17]

Lilly finally prepared estimates for the construction of the fort in the spring of 1730. The amount needed to complete the structure was £7,351, but the Jamaica assembly voted only £3,000. The work proceeded, but governor and engineer knew that without more funds the fort could not be completed. Hunter, despairing of Lilly's commitment and aware that the engineer preferred to spend his time amidst the relative luxuries of Kingston than in the rugged wilderness of Port Antonio, appointed Colonel Robert Nedham, a planter, as on-site overseer at Titchfield. Nedham was particularly anxious to finish the fort because he had personally suffered a severe financial loss in March of 1730, when Maroons burned his new plantation near Port Antonio.[18]

In 1730, Hunter decided to supplement the Titchfield fort with an islandwide communications and defense system. These tactics had been employed by the British government in the 1690s against the Highlanders. Hunter had, of course, been part of the Highland pacification program. He had ample reason to believe "that the sure way to destroy these rebels, or distress them at least so as to make them embrace any terms you may think fit to offer them, will be to take post in the several passes in the mountains in proper places so as they may have easy communication with the settlements on either side of the island, or with one another." Hunter, therefore, ordered small barracks to be built and initiated the construction of a network of roads through the mountains to link north and south sides. Such a road system was being built through the Scottish Highlands by General George Wade for the British government between 1726 and 1738. Both in Scotland and Jamaica, the hill posts and roads permitted coordinated military action by serving as a communication network while at the same time impeding enemy movements. The similarities between the Maroon War and the Highland fighting was grasped by other Jamaicans in addition to Hunter. In 1731, a proposal was made to import one hundred Highlanders to fight the Maroons. The theory apparently was that the Highlanders, familiar with mountain fighting, could subdue the rebels.[19]

"The magna Carta of Jamaica"

His military function was only one aspect of Hunter's gubernatorial duties in Jamaica. He was also head of the legislature, and one of his first acts after arriving was to issue writs to convene an assembly. The forty-one representatives, two from each parish and three from each of the three major cities, met in Spanish Town on March 21, 1728. Hunter, who remembered the obstinacy he encountered from his first assembly meeting in New York, was pleased to see signs of cooperation in his first Jamaica assembly, despite dissension between the assembly and council. Part of the reason for the assembly's spirit of cooperation lay in Jamaica's history. Like New York, Jamaica was a conquered province. Unlike New York, however, where the predominantly Dutch preconquest population, with established customs, laws, and traditions, remained to form an alien cultural and ethnic backbone of the new English colony, the Spaniards in Jamaica had all fled by 1660 and left behind no social heritage, no opponents of anglicization. In addition, Jamaica was precisely in the middle of the Spanish Main, seized by the English from a nation that claimed absolute sovereignty in the West Indies, and in North, Central, and part of South America. Spain based her claim on a 1493 ruling made by Pope Alexander VI which divided the New World between Spain and Portugal. Spain felt this ruling gave her the right to protect her property beyond the papal line by the use of force. The French, the Dutch, and the English all denied Spanish sovereignty, all tried to shake Spain's control of New World territory and New World precious metals. Neither Spain nor the English, French, and Dutch contenders for her empire recognized any restraints on their behavior in what remained for decades a lawless frontier centered on Jamaica.[20]

This lawlessness was reflected in the immediate post-conquest government of Jamaica. The nearness of the hostile Spaniards and the rough character of the English colonists on Jamaica necessitated at first the maintenance of a military regime. As the English became more secure and somewhat settled, the king-in-council established in Jamaica the type of government typical of any royal colony: the crown appointed the governor-general, who nominated the council members, subject to the approval of the crown. There was also a representative assembly, which met for the first time in 1664. Yet, Jamaica's laws were only in effect for two years and then expired. Nor was the Jamaica assembly permitted to adopt en masse the laws of England, a long-established society, whose laws were based on tradition and custom. Jamaica was a violent, new society of outcasts without either tradition or custom. Unable to secure English law en bloc, the Jamaica assembly was permitted to pass laws based on English precedent, but they would be confirmed or rejected in England.[21]

The Jamaica assembly, whose crown-assigned function, like that in any other royal colony was to raise money for government expenses, soon began to use its control over finances to ameliorate the colony's legal inferiority and to enhance its own power at the expense of the royal prerogative. They accomplished this by trading revenue bills for legal and political concessions from the governors-general and the crown. The assembly's first significant attempt to gain power came in 1675, during the administration of John lord Vaughan. The assembly at that time demanded a wholesale adoption of English law, attempted to appropriate all money raised by revenue bills for the colony's exclusive use, and tried to limit the control of the governor-general over Jamaica's militia. The assembly also attempted to usurp Vaughan's control over taxation, revised all the colony's laws every session, and sent home copies of bills only after they had expired. Their actions finally forced the home government to consider Vaughan's mismanagement of the island. Vaughan was recalled and Poynings' Law extended to Jamaica, still considered a conquered province. The imposition of Poynings' Law, the "Irish Constitution," meant that all Jamaica's laws would be drafted by the crown in England and that assemblies would be convened in Jamaica to accept these laws only at the king's orders.[22]

In 1681, after a crisis in Anglo-American politics highlighted by the Popish Plot, the crown abandoned its authoritarian rule of Jamaica. The assembly then agreed to vote a seven-year revenue because it wanted to avoid the reimposition of Poynings' Law and believed rightly that the confirmation of its laws for an extended period of time would confer immunity from home government interference during that time. In return for the bill, the king-in-council confirmed the island's laws for the same period. In 1684, a compromise of even longer duration was achieved. In that year, in exchange for a twenty-one-year revenue act, Jamaica's laws were confirmed for the same number of years. Another such act was passed in 1703 for another twenty-one years. In 1722, when that act was about to expire, the governor-general, Portland, was ordered to secure a permanent revenue act. The Jamaica assembly approved such a measure in March of 1723, but the bill was disallowed in England in August of that same year because Portland had ignored his instructions and assented to the act without first submitting it to the home government.[23]

With Portland's bill rejected, the 1703 act expired in 1724, but the home government issued an order that all acts would remain in force for an additional year. Although government continued to function after 1725, all Jamaica's laws expired with the 1703 act, including those governing the number of assemblymen, those regulating law courts, and acts for raising the militia. Jamaicans particularly feared that the home government would take advantage of the absence of laws to take away hard-won privileges of self-determination and once again impose an arbitrary government on the island.[24]

Hunter's instructions regarding the Jamaica revenue were substantially different than those given to Portland. The home government had insisted Portland first submit the act to it before giving his approval. The crown also insisted that money be included in the revenue act for the extraordinary costs of the two independent companies stationed in

Jamaica. These companies, each of which consisted of one hundred men and their commissioned and noncommissioned officers, were supported by the home government at an annual cost of £3,653. The crown, however, required that the Jamaica assembly vote an additional salary for officers and men to compensate them for the high cost of island living. When Hunter was commissioned governor-general in 1727, the crown did not insist on either prior approval or military funds. Hunter was instead told that for government expenses he was free "to give your Assent to any Act which shall be prepared by the Assembly of that Our Island. . . . " Hunter could then "assent to any Seperate Act" for the subsistence of the independent companies. Hunter, therefore, had far more leeway than did Portland in negotiating a revenue act.[25]

When Hunter met his first Jamaica assembly in March of 1728, he urged them to prepare a bill "for reviving and perpetuating your Laws, expired by their own Limitation, and for Establishing and perpetuating a Revenue for the Support of his [Majesty's] Government. . . . " The assembly, aware that the confirmation of the island's laws hinged on the establishment of a permanent revenue, quickly voted a sum of £8,000 a year. The king's quit rents, which yielded about £4,000 in 1728, usually brought in less than half this money; the rest was to be raised by duties on wines and a few other commodities. Of the £8,000 revenue, £2,500 was for General Hunter's salary (the amount of Hunter's salary was set by the crown and was half the sum the crown allowed the impoverished, entitled duke of Portland). Of the remainder, £1,250 was appropriated for forts and fortifications; the rest was for the salaries of government officials. All money was to be issued on the governor-general's warrant with the receiver-general accountable to the governor, council, and assembly.[26]

The amount of £8,000 was adequate as long as there were no extraordinary government expenditures. In the event of war or rebellion, however, the £1,250 slated for forts and fortifications would not cover even the necessary repairs for the island's defenses, much less the price of subsisting and paying military forces. Such forces would have to be paid by annual additional duty bills. This increased the assembly's control over the pursestrings, because while the deployment of money raised by the permanent revenue was under the control of the governor-general and the council, the assembly alone controlled disbursement of money raised by additional taxes.[27]

In return for the guaranteed support of government, Jamaica received confirmation of all its existing laws with the very last clause of the revenue bill—the "great charter" or the "magna Carta of Jamaica." This clause provided that "all the Acts and Laws of this Island... shall be and are hereby revived, and hereby declared to be and continue Laws of this His Majesty's Island of Jamaica for ever." Jamaicans "had been... without Courts of Justice almost two years, and were apprehensive of an Alteration being intended in their Constitution or form of Government, but being now restored to their rights & Priviledges, as well as their Laws, their minds were quieted and made easy." The revenue act was confirmed by the king-in-council on May 22, 1729.[28]

The revenue act, secured after Hunter had been on Jamaica only a few months, has rightly been termed the high point of Hunter's Jamaica gubernatorial career. All royal governors-general were instructed to secure permanent revenues from their assemblies, yet Hunter was the only one to do so after 1700. He himself had failed to coerce either the New York or the New Jersey assemblies into voting similar measures during the nine years in residence as governor-general there. The laws of New York and New Jersey did not, however, expire after a predetermined number of years, as did those of Jamaica. The reason Hunter was successful in securing a revenue in Jamaica, when he and all other governors-general had failed elsewhere, was because Jamaica had more to gain by voting such a measure: in exchange for the bill, the island received permanent confirmation of all its previously enacted laws. The assembly had indeed won a good deal constitutionally, putting Jamaica at last on an equal footing with other colonies and ending the legal stigma of conquest. Yet the assembly also managed to retain a voice in colonial finance by voting a sum of money for the support of government which they knew would be inadequate in any emergency. They assured Hunter's approval of this favorable bargain by giving him a substantial bribe.[29]

The bribe to Hunter was a bill, passed by the assembly on April 12, 1728, "to raise an additional salary for me," as Hunter wrote. Hunter was granted a £6,000 gift, over and above his salary of £2,500. He had indignantly refused proffered presents from the New York assembly, but accepted the Jamaica money with alacrity, despite his thirty-first instruction which prohibited him from accepting gifts. Hunter, however, believed his acceptance of the gift was covered by his thirty-second instruction by which he was permitted to accept an additional "annual allowance" from the assembly to maintain the dignity of His Majesty's government. Hunter further rationalized his acceptance of the gift by explaining to the Board of Trade that the £6,000 would make him financially independent of the assembly. The board and its attorney, Francis Fane, agreed, and they successfully recommended to the king-in-council that Hunter be permitted to keep the gift.[30]

The £6,000 made a nice addition to Hunter's income. As in New York and New Jersey, however, Jamaican salaries, both annual and occasional, were but a small part of the money the governor-general received. The money from official perquisites such as fees and commissions amounted to another £6,000 a year. Besides these legitimate fees, there were also unofficial doceurs such as the welcoming purse from Kingston residents and an annual purse from Jamaica's Jews. As in New York, General Hunter continued to collect his share of subsistence money for the two Jamaican-based independent companies of soldiers (approximately £1,400 a year), his pay as captain of one of these companies (about 12s per day), and his half pay as major general of the royal army (£1 per day), a promotion received simultaneously with his commission to command Jamaica. Jamaica was truly a choice post, from a financial standpoint at least.[31]

Despite the prospect of such easy money, Hunter soon learned the Jamaica post was not trouble free. Opposition came both from factions on the island and at home. Just as Jamaica was richer than most colonies, so the parties to its Anglo-American politics were more powerful and determined than they were in such relatively "impoverished" commands as New York or New Jersey. Perhaps the most powerful of Anglo-American interest groups was the South Sea Company. During Hunter's first assembly session in the spring of 1728, a bill was passed by the assembly placing a duty on slaves sold in Jamaica by the South Sea Company. When transmitting the bill to the Board of Trade, Hunter noted that he had only with the greatest difficulty prevented the assembly from passing an act to place a duty on slaves landed temporarily in Jamaica to be resold to the Spanish. Such a duty was specifically forbidden by his instruction of November 13, 1727. After 1728, however, the assembly, forced to finance increasingly expensive expeditions against the Maroons, proposed, and Hunter approved, taxes on both imported and exported slaves. The Board of Trade ignored these taxes on exported slaves, even though they were approved by Hunter in violation of his instruction, as long as, but no longer than, the South Sea Company bore them in silence.[32]

Although Hunter found the legislature cooperative during the assembly's first session, dissension was more pronounced when the assembly reconvened in July of 1728. In July, the representatives passed a bill which made sugar lawful tender for the payment of debts. Hunter, on the advice of his council, refused to give his assent to the measure because he feared creditors would be cheated. The assembly, which may have believed it had paid for the governor-general's continuing compliance with a £6,000 gift, resented Hunter's objections to the bill and refused to enact any other measures. Hunter prorogued them until January of 1729, with the hope that "as the weather grows cooler so I hope their passions and little resentments at one another will abate. . . . "[33]

Hunter suspected senior councillor John Ayscough of promoting the passage of the sugar bill through the assembly with the connivance of representative Dennis Kelly. Ayscough, as senior councillor, had headed the government following the death of the duke of Portland and was slated to do so again in the event of Hunter's death or absence. Judge Dennis Kelly was the leader of a small faction of Irish lawyers who opposed Hunter throughout his tenure. Hunter also suspected Ayscough of promoting dissension between the council and the assembly.[34]

Hunter, faced with an opponent on his council, sought to apply in Jamaica the same solution that he had used in New Jersey where he had removed dissidents from office. In May of 1728, Hunter asked the duke of Newcastle to issue a dormant commission to Ezekial Gommersell to serve as acting governor. Hunter also asked permission to remove Ayscough, "a man of such passions and resentment," from the Jamaica council. The duke and the board agreed to pass over Ayscough as far as the succession was concerned, but he continued on Jamaica's council until 1730, when ill health forced him to return to England. Hunter, believing Ayscough gone for good, replaced him on the council, but with or without Ayscough's assistance, the Kelly-led Irish lawyers in the assembly remained a thorn in Hunter's side.[35]

"I have a Longing to Lodge In't"

Despite Ayscough's and Kelly's opposition, Hunter's first few years in Jamaica were relatively happy, partly because Jamaica's warm, humid climate had had its desired effect. As the governor put it, "I Injoy perfect health here." Hunter also enjoyed the companionship of his sons, Charles and Thomas, who had grown "as tall as I am almost." Tom had gone to sea at his own request. Hunter agreed with his son's decision and believed Tom was "Indeed well Suited for a Camp or Fleet." Tom's decision may also have been prompted by frustration, because his brother "Charles had so much The heels of him In all other points of Learning except ye Mathmatical that ye boy was Quite discouraged." Charles had apparently given Hunter much pleasure. In a letter to James Alexander, the governor noted that "Charles is one of ye most hopefull youths I ever Knew of his years, & a Comfort & pleasure to me."[36]

Hunter also had good news in the summer of 1728, when Alexander told him he had repurchased his old house in Amboy from William Burnet. Hunter was "much pleas'd" at the purchase and admitted to Alexander that he entertained "a sort of Impulse or Inclination of Laying my bones In that Country [New Jersey]." There, he said, "I hop'd to Live retir'd from all buss'nesse In ye latter part of my life."[37]

Nor was that hope "quite lost as yet," Hunter wrote, but the businessman in him was tempted to sell out his American holdings and hopes. As Hunter told Alexander, he had received an offer from "One Orgyle a gentleman of the Country [Jamaica]," who wanted to move to North America. Hunter proposed that he would exchange "What I have in N[ew] York or New Jersey" for Orgyle's estate in Jamaica, "which makes at present 80 hhd of Sugar a year. . . . " Hunter, the eternal Scot, was not as yet quite certain if he was getting a "bargan" so he asked Alexander to send him a list of his "houses Lotts or Land in N. York or N. Jersey wt a guess of your own at ye Value that I may make Some Judgment as to ye Expediency of My Closing wt his Offer." The deal fell through because Hunter retained his North American property until his death.[38]

It seems that Hunter was pleased that the land swap with Orgyle had not worked out and that he retained a claim to a continental base. The desire to return to his home in New Jersey (and perhaps to Betty Holland) pervaded his future correspondence with Alexander. "I assure You," he told Alexander in July of 1729, "I have a Longing to Lodge In't [the Amboy house] and when I go to Europe, If I ever go, I am determin'd to make New York My Route."

"The publick Safety"

Despite the pleasant anticipation of a visit to old friends in New York and New Jersey, Hunter in Jamaica was beset by external, as well as internal enemies. At the time of his promotion to major general and governor-general of Jamaica in 1727, another full-fledged war between England and Spain seemed likely. Indeed, Spain, with Austria's help, blockaded both Gibraltar and Minorca. Britain and Spain sought to end hostilities, however, and in March of 1728, diplomats from both countries met in Seville to discuss a treaty. On February 17, 1729, despite the continuing peace talks, Newcastle wrote to Hunter in the greatest urgency to warn him that "His Majesty. . . hath fresh intelligence that the Court of Spain have a design . . . to make an attempt upon Jamaica with a strong squadron. . . . " Newcastle ordered Hunter and Commodore John St. Loe to "take the necessary measures for the defence of a Colony of so great importance to the Trade and Navigation of H.M. Dominions."[39]

Hunter promptly summoned his field officers, who, together with his council, constituted a council of war. Acting under General Hunter's presidency, the council promptly declared martial law, called out the militia, and placed an embargo on shipping "to keep their seafaring men at home."[40]

Even though near death, Commodore St. Loe ordered the deployment of his fleet at the entrance of Port Royal Harbor. Six armed merchantmen were also deployed at the head of Kingston Harbor. General Hunter then recruited sailors from the merchant ships and assigned them to carry materials where needed. The sailors also assisted in strengthening the island's fortifications.[41]

Jamaica was to be primarily defended by its militia, whose rank and file was composed of slaves, freed slaves, and white indentured servants. After deploying his forces, Hunter became convinced that Jamaica's three-thousand-man militia was fundamentally flawed. The officers, for instance, were largely incompetent men, many of whom, prior to Hunter's administration, had bribed former governors-general to get their commissions. Hunter purged the officer corps, as he had in New York and New Jersey, but because of the small number of whites on the island, and "the exemption by law of great numbers" of these from military service, he had a very small pool of qualified men from which to draw. The large number of exempt officers was caused by an act passed in 1681, which stated that any commissioned officer who had resigned or been superseded could not be forced to serve in any rank lower than that he had previously held. Since the turnover among officers was great, a large percentage of Jamaica's ruling elite were "reformed" officers who were virtually excused from service. Hunter did, however, insist they serve in times of national emergencies, such as the threatened Spanish attack.[42]

Hunter soon found that the blacks in the militia were trustworthy soldiers, despite attempts by the rebels to have them desert. The Maroons often crept within hailing distance of the soldiers' campfires. They then taunted the slaves for helping their white masters kill fellow blacks, just as the rebel Highlanders had taunted Lowland soldiers in the 1690s. Some slaves did desert to the Maroons, but blacks were usually more loyal than the largely Irish Catholic servants who composed the bulk of the militia. Hunter believed these whites were "not to be trusted with arms," especially because they had often been overheard to say "they had no Quarrel with the Spaniard and would not fight against them." Hunter deployed the white militiamen in the north, but ordered "a reserve of negroes in the rear to knock down any man who should desert or flye from his ranks. . . . "[43]

The Spanish enemy did not appear but the mobilization convinced Hunter that the risk presented by the Irish in Jamaica must be reduced by an act of the legislature. Yet even this body was influenced by the Irish enemy, or so Hunter told the Board of Trade. Hunter reported the assembly was disturbed by a "restless faction" whose "Arts and Endeavours have been Lay'd out In opposing or defeating what ever was propos'd for the publick Safety. I mean a Sett of Irish lawyers, for 'tis time to speake out." This faction "E'n before my arrivall had disclosed an avertion to me, and who have ever Since Sett themselves against ev'rything proposed or offer'd for the public Safety makes be believe what I was indeed told, that their Plott was much deeper than I imagin'd." Hunter suspected the Irish faction, particularly Irish Catholics, of supplying the Spaniards in Cuba with information about Jamaica.[44]

The assembly was by no means controlled by Irish lawyers at this time, nor were any of them Catholics. Hunter was libelling his political enemies, as he had in New York and New Jersey, with allegations of treason and conspiracy because he, like all the rulers of his century, conceived of opposition as illegitimate. Prodded by the governor-general, in August of 1729, the assembly passed a measure specifically designed to halt the immigration of Irish Catholics, the so-called "Protestant Act." By it Hunter hoped to discourage the importation of Irish Catholic servants, "a lazy useless people who come cheap and serve for deficiencys," that is, to fill planters' quotas of white servants to black slaves. The act set a fine of £50 on the importer or the buyer of Catholic servants. The majority of the assembly and all of the council were in accord with Hunter in supporting this measure. Hunter reported it passed both bodies with "but one dissenting vote (one of the Kellys). . . . "[45]

The Protestant Act, which was confirmed by the king-in-council, provided that no Catholic could hold, exercise, use, or enjoy any civil or military office in Jamaica, or find employment in any civil or military capacity, or work as an overseer on any plantation where there were more than ten slaves. Every Irish person who claimed to be a Protestant and had been on Jamaica for less than ten years was required to secure a certificate from his minister in Ireland, counter-signed by a senior secretary of state, confirming that he was a member in good standing of the Church of England. The act also imposed severe penalties on any Roman Catholic priest who attempted to conduct services in Jamaica and on any Jamaicans who attended these services. The proponent of the act, Governor-General

Hunter, had been familiar with this sort of politicoreligious discrimination since childhood. The Protestant Act was similar in intent and purpose, if not in actual content, to the 1661 Ecclesiastical Settlement and the 1680 Test Act, both tools used by Charles II and the duke of York to subdue militant religious dissidents in Scotland.[46]

Possible Catholic aid to the Spanish was cause for concern, but a more pressing problem was Jamaica's large slave population. Despite the fact that Hunter found blacks more reliable than whites in the militia, he, like all Jamaicans, lived in constant fear of a slave uprising. The many Negroes on the island, so many more in proportion to the white population than in New York, where there were three whites to every black, caused Hunter to change his attitude toward the manumission of slaves. After the 1712 New York slave uprising, Hunter had not only denounced the barbarous punishments inflicted by the colonial courts on condemned slaves, but he had only with the greatest reluctance passed a bill which discouraged the manumission of slaves. Hunter feared the passage of this act would cut "off all hopes" and in the end would only serve to heighten discontent among slaves. As he pointed out to the Board of Trade in 1712, hopelessness "will make 'em [slaves] not only careless servants, but excit 'em to insurrections more bloody than any they have yet attempted, seeing that by the Act death is made more eligible than life, for the longer they live the longer they are slaves. . . . "[47]

By the time Hunter had lived in Jamaica for two years, however, the number of slaves, the impossibility of absorbing freed slaves into white society, the need for a large, permanent work force, and the fact that freed slaves supplied the rebels with arms and ammunition, had convinced him that freed slaves were a threat to white society and that the perpetual servitude of blacks was inevitable. He, therefore, willingly approved an act which imposed crippling limitations on the occupations, movements, and activities of freed blacks. The act brought an added plus. Hunter was assured he would have the military service of freed slaves who were now required to register with local officials so they could be hastily summoned to supplement military expeditions.[48]

Hunter not only approved the act, but wanted to make it even more stringent and more like the New York act he had previously deplored. He commented to the board in 1730 that "tho' this law is thought by some to be severe, yet for my own part I think it a good one, and could have wish'd that a clause had been incerted in it, that no mulatoo, Indian, or Negro should hereafter be made free, unless the owner allotted them a sufficient maintenance during life." The Board of Trade did not agree. In response to Hunter's letter, they virtually quoted Hunter's own words to him, written following the 1712 New York slave uprising. The board believed the 1730 Jamaica act undermined "the integrity of slaves and the industry of freed slaves" and refused to recommend its confirmation to the king-in-council. The act was disallowed on November 25, 1731.[49]

Hunter's attention was diverted from manumitted slaves, domestic dissidents, crypto-Catholics, and obstreperous assemblymen in August of 1729, when he received word of English merchant opposition to his government. Newcastle told Hunter the merchants objected to the embargo the governor-general had placed on shipping in the spring. This, they claimed, interfered with their trade. Newcastle added that he wished Hunter had not raised so great an alarm over the invasion scare. Since the Spanish danger seemed over for the moment, Newcastle ordered Hunter to lift the embargo so the merchantmen could sail. Hunter, who remembered the strong backing he had received from the home government in his struggles with the New York and London merchants over the 1717 Debt Bill, must have been surprised by the condemning tone of Newcastle's letter. Nevertheless, he promptly replied that he had lifted the embargo nearly three months previously, on May 29th. Few ships, if any, he told Newcastle, had been prevented from sailing during the month-long embargo.[50]

Hunter also found opposition closer to home. The Protestant Act antagonized Jamaica's Irish population. The assembly, which met in the fall of 1730, was influenced by the Kelly-led lawyers who "had got such an ascendant over the thoughtless planters, that they have the chief influence in the election of Assemblymen, and great influence in that House to the obstruction of publick business, . . ." as Hunter told the board. The Irish faction pushed through a bill for repealing the Protestant Act which Hunter, amazingly, approved. This, in spite of his judgement that the act was a necessary measure.[51]

Hunter's approval of the repeal was undoubtedly the price the assembly demanded for voting defense appropriations. The Maroon raids had persisted and were so devastating that in the summer of 1730, the assembly was forced to support two expeditions. Indeed, from 1729 to 1734, more than £105,000 was spent by Jamaica on military operations directed against the Maroons, every penny of which had to be raised by special acts of the assembly. To obtain the money he desperately needed for defense measures, Hunter had to make concessions to the assembly. Hunter well knew, however, that colonial acts were subject to confirmation or rejection by the king-in-council. While he was forced to approve the bill in Jamaica, Hunter could block its confirmation in London. In October and November of 1731, Hunter wrote to the duke of Newcastle to request he "advise H.M. to reject the Act repealing the Protestant act, as 'tis call'd." Hunter warned that if the repeal were approved, "it will give much matter of triumph to that party [the Irish lawyers] that all my endeavours ... may be rendred'd of little use...." The repeal was not approved by the king.[52]

By the autumn of 1730, all the issues the Hunter administration would face in Jamaica were apparent. The rivalry between council and assembly would accelerate to hamper legislative action as each body defended its sphere of influence against encroachments by the other. The determination of the governor-general to defend the royal prerogative would lead to more bickering over petty issues as the assembly defended what Hunter termed its "presumed rights." All the executive's political problems were intensified by the nearness of the hostile Spaniards, the depressed sugar market, the racial imbalance exacerbated by the continuing exodus of whites and the growing number of blacks. On top of all these problems, the Maroons' savage attacks called for defense measures which the assembly financed only with great reluctance and at the price of continued political concessions.

In the autumn of 1730, Robert Hunter realized that the problems he would face in Jamaica were, if anything, more severe and persistent than those he encountered in New York and New Jersey. Nevertheless, he was still in good health and retained his youthful vigor. At sixty-four years of age, Robert Hunter was determined to make his last governorship a success.

ⒺⓈ *9* ⒺⓈ

"Bad Spirits, and Innumerable Griefs"

September 1730– March 1734

> *...old age, which no one wants, gets one before he makes his*
> *goal. Painful diseases wear down some; others are killed in battle, and*
> *death takes them under the dark earth*
> *...Thus, no evil thing is missing. In their thousands stand bad*
> *spirits, and innumerable griefs, and pains about our life.*
>   Semonides of Amorgos
>   "The Vanity of Human Wishes"

"The spirit of piracy"

ALTHOUGH Robert Hunter was three thousand miles away from the center of the British Empire, he was constantly influenced and affected by European events. Britain's prime minister, Robert Walpole, was anxious to secure peace with Spain so that he could implement his program of prosperity built on trade. He therefore worked with Southern Secretary Newcastle to conclude the Treaty of Seville, signed in November of 1729. Hostilities between Spanish and English colonists in the West Indies could well disturb Walpole's peace, so, in December of 1729, George II issued an order to all governors-general to halt privateering and to restore all Spanish prizes taken after June 22, 1728.[1]

Governor-General Hunter in Jamaica was particularly affected by the king's order to halt privateering, because he commanded a pirates' paradise. Despite strenuous efforts by the governors of Jamaica, the Leeward Islands, South Carolina, and Virginia, all of whom captured and hanged pirates, buccaneering persisted among the British.[2]

The Spanish were as lawless as the English. The Spanish guard-acosta, which was supposed to prevent depredations, instead joined in illegal seizures of English ships and raids on English colonies, including

Jamaica. After the signing of the 1729 Treaty of Seville, the official policy of both Great Britain and Spain was clear: buccaneering was to halt, and the West Indies were to enter the comity of nations. General Hunter and the admiral of the Jamaica station, Charles Stewart, were in agreement that British depredations against the Spanish would halt. Their determination was, however, not shared by the British king, the southern secretary, or Jamaican buccaneers.[3]

In August of 1730, Hunter and Stewart were at Port Antonio when they received word that a Spanish man-of-war, the *Genoesa*, with a great treasure on board, was stranded about ten to twelve leagues south of Jamaica on the Pedro shoals. Hunter and Stewart immediately returned to Port Royal to make arrangements to guard the wreck and to help the Spanish fish up the treasure. Soon after his arrival, Hunter issued a proclamation for the arrest of anyone who took treasure illicitly. Well before the proclamation was issued, however, the *Genoesa* was plundered by several adventurous Jamaicans who had not forgotten the quick profits to be made from buccaneering.[4]

The taking up of treasure, both legally by ships of the Royal Navy and illegally by buccaneers, continued through the autumn of 1730. By October 22nd, the treasure retrieved by the British military units under Hunter's command amounted to almost £70,000 sterling. The *Experiment* mounted an almost constant guard at the site, yet the buccaneers made repeated and successful attempts to seize treasure. As an unknown correspondent wrote to a friend in England, "the spirit of piracy is much revived here.... and all think they have a right to plunder."[5]

By November 9, 1730, word of the wreck had reached London. Newcastle wrote to Hunter "in the utmost secrecy" about the wreck. Newcastle ordered General Hunter to take all recovered specie into his own custody and to make exact inventories of the treasure in the presence of the Spanish officers. He further instructed Hunter to keep the treasure safe until he received orders from home for its disposition. Newcastle's intention to appropriate the treasure from the Spanish now became apparent. He instructed Hunter that "when the Spanish Officer shall apply to You (as undoubtedly he will) for the release of the effects, you are to tell him, that you will send the King an account of what has happened." Newcastle continued that "on no account" was Hunter to part with the treasure without the king's orders. The Spaniards could come or go as they pleased, but Hunter was not to permit them "to convey away any part of their effects."[6]

Newcastle's letter did not arrive in Jamaica until after the treasure had left the island. The pieces of eight had been shipped on board H.M.S.

Adventure, Lord Muskery commanding, on December 26, 1730, bound for Cadiz. Thus, 256,992 Spanish dollars (Hunter retained 21,404 dollars to pay salvaging expenses), were being delivered by an English ship to the past and future enemy—Spain.[7]

On receiving Newcastle's letter, a worried Hunter assured the duke that he "had no share in the advice of sending it [the treasure] that or any other way till H.M. pleasure was known." Hunter may not have had any share in Stewart's decision to ship the treasure as promptly as he did (admirals on the Jamaica station were notoriously unwilling to take orders from the island's governors-general), but he had certainly encouraged the salvage of the treasure and its return to the Spaniards.[8]

Robert Hunter as governor-general and Charles Stewart as admiral were apparently more inclined to enforce imperial policy than was the southern secretary (and perhaps the king, as well). Hunter and Stewart were military imperialists who were not only trained to follow orders but also to consider the interests of the empire before their own. The ministry at home had succumbed to the commercial imperialism of the Walpole era, which put profit ahead of almost any other consideration. The theft of several thousand pounds worth of treasure would infuriate the Spanish. The ministry must have been aware that such a move would endanger the peace Walpole desired, but greed had triumphed in London. Despite continued depredations by both British and Spanish seamen, peace was preserved for the moment in the West Indies because the governor and the admiral had obeyed their orders.[9]

"I have left no thing undone"

Despite continued harrassment by Spanish buccaneers, the immediate foreign threat to Jamaica was reduced by the signing of the 1729 Treaty of Seville. The menace of the Maroons, however, continued to trouble Hunter's administration. The constant attacks by the rebels on the growing settlements in Portland Parish increased Hunter's determination to complete the fort there. Engineer Lilly, however, continued to procrastinate and refused to leave Kingston. Lilly's indifference to his job was perhaps caused by the limited opportunities for graft presented by the Portland project, a distinct difference from most army engineering assignments. Without a completed fort and without the presence of an engineer to supervise the work, rebel attacks on Portland plantations accelerated. Plantation owners occasionally killed a few rebels and then sent their severed ears back to town. Most Maroons, however, invariably escaped back to their mountain retreats.[10]

In March of 1730, the frequency of the rebels' attacks caused Hunter to ask the Board of Trade and Newcastle for additional troops to use against the Maroons. The Jamaica assembly did not believe these troops were necessary and had in fact rejected a suggestion from their own committee that they make such a request to the home government. While the assembly, wary of expenses, refused to request additional forces, they did provide funds for yet another "country" expedition of militiamen. This raiding party, sent out in June of 1730 to attack the main rebel village of Nanny Town, was routed by the Maroons and fled back to Port Antonio.[11]

News of the continuing Maroon raids on white plantations, the difficulty of persuading competent white Jamaicans to serve in the militia, and Hunter's claim that he needed military assistance to defend the island, prompted the home government to send two regiments with a total of eight hundred men from Gibraltar to Jamaica. The regiments, despatched on October 12, 1730, were commanded by Brigadier General Richard Newton and Colonel Robert Hayes. Newcastle suggested Hunter urge the soldiers to remain in Jamaica by offering them some of the land now occupied by the rebels, just as the post-conquest government had tempted soldiers to remain in Jamaica in 1658.[12]

After the defeat of yet another raiding party in the autumn of 1730, Hunter was pleased to welcome the regiments which arrived in February of 1731. Hunter ordered some soldiers quartered among the residents of Port Royal and Kingston, while six companies were sent directly to Port Antonio, the site from which almost all attacks against the rebels would be mounted. Other companies were later deployed by Hunter throughout the island.[13]

Within a month after their arrival, the commanding officers of the regiments reported deaths among the troops. By March 17, 1731, four officers were also dead. The deaths of so many officers proved momentarily advantageous to Roger Sterne, Laurence Sterne's father, who had been in the army since 1708 as an ensign in Colonel Hayes's regiment. In March of 1731, Hunter recommended Sterne's promotion to a long-awaited lieutenancy. Sterne did not live to enjoy his new responsibilities, however, for he fell ill of "the country fever, which took away his senses first, and made a child of him, and then, in a month or two, walking about continually without complaining, till the moment he sat down in an arm chair, and breathed his last" on July 31, 1731. It is not known if Sterne's ordeal was typical of the sufferings of most other soldiers, but the ranks of the regiments were quickly depleted. Most deaths among the soldiers, according to Hunter, were not caused by "country fevers," but rather by the soldiers' high consumption of rum. In fact, although contemporaries did not know it, the men died not of alcohol, but rather of lead poisoning, since rum was processed through lead pipes and in lead vessels.[14]

By late March of 1731, Colonel Hayes was also dead. Hunter immediately wrote to Newcastle to inform him of Hayes's death and to "most humbly intreat and hope for your Grace's recommendation to H.M. for the command of that Regiment. I think I am the only Genll. Officer in actual service without one, and if a great deale of additional trouble and expens can add weight to my clame I assure your Grace I have both. . . . " Hunter repeated his request in April, and warned Newcastle that "A disappointment in this may lessen the authority my rank and station require amongst the souldiery. . . . " Hunter was never given the command.[15]

The governor-general was right to fear the lessening of his authority with the officers and men. A generation or more younger than he, they were, for the most part, unseasoned and inexperienced in warfare. Ignorant of Hunter's role in the war that brought Britain its empire, the officers resented taking orders from a man who had no direct command over any of them. Hunter, for his part, felt a barely disguised scorn for these military novices who had neither fought pitched battles in Europe nor shared his New World experiences. They were, therefore, incapable of adapting to the tactics of guerilla warfare. The officers, for instance, wanted to attack the Maroons with large bodies of men, whereas Hunter knew that many men were useless in the mountains and were actually an "encumbrance" for the "rear hitherto has commonly given away whilst the front was engag'd. . . . "[16]

The elusiveness of the Maroon enemy was another source of friction between officers and governor-general. The officers, who did not see the Maroons, believed Hunter had exaggerated the seriousness of the rebel threat. This belief was reinforced soon after they landed when a band of militiamen took, plundered, and burned Nanny Town. The officers thought they might "now naturally conclude the war is over in this country." The rebels were far from defeated, however, for the militia abandoned the town after three days. The Maroons promptly reoccupied the site and began to rebuild the town.[17]

The officers' desire to leave Jamaica was prompted by more than their mistaken belief that they were not needed. They hated the hot, humid climate, the limited and expensive accommodations, and the high death rate. By June of 1731, indignant letters which they had written to friends and relatives in England began to reach London, as did Hunter's reports.

When the correspondence was read to the privy council, the councillors could not help but notice the discrepancy in the accounts between the officers and the governor-general: the officers believed the Maroon threat had been eliminated with the capture of Nanny Town; the governor-general insisted the Maroons were still active and dangerous. In addition, the officers emphasized the number of deaths among the men, while Hunter was inclined to minimize the number of dead.[18]

On the basis of these conflicting reports, the Board of Trade, on July 15, 1731, concluded that Hunter had misrepresented the extent of the danger to Jamaica. The board suggested to the king-in-council that at least one of the regiments be withdrawn from Jamaica. Newcastle, as southern secretary, might well have championed Hunter's cause when the issue was considered by the king. The duke, however, shunned criticism and craved approbation. He would not take a public stance to advocate an unpopular cause. Unpopular it was, especially after the king received a message from the financially strapped Jamaica assembly in which that body expressed its "opinion that the regts. were not necessary for the safety of the island. ... " The message was accepted at face value in England. On September 16, 1731, Newcastle informed Hunter that the king-in-council had decided to withdraw the regiments. Hunter was urged, however, to encourage the soldiers to voluntarily remain in Jamaica by offering them a bounty of £10 per man. Newcastle also told Hunter that the king had received the assembly's message and was displeased that Hunter had not conveyed to him the true state of conditions on the island.[19]

Hunter promptly responded that he had accurately represented the "impotence under which it [Jamaica] suffers of defending its self even against their own slaves in rebellion, not to mention invasion from abroad. ... " He told Newcastle he had known nothing of the assembly's message "'til I saw it in the Minutes of the day and the Council...thought it best to take no notice of it. ... " As he bitterly pointed out to Newcastle, he had "left no thing undone that was in my power to do, to make them [Jamaicans] easie," even to the point of sacrificing his own health for the islanders' interests.[20]

In the autumn of 1731, still unaware that the regiments would be withdrawn, Hunter ordered a group of regular soldiers to supplement a force of black and white volunteers and militiamen in a raid on Nanny Town. The attack force, after being delayed by flood and weakened by illness, was badly defeated, with eight killed and several wounded. The defeat was shameful, because "most of the soldiers and negroes had run away on the enemies first fire.... " Captain DelaMillier, who commanded one of the companies, reported to Hunter that the men fell into confusion and retreated in great disorder when attacked by about two hundred rebels. The difficulty of guerilla warfare was borne in on the captain, for he reported to Hunter, "the road we went on is such that in a hundred different places, ten resolute men are sufficient to stop a thousand."[21]

Fears of the Maroons increased among white Jamaicans as the new year of 1732 began, perhaps because of an old prophecy that in that year the island would be in the possession of the rebel Negroes. Despite these fears, and the continued failure of the expeditions against the Maroons, the regiments had to be sent home as ordered. The assembly agreed to offer the men both cash bounties and land in Jamaica if they would remain. About two hundred soldiers, or most of the surviving enlisted men, volunteered to remain in Jamaica to become settlers or to complete the ranks of the two independent companies.[22]

The additional strength provided by the volunteers from the regiments enabled Hunter to send out two expeditions in March of 1732. This spring offensive was successful. Hunter soon received reports that Nanny Town, Molly's Town, and Diana's Town had been taken. It seemed a complete victory for the government soldiers, but rather than pursue the enemy, the officers decided to keep their troops in the rebel towns. Thus "slipt the opportunity of immediately improving the first blow. . . . " Then the provincial soldiers began to desert from the towns. The government forces held on to Nanny Town, however, and in September of 1732, Hunter reported to the Board of Trade that "A Defensible House or Barrack capable to lodge fifty men at the Great Negro Town (as it is Call'd) lately taken is finish'd all to the Roof. . . ." This garrison at Nanny Town was only one of a series of barracks "which had been built by the several parishes at a great expense" at Hunter's orders. These garrisons did much to weaken the Maroons by hindering their movements and preventing runaway slaves from swelling their ranks. The encirclement of the Maroons by the garrisons planned by General Hunter led them, in 1739, to come to terms with the British.[23]

"Adhere more strictly to your Instructions"

Hunter was well aware that the military imperialism of the Marlborough era had yielded to the commercial imperialism of the Walpole era. Walpole sought to extend the empire by trade. For Walpole to remain in power, Britain's economy had to grow and prosper. The desire for mercantile prosperity and Walpole's need for merchant support at the polls, led the administration to be particularly responsive to complaints by large trading companies, as Hunter found when the South Sea Company attacked his policies in Jamaica.

The South Sea Company's displeasure with Hunter arose over assembly acts passed in February of 1731 to subsist the two regiments sent to Jamaica. The island's high cost of living meant that all soldiers needed an additional allowance for subsistence. The assembly agreed to bear this expense by passing several acts to appropriate and apply such money. Subsistence money was partially raised by a poll tax and a "Deficiency" act. The funds raised by other acts were to be used to construct housing for the soldiers and to pay each soldier a reward of £10 for each rebel Negro killed or captured. These acts, however, raised only part of the money needed to subsist the regiments. The major part of the funds was raised by other acts which imposed a tax of £1,000 on Jamaica's Jews; placed a duty of £100 on every convict imported into the island from Great Britain; and taxed the South Sea Company 15s on every Negro imported into Jamaica and 30s on every Negro exported from the island.[24]

Because the regiments had to be supported, the governor approved the measures and forwarded the acts to the Board of Trade. Hunter was aware that legal or commercial objections might be raised at home. He reminded the board that none of the acts were of an extraordinary nature. He particularly pointed out that the act imposing tariffs on the South Sea Company differed "little in substance from the annual bills" usually passed by the assembly. This was true, but there was one significant difference in that the amount of duty imposed on the company had been raised substantially. In the past, the South Sea Company had paid only 10s a head on imported Negroes and 20s a head on exported Negroes. It remained to be seen if the company would bear the increased burden in silence.[25]

Hunter soon found that his fears concerning the company were well founded. On receipt of the bill which raised the duties on exported and imported slaves, the Board of Trade informed Hunter that he had violated his additional instruction of November 13, 1727, which prohibited him from approving any such act. (The board had, however, ignored Hunter's assent to similar acts in 1728, 1729, and 1730.)[26]

The board probably objected to the increased tax at the insistence of Walpole and Newcastle, who did not wish to alienate powerful mercantile interests. In addition, the South Sea Company had legal justification for its objections to the bill, confirmed by Board of Trade attorney, Francis Fane, because Hunter had passed the measure in violation of his instruction. The Board of Trade advised the king that although the Jamaica assembly had been allowed to tax Negroes in the past "as they should think fit, yet this indulgence was never designed to be extended to the present case."[27]

The Board of Trade recommended that the king reject the revenue bill. They also noted, however, that since the measure would expire in February of 1732, it might be better to table the veto message until that time because the money raised by the act was needed to subsist the regiments. They strongly advised, and the king agreed, that to prevent similar measures from being passed in the future, Hunter be admonished "to adhere more strictly to his instructions. . . . " In essence, the board and the king-in-council decided to allow the substance of the act so as to support the army, but the measure itself was to be vetoed after it expired. This, and the slap on the wrist delivered to Hunter, would satisfy mercantile interests in Britain. The board had indeed come up with the best of all possible solutions, except for Hunter, who was admonished by the king "on pain of Our highest displeasure, and of being recalled from that Our government, to adhere more strictly to your Instructions. . . . " The king also ordered Hunter not to approve any similar bill in the future. The king's order, forwarded by the Board of Trade, was received in Jamaica on February 6, 1732. Hunter quickly replied that on January 29, 1732, he had given his assent to yet another Additional Duty Act to tax the South Sea Company's slaves. This act, he explained to the board, laid "no other or higher dutys on slaves then what had been for many years past without complaint." The South Sea Company, assured on government support, would not pay the duties.[28]

The mercantile selfishness, so abhorred by Robert Hunter and his imperialist ilk, could have no more lurid example than that provided by the South Sea Company's management. The company refused to pay duties on slaves because they claimed they lost money on the slave trade, a statement confirmed by their public books. The secret books of the company, however, showed that their profit on illegal commerce with the Spanish colonies was £1,000,000 sterling annually in 1730 and in 1731, £750,000 in 1732, and more than £500,000 sterling each year from 1735 to 1739. The company could undoubtedly have afforded the few thousand pounds in duty demanded by the Jamaica assembly. The money was, after all, for the support of the troops who protected the South Sea Company's Jamaica entrepôt. Nevertheless, the company vigorously protested the act and demanded that the Board of Trade investigate Hunter's actions.[29]

The board did conduct an investigation, but Hunter was not recalled because he had approved the most recent Additional Duty Bill before receipt of the king's order forbidding this practice. The larger issues implicit in the bill of military defense versus mercantile profit and of assembly authority over metropolitan monopolies were still unresolved. The board warned Hunter they had sent the bill laying duties on slaves to the king for his opinion. George II, or Walpole, agreed with the Board of

Trade that the mercantile interests of Great Britain should predominate over local concerns and imperial/military considerations. On October 13, 1732, the king ordered the instruction to Hunter not to impose duties on slaves to remain in effect, although the loss of revenue to Jamaica was considerable.[30]

The king's decision meant that the assembly's reluctance to support provincial military expeditions would continue, if not worsen, for there were few other sources of income on the island. The larger significance of the king's decision was that the continuing need of the governor-general for funds would cause him to make more and more concessions to an assembly which did not want to vote defense funds. Thus, the end result of this measure, along with countless other decisions of the Walpole era, was to increase the power of the provincial assembly at the expense of the royal prerogative.

"I would fain live a little for my self before I dye"

Criticism from the king and southern secretary, and opposition from the provincial legislatures, awakened in Hunter a strong desire to escape from Jamaica. He missed his New York and New Jersey friends and still hoped to visit them. "I do not despair," he assured James Alexander, "of Spending some part of the remains of Life In ye Society of So Sincere ones. I have had many of another Kind since I parted with them. I have lab'd for others and to Some purpose hitherto. I would fain live a little for my self before I dye." The statement was confirmation that the Jamaica governor-generalship had proven to be a burden. But more important was Hunter's conviction that he had led a successful life.[31]

An inner conviction of a worthwhile life was the best balm for the illness that struck Hunter in the late autumn of 1731. Hunter, still ill in January of 1732, asked the Board of Trade for a six-month leave of absence. The home government granted his request in May of 1732.[32]

While waiting to hear if his request for a leave had been granted, Hunter continued his correspondence with Alexander. On June 13, 1732, he asked Alexander about his New York and New Jersey property. He was particularly anxious to know if a tenant had been found for his Raritan acreage and wanted to buy still more land. Despite his acquisitive nature, Hunter did not add to his North American holdings because his desire to increase his estate was reduced by a personal tragedy.[33]

During the troubled years of his Jamaican governorship, Hunter had been partially consoled for the persistent annoyances he met by the presence of his sons, Charles and Thomas. His elder son, Charles, had apparently decided on a military career. On July 22, 1731, Hunter issued a commission to Charles to fill a vacancy in his independent company. Charles was on the half-pay list in England and was well qualified for the post, according to his father, who was naturally biased in his favor. Unfortunately, Charles did not have a chance to develop his capabilities. Sometime between Hunter's letter to Alexander of June 13, 1732, and his next letter of August 18, 1732, Charles Orby Hunter died. The death may have been caused by smallpox, because there was an epidemic in Jamaica during the summer of 1732. Charles was his father's favorite, "one of ye most hopefull youths I ever Knew of his years, & a Comfort & pleasure to me." No matter how close Hunter felt to his remaining son, Thomas, or to his three daughters in England, they coult not compensate him for the loss of Charles, with whom he had shared an affinity of spirit.[34]

Most of Hunter's will to live was buried with his son in the church-yard of St. Jago de la Vega. After the summer of 1732 (except for a brief recovery in the winter of 1733–1734), Hunter merely went through the motions of living. By August, when the bereft father learned that his leave was approved, he had decided he could not leave Jamaica immediately, because he believed he was not in good enough physical condition to risk a winter crossing. His need to escape from Jamaica and the unhappiness he had endured there was so great, however, that he considered the possibility of sailing as far as Carolina and waiting there for better weather to complete the trip to Great Britain. He wrote to Alexander in New York that he would visit him on his way back to England: "I have a strong Inclination to See New York, once more before I dye."[35]

Knowing and not caring that his own life was almost over, Hunter now desired to consolidate his estate. Therefore, he asked Alexander to sell whatever property he could in New York and New Jersey. He now wanted his "affairs within a narrow compasse," a request which he repeated frequently in the autumn of 1732. By November of that year, Hunter finally felt a bit better, but he had little strength. His failing health led Hunter to draw another will on January 4, 1733.[36]

The bulk of Hunter's estate, including the New York, New Jersey, and Jamaica property, Croyland, Burton Pedwardine, Chertsey, and the London houses in England, were left to his son, Thomas Orby Hunter, in keeping with the custom of primogeniture. The property was left to Thomas, however, only on the condition he did not "marry contract Marriage or enter into matrimony with Sarah Kelly widow of Charles Kelly of the parish of St. Katharines in Jamaica...." If Thomas persisted in his desire to wed the widow Kelly, whose late husband's family consistently and maliciously opposed Hunter in the assembly, the estate was to be divided equally among Hunter's daughters, Henrietta, Katharine, and Charlotte. Hunter had already settled "a portion of Six Thousand pounds" on Katharine at the time of her 1727 marriage. Henrietta and Charlotte were to receive £5,000 sterling each when they married or reached the age of twenty-one. Hunter also mentioned in his will the debt still due him from "the crown for subsisting the palatines sent to New York by her late Majesty Queen Anne . . . amounting to the Sume of Twenty one Thousand pounds and upward principal as it was duly and Regularly Stated audited and Reported by Mr. Auditor Harley. . . ."[37]

His will made, Hunter again thought of leaving Jamaica. The press of official business caused him to delay his departure, however, until it was finally too late in the summer of 1733 to sail. Hunter remained in frequent correspondence with James Alexander during this period. In one letter written on August 27, 1733, Hunter told Alexander he would wait until the next spring to go home unless a particularly good man-of-war was available. He then mentioned routine business matters and finally, at the end of the letter, commented to Alexander that he had "had Letters from Betty Holland and her daughter, I beg of you as a Sincere friend to Send me Some acct of both, as to their way of Living or Character, and Keep nothing from me that you may know or have come to your knowledge."[38]

Alexander responded quickly to Hunter's request for information about his former mistress. Betty Holland had made a small livelihood by "mantua making and other womans work." Her eyesight had grown weak, however, and she could no longer sew, but was now helped in her trade by her daughter, Elizabeth Hunter. Both lived with Betty's mother, now the chief support of the family, still employed "by the best people in town as a Nurse." Alexander pointed out to Hunter that the family was very poor and urged Hunter to "bestow some small matter annually upon them . . . ." The young girl, Elizabeth Hunter, often came into the shop owned by Alexander's wife (the former widow Provoost) and was "always nicely dressed & of a modest Genteel behaviour." Alexander told Hunter that his daughter had been well cared for and that "the mother & grandmother have Spared nothing in their small power to bestow upon her." Hunter was touched by Alexander's account and made arrangements with him to pay a small annuity "for the maintenance & Education of Elizabeth Hunter. . . ."[39]

"Not so much the Governors as Government"

Despite concern for his children, Hunter had to govern the province. His frustrations increased on May 31, 1731, when the crown chose to ignore his recommendation that John Ayscough, who was still in England, be kept off the council. The king ordered Ayscough's restoration and also instructed Hunter that Ayscough was to take over the government in the event of the governor's death or absence. Ayscough, with mission accomplished and health restored, returned to Jamaica. Undoubtedly with much satisfaction, he resumed his place at the council table. Hunter, embarrassed and annoyed with Ayscough's triumphant return, probably urged the appointment of James Lawes as lieutenant-governor. Lawes, appointed by the king on March 28, 1733, would be next in line to head the government.[40]

In addition to coping with annoying councilmen, Hunter also had to deal with recalcitrant assemblymen. The governor-general was forced to swallow many of the assembly's insults because he needed their votes to support bills to finance military raids against the Maroons. In January of 1732, for instance, Hunter sent the provost marshal to the assembly chamber to convey his order that all assembly members should go immediately to the council chamber where he wished to address them. The assembly, who were in committee, refused to admit the marshal. The next day, Hunter addressed the assembly sharply, scolding them for this "encroachment on H.M. royal prerogative, never before attempted or aimed at in any of H.M. Dominions." The house not only refused to accept the rebuff, but further disagreed with Hunter that their action was unprecedented. As proof, they cited an incident in 1629 when the English House of Commons had refused to admit Black Rod, sent by Charles I to dissolve the house. The practice of citing seventeenth-century English examples to justify eighteenth-century colonial opposition was to become a familiar one in America. Although Hunter was annoyed with such legislative extremism and threatened the assembly with retaliation for their rudeness and defiance, he admitted he could do nothing because of "the present exigency of the publick...."[41]

Bickering between council and assembly also impeded legislative action and hampered military defense as well. On January 13, 1733, Hunter reported to the Board of Trade that not one act had been passed in the last session of the assembly. Consequently, with the advice of the council, he had dissolved the assembly and a new body of representatives met on March 13, 1733. Hunter at first thought he saw signs of conciliation among the assemblymen but was still suspicious that "the artifices of a few may prevail at this time as they have done formerly in clogging the bills or throwing rubs in the way...."[42]

Hunter was right to expect trouble, because the perennial rivalry between legislative branches, familiar to all governors-general of royal colonies, erupted once more. As Hunter observed, the contention sprang from the assembly's determination "to assume what does not belong to them," while the council, "tenatious of their own rights," protected their sphere of influence. During the spring 1733 session, the assembly persisted in sending bills to the council which that body could not accept. If the council suggested alterations, the assembly would then refuse to proceed further with the bills.[43]

The Jamaica assembly was particularly pugnacious during this spring session because Hunter was forced to ask them for more money with which to finish the fort at Titchfield. The assembly, which had already voted large sums of money to support several military maneuvers against the rebels, was reluctant to raise still more money for the fort. Their reluctance led them to assume that the funds already voted had been misappropriated. They, therefore, demanded an investigation into the conduct of the commanding officer at Titchfield, Major Jasper Ashworth, whom they suspected of embezzling funds. Hunter was furious that the assembly attacked Ashworth, a man whom he considered loyal and honest. The governor-general informed the representatives that he considered their investigation of the major to be a personal attack on him as well as an assault on the royal prerogative he represented. The assembly was unmoved by Hunter's rhetoric and continued their fruitless investigation of Ashworth. Their inability to prove Ashworth's guilt did not, however, lead them to vote funds for the fort.[44]

The rift between the assembly and the governor and his council widened when the assembly reconvened in July of 1733. The Maroon threat continued, all white Jamaicans lived in daily fear of a slave uprising, and the islanders were unable to defend themselves. Yet when the council proposed to the assembly that they request the home government to send eight companies to Jamaica, the assembly refused, raising the popular and perennial English argument against standing armies. The assembly did, however, send up a bill for building additional barracks in wilderness areas and for sending out "flying parties." The governor-in-council rejected the bill because it placed the management of the colony's military activities almost exclusively under the control of the assembly. The bill "tended in general to wrest the power out of the hands of the Governor and fix it in Commissioners who consisted chiefly of members of their own House . . . vested with authority to hold Court Martials and to try for capitall cases by a Quorum . . . and this without the knowledge or direction of the Commander-in-Chief, and in no way accountable to him for their proceedings."[45]

The net result of such bickering for the island of Jamaica was decreased military capability. Defense measures were postponed or rejected out of personal resentment. So much was evident when the assembly met again in October of 1733. At that time "in a conference with the Council they [the assembly] agree'd to what I had long ago and now again propos'd," Hunter reported, "as to a defensible barrack," or fort, about halfway between Port Antonio and Nanny Town to protect settlements and facilitate future expeditions. The assembly prepared two barracks bills, but both were rejected by the council because they again wrested authority for military operations away from the governor-general. The barracks remained unbuilt and the Maroons undefeated.[46]

This assembly session convinced Hunter that Jamaicans were "runing headlong to ruin with their eyes open." As the governor realized, the problems of Jamaica were fundamental. They concerned the islanders' desire for political autonomy and the selfish character of the men who comprised the provincial legislature. As Hunter noted, it was "not so much the Governors as Government that has been disagreeable to the Assembly. How can it be otherwise, when the men of greatest substance and best education have ever made it their choice to ly by at their ease," or instead go home to England. Hunter controlled assembly elections in Jamaica to a far lesser degree than he had in New York or New Jersey because, despite his powers of patronage, he found it difficult to persuade the few competent men on the island to run for public office. Lazy, absent, or disinterested wealthy whites would not serve in government, but the assembly was encumbered by those who chose to run simply "for protection of their persons," that is, to avoid imprisonment for debt. There were still others who sought assembly seats because of "private resentments" or merely "to embroil matters and perplex the administration...." The lack of competent politicians was familiar throughout the colonies because there was no traditional ruling elite in America. The situation was, of course, worse in sugar colonies such as Jamaica where there were few whites. By December of 1733, the largely self-serving men who composed Jamaica's assembly had brought government virtually to an impasse. The "Negroes in rebellion" were growing stronger and bolder. Hunter was unable to defend the island because the home government was reluctant to bear the expense of maintaining additional troops there and the island government did not want to support military forces except under their own terms.[47]

Another cause for Hunter's depression was the death on December 28, 1733, of the lieutenant-governor, James Lawes. John Ayscough, who held a dormant commission to take over the government in the event of Hunter's death or absence, was again in line to succeed him. Hunter could neither resign himself to Ayscough's succession nor would be willingly leave Jamaica while Ayscough was next in line. On December 29th, Hunter wrote to both the Board of Trade and to the duke of Newcastle to request that Richard Mill be given a commission to head the government. Until he received word that Mill had been appointed, Hunter was determined to remain on Jamaica.[48]

"Rum, the ruin of this island"

The Maroon War continued to be as much of a concern to Hunter as were his legislative battles. In March of 1733, yet another party of 250 men, "compleatly arm'd and victual'd" by Hunter, "march'd off by different routes" to attack the rebels who again held Nanny Town and the newly built barrack there. Sir Chaloner Ogle, who replaced Stewart as admiral of the Jamaica station, helped Hunter to provision and equip the black and white men who formed the expeditionary force. Much to Hunter's disgust, however, the soldiers retreated from the mountains without ever seeing the enemy.[49]

The reason for the soldiers' cowardly disregard for orders, according to Hunter, was because he "could not obtain any other punishment for disobedience, mutiny, or desertion to be inflicted by their lawe than such as their slaves and servants, of which this body is chiefly made up, are inur'd to every day of their lives, and value not." Part of the problem was also that the men were "drunken and disorderly, for rum, the ruin of this island, is easier to come at here than small beer in England." Servants and slaves may indeed have been drunk and inured to physical punishment, but a more obvious reason for their lack of enthusiasm in engaging in battle with the Maroons was that they saw little reason to risk their lives for the interests of wealthy white planters and merchants. Hunter, of course, was aware of the civic and military disinterest of "hir'd servants and free negros who have no obligations either of honor or interest for the defence of their master's propertys."[50]

Another volunteer force, raised by Captains Ebenezer Lambe and Henry Williams, attacked the rebels in June of 1733. The expedition was somewhat delayed, because the men refused to march until they received the month's pay which the assembly had promised them but then refused to pay. Hunter got a loan for the amount, saw that the men were paid, and then sent the expedition off from Port Antonio on June 15th.[51]

The government forces beat the rebels in a mountain pass and entered one of the rebel towns which the Maroons set afire before fleeing into the Blue Mountains. The soldiers followed them, but were beaten back. The raiding party held the town for a few days and then "shamefully abandon'd the place," not even bringing back "one Ear of a Rebellious Negro." Hunter was furious with the leaders of the expedition for leaving the town against orders. He had Lambe and Williams examined by the council before jailing them. Both men were subsequently released on the condition they volunteer for another foray. Lambe, at least, did nothing to exonerate himself on the next expedition. At least, so reported Lieutenant James Draper of the independent company, who said that Lambe had been jailed again because he "grossly misbehaved" after joining the troops.[52]

After the June attack, Hunter decided to launch another raid immediately, especially since the rebels "have done much mischief of late and flusht with success have ventur'd to plunder a plantation within sight of the town of Titchfield." The reason the rebels had been so bold as to come near Titchfield was because the fort remained unfinished. Without funds, and without a dedicated supervisor, Hunter was powerless to compel its completion. He could, however, attack engineer Christian Lilly, who had been remiss in his duties. On August 20, 1733, Hunter issued an order suspending the engineer from his military office "for repeated disobedience to my Orders, habitual neglect of your Duty and disregard to your Superiours."[53]

Lilly's dismissal may have satisfied Hunter's sense of justice, but it did nothing to thwart the rebels. In July of 1733, the assembly sent a request to Sir Chaloner Ogle for permission to recruit 130 volunteers from the seamen aboard his fleet to supplement the island's forces. Ogle agreed, and 200 seamen were recruited. The sailors were of immediate use because before the expedition set out, "the Soldiers of the Country Mutinied and were forced to be reduced to obedience by the Sailors, who were drawn up in a Body against them with orders to Fire upon them, if they did not Submit. . . . " The soldiers capitulated and left on the march, but their discontent and disinterest were infectious.[54]

The soldiers and sailors left Port Antonio on August 18, 1733. By September, Hunter had heard the disgraceful story of their defeat and flight. About two miles from one of the rebel towns, one of the companies was attacked. The men held briefly, but then the sailors panicked, turned, and fled. They were promptly joined by the soldiers. None of the men fled so fast, however, that they were blind to plunder. As they approached their own baggage Negroes, they told them the officers were all dead and that they were to lay down their burdens and run away. The Negroes did as they were told, and the sailors and soldiers broke, stole, or destroyed "every individual bag, and box broke and threw away all the Surgeon's instruments and medecines and pulled the beef and bread all out of the baggs and hove them down the precipiece. . . . "[55]

Hunter demanded severe penalties. Most of the soldiers were rounded up, two of them court martialled and executed, "one for the plundering the baggage, the other, a Guide for perswading the sailors to run away. . . ." The seamen, however, escaped punishment because of an "act of Assembly [which] exempted [them] from the rules and articles of war to which the rest were subjected, tho' the disorder begun with them I can not proceed further," a discouraged Hunter wrote.[56]

The rebels were emboldened by the aborted attack, or perhaps they were better armed by the unexpected bounty of guns and ammunition which the fleeing soldiers and sailors could not carry away. They soon increased their attacks on white settlements. Hunter told Newcastle that on January 11, 1734, some 250 rebels had gone so far as to attack a military "post called Brest Work where we were building a barrack." The planters were terrified by the increased belligerency of the rebels, especially because many of their slaves seized the opportunity to join the outlaws. The runaways included twenty-nine Negroes who belonged to the king, purchased by the admiralty to clear Lynch's Island. The desire for freedom among the slaves was persistent, but equally persistent was the fear this desire generated among the island's whites. The resulting apprehension was sufficient to convince the assemblymen they must put personal animosities aside to work for the defense of the island.[57]

"Life is a tragedy"

In February of 1734, Hunter oversaw another assembly session. On March 9, 1734, he told the Board of Trade that the representatives, who had refused to ask for troops from the home government in August of 1733, were now almost wild with fear after the last attack by the rebels on "the Brest Work." The assemblymen hastily prepared a representation to the king asking for military "assistance in their distresse." The assembly's awakening to the threat posed by the Maroons led Hunter to gloat to the Board of Trade that "Nothing has happen'd that has not been foretold to them, but it seems feeling only is believing here." As he tended to Jamaica's defense against the Maroons in the late winter of 1734, Hunter seemed almost his old and vigorous self. One of the last measures he signed was a bill to cut additional roads and build more barracks in the eastern half of Jamaica. His last official appearance was at a council meeting held on March 19, 1734, at which time plans were laid to draft men to mount another offensive against the Maroons. Hunter thus ended his public life as he had begun it in 1688, involved in the planning and execution of a military expedition.[58]

Jonathan Swift in 1727 had commented that "life is a tragedy, wherein we sit as spectators awhile, and then act our own part in it." Hunter had been a spectator at many of life's tragedies: his parents, friends, relatives, wife, and son had all died before him; as an officer and governor-general, Hunter had seen many men killed, had sent many more to their deaths, and killed other men himself. In March of 1734, still active, with an alert and lucid mind, Hunter was called upon to play his own part in the tragedy. The governor-general had "for some time laboured under a Complication of Distempers, though to outward appearance He was as well and as Active as could be expected from a Man of His Age. . . ." Hunter "was taken ill the 17th and died the 31st of March 1734 in the 67 year of His Age and the 6th of His Administrations."[59]

Robert Hunter was buried the next day in the churchyard of the Anglican Church at St. Jago de la Vega, while his independent company formed an honor guard and a sixty-one-gun salute was fired in the background. No trace of his grave survives, but his epitaph has been preserved:

Here lie the dear remains of Robert Hunter late governor of this island, who borrowing nothing from his forefathers' glory shone with the worth of his own nobility. To remarkable personal beauty he joined a kindly disposition and to great practical and literary knowledge courteous manners. Renowned in war, and no less distinguished in peace he passed his days of active service with wisdom and courage, those of leisure with dignity and refinement. Here, therefore, good reader, at the dead man's tomb pay the tribute of respect which his modesty when he lived could not bear to receive. And ye who come after pay with a flood of tears the debt of sorrow due to him who was careful of the people's health and destroyed his own.

Immediately after the burial service, Robert Hunter's son and heir, Thomas, took the first available man-of-war back to England and to the landed, parliamentary future his father had prepared for him. The body of Robert Hunter remained in Jamaica to become part of the island and the empire he helped to create.[60]

⬦ CONCLUSION ⬦

"A Sound Man"

𝓡OBERT HUNTER had generally made positive and profitable decisions throughout his career. He had achieved his youthful ambition to attain property, power, and position. Hunter, who began life as a penniless Scot, had enjoyed a highly successful military career. He served in the best regiments and under the best commanders in the British army, participated in most of the major battles and sieges of the War of the Spanish Succession, personally and faithfully served the duke of Marlborough, and was fortunate enough to emerge unscathed from combat. By 1705, Hunter had been promoted to the rank of colonel. His final promotion in 1727 was to the rank of major general.

Hunter's reputation as a skilled army officer and his personality made him an eligible suitor for the hand (and the land) of his former commander's wealthy widow, Elizabeth Orby, Lady Hay. Through this fortunate marriage, Hunter acquired estates in Croyland, Burton Pedwardine, Chertsey, and Jamaica. To this extensive acreage, Hunter added land he purchased in New York, New Jersey, and Jamaica. Hunter apparently led a happy life with Lady Hay. He also enjoyed the companionship of his five children, all of whom, in an era of high infant mortality, grew to adulthood. Hunter himself enjoyed a long and comparatively healthy life and remained active until just a few days prior to his death.

In addition to a rewarding personal life and successful military career, Hunter was also an accomplished politician. Well might he boast at the end of his life that he had "lab'd for others and to Some purpose...." Hunter's New York and New Jersey administrations would later be regarded as something of a golden era in American colonial history. Hunter's Jamaica administration was also successful. Despite the limitations of age and illness under which Hunter labored, he controlled the rebels who presented the most significant threat to stable government during his tenure of office. In addition, his strategic plans for the island's defense were the ultimate cause for the rebels' capitulation.[1]

Along with wealth and power, Hunter had acquired the patronage or friendship of the most politically influential and culturally powerful Britons of his day. His patrons included the dukes of Marlborough and Argyll, the earls of Stair and Mar, the politicians Godolphin, Oxford, Sunderland, Somers, Stanhope, Bolingbroke, Dartmouth, Carteret, Townshend, Newcastle, and Walpole.

Hunter included among his friends the creative geniuses of his era, poets and playwrights, artists and musicians, such as Swift, Gay, Congreve, Addison, Steele, Pope, Kneller, and Handel. Hunter brought colonists into contact with the thoughts, words, attitudes, and deeds of these exceptional artists of England's Augustan age. English culture, transplanted to the New World by governors-general such as Hunter, awakened a respect for learning and a scientific curiosity in provincials.

Hunter and other governors-general of the early eighteenth century had also carried English imperial values to America. These values demanded that Governor-General Hunter defend, preserve, and extend the outer limits of Great Britain's empire while maintaining social stability, tranquility, and prosperity within the colonies under his command. It was a formidable task, but Hunter and other governors-general had several weighty weapons at their command. One such weapon was the Church of England, the ideological mainstay of the state and, in New York, the means by which Hunter hoped to secure the powerful Iroquois to the British cause. One way to guarantee their allegiance was to bind them to the English by the shared cultural ties of religion and language. Hunter therefore urged the Society for the Propagation of the Gospel to send missionaries to New York not only to instruct Iroquois children in religion, but also to teach them to read and write English. Hunter explained his imperial prescription for native Americans by reference to the native Britons, "our Scotch Highlanders who keep to their ancient language, habits and customs, but yet have little more of Christianity besides the name than they had in St. Columbs day." Hunter's solution for the North American Indian was the same as that used by the English government in the Highlands. English culture was extended to both provinces to bring together diverse people by minimizing differences, and hence, possible sources of conflict.[2]

Hunter also believed that strengthening the church meant strengthening the provincial government. The commonly held belief of the time was that religious diversity divided society and demoralized government. Hunter, therefore, repeatedly urged the society to send out competent missionaries, not only to anglicize natives, but also to persuade Europeans to a "uniformity in worship." Yet Hunter, although he applauded missionary achievements among the Mohawk, did not blame the missionaries for their lack of success among British nonconformists and continental Europeans. As Hunter pointed out, colonists were "generally obstinate, the whimsical & factious who flock hither for elbow room to exert their talents."[3]

As a secular Whig, Hunter was personally tolerant of reformed Protestant sects. His religious toleration did not, however, extend to either Roman Catholics or Jews, at least not in Jamaica, where he suspected that both Catholics and Jews were intriguing with the Spaniards in Cuba and supplying the island's rebel Negroes with arms and ammunition. Hunter sought to reduce the threat to Jamaica by halting the continuing immigration of Catholics to the island from Ireland. The Jewish immigration to Jamaica had halted. Jews irritated Hunter, however, because their religion excused them from the burden of holding public office. Hunter used this as an excuse for approving the exorbitant taxes imposed on them yearly by the assembly. His dislike of the Jews as an ethnic and religious group did not prevent Hunter from accepting from them a well-filled yearly purse.

While Hunter believed in religion as a means of social discipline, his own personal attitude toward the Church of England was ambiguous. It is evident that Hunter lacked any strong conviction or attachment to the church, perhaps because his nature was irreligious to begin with or perhaps because his early attachment had been to Presbyterianism, incompatible with an Anglican empire. Whatever the depth of his childhood commitment to the religion of his native Lowlands, Hunter was willing to make compromises with his conscience, just as his uncle, John Spalding, had in 1670. There was probably more than a grain of truth in the 1712 statement of Long Island Presbyterian, John Coe, who claimed that Hunter asked him, "Why do not you Conform as I, I am as you are though I hear the prayers and Receive the Sacrament...." Later, probably at Hunter's insistence, Coe retracted his statement, but the suspicion remains that Hunter actually urged nominal and occasional conformity on others and practiced it himself.[4]

The authority of a governor-general was reinforced by the Anglican Church, but its most obvious manifestation was military. Hunter never retired from the army, but received promotions and collected half pay until he died still on duty in imperial government. Hunter was as much of a military officer in command of New York, New Jersey, and Jamaica, all conquered provinces, as he had been in the garrisons of Ireland and Scotland or in the wars and towns of the continent. And Hunter had regular army units under his command both in New York and in Jamaica. In each colony, he held a commission as captain of one of the independent companies of regular troops in the garrison he commanded. In addition, like all other governors-general, Hunter also commanded the militia. In

New York, Hunter lived in the fort with his soldiers, surgeon, chaplain, and staff officers, much as a Cromwellian military governor would have done. His Jamaican capital, St. Jago de la Vega, itself organized and governed on a Cromwellian model, was garrisoned by regular soldiers. In New York, New Jersey, and Jamaica, these regular military forces were increased by volunteers raised for specific purposes, such as the 1711 Canadian expedition and the Maroon War. The governor-general also had the power to call up the militia and, with the advice of a council of war, to declare a state of martial law.

American colonists generally recognized that the British troops were useful protectors and policemen, although Jamaicans especially resented having to compensate the soldiers for the high cost of island living. New York did not contribute to the soldiers' support, but the assembly was expected to vote funds to maintain and repair the colony's forts and fortifications. The strategic positioning of these forts permitted New York's soldiers to protect frontier settlers and the Iroquois, whose geographical proximity to Canada left them vulnerable to attack by the French and their Indian allies. The redcoats certainly helped not only to protect but also to impose political order and social stability on the royal colonies. So much was seen in New York in 1711, when soldiers put down the rebellious Palatines. Troops were then quartered in the Palatine villages where they maintained the system of military rule Hunter dictated to the immigrants. In New York City, the regular redcoats and the militia helped suppress the 1712 Negro uprising. Regular soldiers were needed even more in Jamaica, where they helped to control the rebel Maroons, protected frontier settlements, and discouraged Spanish attempts to re-take the island.

Whether militarily imposed or locally produced, social order and political stability had not been characteristic of New York, New Jersey, or Jamaica prior to Hunter's command. Almost as soon as Hunter landed in New York in June of 1710, he found himself in the middle of the bitter factionalism and partisan politics which had characterized that province's society since Leisler's 1689 rebellion divided the colony into Leislerians and Anti-Leislerians. New Jersey was also rent by political and religious factions which had formed the Proprietary and Anti-Proprietary parties. In New York and New Jersey, the leaders of local parties not only vied for the political patronage and personal favor of each succeeding governor-general, but represented the divergent class interests of merchants and landowners. Each group was determined to secure the governor-general's assistance in protecting their profits, often by playing on the governor-general's need for funds to secure favorable legislation.

All New York governors needed the support of one or the other party or faction and so were forced to choose sides. In New York, like his Whig

CONCLUSION, "A SOUND MAN"   221

predecessor, Bellomont, Hunter chose to ally with the revolutionary Leislerians; in New Jersey, unlike his Tory predecessor, Cornbury, Hunter allied with the Scots-based Proprietary party. In both colonies, Hunter favored the interests of landowners over those of merchants, whom he despised as a class. To control his opposition, Hunter used both political coercion and personal conciliation to achieve a relatively stable administration.

In addition to taking sides in political factionalism and elite rivalry, Hunter also had to moderate the constitutional struggles with the New York and New Jersey (and later the Jamaica) legislatures, as the councils and the assemblies vied for power. When the form of royal government was established in the seventeenth century, it was the intent of the crown that the governor would be assisted in the legislative functions of government by a council and an assembly. The former, nominated by the governor-general and confirmed by the crown, was to act as an upper house to the governor, its role similar in some respects to that of the House of Lords. Unlike the lords, the council had crown-conferred power to pass, amend, or reject money bills. The assembly, on the other hand, was to be elected by colonists. Like the English House of Commons, it was to have the assigned function of providing funds for the maintenance of the government. Despite some superficial similarities, rulers in Great Britain did not recognize the colonial assembly to be the equivalent of the House of Commons. Nor were colonial councils admitted to be equivalent to the House of Lords. Colonists, however, persisted in drawing comparisons between metropolitan and provincial legislatures. This led assemblymen to challenge the councils' attempts to amend all legislation, including money bills. The rationale of representatives was that the English upper house had no similar voice in amending parliamentary fiscal legislation in Great Britain.

By 1710, the New York assembly was already a defiant body whose power had grown consistently, partially because of its control over finances. Despite its brief existence (New York did not have a representative assembly until 1683; the assembly ceased to exist during the Dominion of New England and was only reintroduced in 1691), by the time Hunter arrived in 1710, the assembly insisted on its right to set fees, including the amount of the governor-general's salary. In addition, that body resented the council's amendments of its money bills, refused to surrender to the crown's representative control of the disbursement of colonial funds, and asserted that the governor-general could not erect courts of chancery without its consent.

Hunter was a rational Augustan gentleman and assumed that once shown the error of its ways, the New York "Assembly might be governed by reason, but experience taught him that it was a vain imagination." Since the faction-ridden assembly was primarily ruled by emotion, its members would not respond to Hunter's common sense and logic. The assembly asserted it had an "inherent Right" to exercise its autonomy, particularly over money issues. This ensured that Hunter, a strong-willed man whose military training had accustomed him to expect obedience from subordinates, would meet aggravating resistance. Hunter was forced to abandon his attempts to use reason and turned to the techniques of coercion and intimidation that he had learned in the army.[5]

Hunter further exacerbated the situation by his unwillingness to make compromises with the merchant-dominated assembly. In 1710, that body sought to buy Hunter's complicity, much as they had that of his predecessor, Lord Cornbury, by offering him a bribe. The assembly was antagonized by Hunter's indignant refusal of the present. The result was that the assembly was alienated from the governor-general, and it was not until November of 1711, that Hunter was voted a salary.

The assembly's antagonism was so intense that the members refused to pass a revenue bill, forcing Hunter to pay all the colony's bills for necessary services. Hunter finally received some money for the province's expenses in 1712. He and other creditors had to wait until 1714, when a major Debt Bill was passed, for full payment. The passage of this bill was an indication that the tide had begun to turn in Hunter's favor. In 1715, Hunter's growing control of the legislature, his willingness to make concessions, and the 1714 accession of George I, enabled him to secure a five-year revenue bill. Hunter finally achieved a proadministration majority in the 1716 assembly, after he had reduced or eliminated the influence of New York's merchant representatives. He accomplished this by securing the allegiance (and votes) of large Hudson River Valley landowners and their tenants, small independent farmers, and small city merchants and artisans, who now supported his candidates at the polls. Voters swung to Hunter's support because he persuaded dedicated and able men to run for office. Their election, and Hunter's appointment of honest judges, competent militia officers, and efficient officeholders, ensured peace and order in a formerly chaotic society. The maintenance of a well-ordered environment endeared Hunter to the affections of "the middling sort," or the more numerous portion of the New York voting population.

Hunter used similar methods and won similar voter support in New Jersey, although the legislative problem in that colony differed from that in New York. In New Jersey, Hunter met opposition from the council, dominated by an anti-Scot and anti-Quaker faction. Hunter quickly allied with the Scot and Quaker Proprietary party and then appointed new councillors. He did not meet the legislature again until he heard that his nominees had been approved by the queen. The expelled councillors won assembly seats, but when they attempted to halt legislative proceedings by absenting themselves from the assembly session, Hunter pronounced them traitors and Jacobites. He then hounded their leaders not only out of New Jersey, but out of America. With his opponents exiled, Hunter achieved a degree of control over all branches of government in New Jersey comparable to that he had achieved in New York.

Hunter rationalized his arbitrary actions in eliminating his provincial opposition by declaring that all who opposed him also opposed the queen (or the king) and were, in effect, traitors. His methods were arbitrary, but while the persecuted colonists could and did complain to the home government, the governor-general ruled supreme within his colonies. North America was three thousand miles in distance and four months in time away from the center of empire. Colonial affairs rarely took priority over European concerns with the home government. As long as Hunter maintained order and stability, he had little reason to worry about government action from a sympathetic Board of Trade and a monarch and privy council predisposed in his favor.

Hunter also enjoyed the support of the home government in Jamaica, but it was in a somewhat diminished form. This was partially because the Board of Trade had lost some of its former vigor. Its members, most of whom had been appointed by Walpole, were also governed by him, as was Southern Secretary Newcastle. Neither board nor Newcastle would take an independent stand against Walpole. Dwindling support from the home government frustrated Hunter's efforts to establish a stable society in Jamaica.

There were also factors in Jamaica that made that colony's ills less capable of solution than had been the case in New York or New Jersey. Part of the problem was the underlying current of terror among the island's inhabitants, which made them fretful and unreasonable. The white ruling elite was outnumbered by their slaves and lived in constant fear of a slave uprising. The Maroon War also produced fear, uncertainty, and turmoil among the island's white population. Economic problems increased uneasiness among Jamaicans. The Jamaica economy was depressed during Hunter's tenure as governor-general because the European market was glutted with sugar. These conditions were clearly beyond Hunter's control, yet provincials wanted order and prosperity and blamed their absence on Hunter. Hunter failed to establish a peaceful, prosperous society because Jamaica's problems were much more severe than those of New York or New

Jersey and less susceptible to local solution. Then too, Hunter was old and sick and preoccupied with the state of his own health and the death of his son.[6]

Hunter's efforts to govern Jamaica were further hampered because the ground rules of imperial administration had changed in the eighteen years that separated the beginning of his New York-New Jersey administrations from his Jamaica governor-generalship. The rise of capitalism and the predominance of mercantilism were well established by the time Hunter arrived in Jamaica. By 1728, the empirewide garrison government implemented by Cromwell, the later Stuart monarchs, and Marlborough was being replaced by the politics of peace and trade advocated by the mercantilists.

In Jamaica, Hunter soon found that Marlborough's apprehension of merchants was well founded, because imperial colonial administration reflected the political philosophy of Robert Walpole. Commerce was now all important, and commercial considerations governed political decisions, at times even military decisions, as Hunter realized after he arrived in Jamaica. Under Walpole, imperial administration entered a new phase of commercially determined colonial management. Political offices in Great Britain and the colonies were given by Walpole to ensure parliamentary support for his policies, often with complete disregard for the qualifications of the potential officeholder. Robert Hunter, a survivor from an earlier imperial era, was one of the best of the Walpolian American appointees. The most likely reason Hunter received the Jamaica post was because Argyll, who exerted a substantial control over Scottish elections, requested it be given to him. Hunter, therefore, was appointed governor-general of Jamaica not so much because of his qualifications for the post, which were considerable in themselves and the traditional, imperial, prerequisites for proconsuls, but because Walpole needed Argyll's continued support.

The poor quality of other Walpolian nominees was reflected in increasingly inept management of colonial affairs. Politics in the early eighteenth century were intensely personal and the success or failure of colonial administration was almost entirely dependent on the governor-general. As can be seen from Hunter's administrations in New York, New Jersey, and Jamaica, the powers of governors-general were extensive and usually sufficient to enforce imperial rule if the man in office was as active, intelligent, dedicated, and competent as was Hunter. No governor-general, however, including Hunter, could resolve all problems. If the governor-general had few of these attributes, provincial autonomy would advance virtually unchecked. As long as colonial officeholders were chosen primarily on the basis of their services to the Walpolian administration and not on the basis of their competence, efficiency, and intelligence, colonial administration would continue to deteriorate.

Walpole's schemes were also imperially unrealistic. Walpole was determined "to seek peace and not empire, to look for prosperity without plunder, to yearn for stability and to shun glory. . . . " Walpole favored the expansion of the empire through peaceful commerce, not by armed conquest. This was impossible in the West Indies because neither the French nor the Spanish were content to maintain the peaceful status quo as long as England held territory Spain claimed and France wanted. In 1728, when Hunter took office in Jamaica, his sense of military duty to protect and discipline his colonial command remained relevant despite Walpolian political predominance, but it had to be exercised within, and was circumscribed by, mercantile values in politics and economics.[7]

Hunter's adaptation to mercantile politics in Jamaica appeared when he abandoned that integrity which had led him to reject the New York assembly's bribe in 1710. Rather than abandon the crown's legislative prerogative in that colony, Hunter did without a salary for more than a year and an adequate government revenue for more than four years. In Jamaica, Hunter sought to reconcile the assembly while enriching himself.

When, in the spring of 1728, the Jamaica assembly passed two significant measures, a permanent revenue bill which also confirmed the island's laws and a present to Hunter of £6,000, Hunter gladly accepted both. In return for the gift, Hunter approved an annual revenue which he realized was insufficient for the needs of the island executive. Governor-General Hunter could, of course, have held out for more money. He had a substantial weapon in that the home government would not confirm the island's laws unless the assembly voted a permanent income judged suitable by him. Hunter did not choose to question the assembly's grant and accepted the inadequate sum. And corruption had its imperial uses, for Hunter thus became the only governor-general to obtain a perpetual revenue from an American assembly after 1700.

Hunter's corrupt compromise in Jamaica in 1728 reflected the methods employed at home by the Walpole ministry. Corruption was reversed in Jamaica. In Britain, the executive bought the legislature; in Jamaica, the legislature bought the executive. This fact, more than any other, illustrates the different sources of power in both Britain and Jamaica. In England, Parliament was sovereign, the dispenser of favors and the controller of destinies, and its members' votes were worth government purchase. In Jamaica, however, the situation was quite different because the supreme control rested with the representative of England, the governor-general, and he was worth buying by the assembly.

Despite Hunter's willingness to compromise, he was unable to avoid contention with the Jamaica assembly. Neither was he able to achieve the degree of control over that body that he had won over the assemblies in New York and New Jersey. One reason Hunter failed to achieve this control was because of the small number of white people on Jamaica. This meant that Hunter had only a shallow pool of men from which to draw alternative officers, civil and military, to replace his opponents. Despite his powers of patronage, therefore, the governor-general could not find or persuade enough proexecutive men to run as representatives to give him control of the Jamaica assembly, while those who did run were often inept or self-serving men.

Hunter also failed to gain control of the legislature because the Jamaica assembly, in existence since 1664, was more experienced in defiance of the royal prerogative and more determined to assert its autonomy than either its New York or New Jersey counterparts, younger institutions staffed by less secure, experienced, or wealthy oligarchs than Jamaica's. After the settling of a permanent revenue in 1728, the Jamaica assembly made few other concessions to Governor-General Hunter. Instead, it continually used its control over militarily essential funds to secure political favors and demanded the sole power to frame the colony's money bills. The assembly also attempted to seize control of the island's militia and military operations from the governor. The New York and New Jersey assemblies, on the other hand, had been prompt to vote the funds needed for the 1711 Canadian expedition and had never attempted to interfere with Hunter's military control of the province.

The Maroon War thus put Hunter at a continual disadvantage in contests with the assembly. Hunter was dependent on that body to pass special money bills each time he wanted to send raiders to the Blue Mountains to attack the rebels. The assembly often baulked at the prospect of raising money. They procrastinated until the governor-general made concessions to get money for defense, his primary concern. To Hunter, any political concessions he made were of secondary importance, given the military priorities of imperial governance. The royal prerogative was slowly reduced, but in the meantime Hunter's methods preserved and extended the British Empire.

Hunter's efforts to conduct the Maroon War were further hindered by that shortage of competent leaders which hampered his political maneuvers. Hunter recognized that the militia suffered from poor leadership and purged the officer class, just as he had that of New York and New

Jersey. In Jamaica, however, for reasons of white flight and veterans' exemptions, Hunter had few men from whom to draw officers. Of those liable to serve, few were willing and fewer were capable. Inadequate leadership was not the only personnel problem, however. The men themselves, whether volunteers or draftees, militia or regulars, were demoralized, even cowardly men, in whom it was impossible to instill any sense of duty or discipline. Despite the weaknesses of these troops on patrol, Hunter checked the rebels by placing soldiers in frontier forts, connected by a system of new roads. Both of these tactics he adapted from contemporary campaigns in the Scottish Highlands. The capitulation of the Maroons was further ensured by the 1734 arrival in Jamaica of six independent companies of one hundred men each, sent out by the home government at Hunter's request. In 1739, five years after Hunter's death, the Maroons finally signed a peace treaty with Governor-General Edward Trelawney, who received the credit for much of what Hunter accomplished.[8]

The governors-general repressed rebels, but they were resisted by representatives. Hard-pressed to obtain money from their assemblies, the viceroys had to concede to civil opponents victories which they denied to the empire's overt enemies. Hunter believed that if the colonial assemblies were permitted to continue to challenge the authority of the crown and Parliament, they would eventually rebel against the home government. His belief that the power of the colonial oligarchs must be contained led Hunter in 1711 to agree with Henry St. John's proposal that all the mainland colonies, including the proprietary and charter colonies, be placed under a central government similar to the old Dominion of New England, a government which had functioned without representative assemblies.

Hunter adapted the arguments of James Harrington relating to colonies, noting that if the assemblies were allowed to usurp the governor's power, it "would bring ye government from Provinciall and dependent, to Nationall and independent. Which is a reflexion that deserves some consideration for ye sake of another from ye same Person [Harrington], to witt: That ye Colonies were infants sucking their mother's breats, but such as, if he was not mistaken, would weane themselves when they came of age."[9]

The colonial objection to empire was fundamental, Hunter argued, observing in New York and Jamaica that it was "not so much Governors as Government that has been disagreeable to the Assemblys." English government itself, rather than the governor-general personally, was indeed resisted and resented in New York, New Jersey, and Jamaica, regardless of the competence of the executive. Therefore, Hunter and his contemporaries in the imperial executive anticipated that the colonies would soon try to throw off the yoke of English control, despite the best, and on the whole, successful, efforts of the governors-general.[10]

Asserting presumed rights to justify political defiance of the imperial crown, the assemblymen believed they were following the antiexecutive tradition established in the preceding century by the English Parliament. Hunter, although a firm believer in the sovereignty of Parliament, had no sympathy with advocates of provincial legislative sovereignty. Like most imperialists, Hunter believed the colonies' interests were to be subordinated to those of the mother country. He felt as had Athenian imperialists in the fifth century B.C.: "we did not found colonies in order to be insulted by them, but rather to retain our leadership and to be treated with proper respect. . . . "[11]

Hunter, the even-tempered Augustan gentleman, was also personally offended by the hysterical rhetoric of militant colonists and representative bodies, whether in North America or in the West Indies. What Hunter especially objected to in the ranting of such alienated colonists as New York's transplanted New Englander Samuel Mulford, was the religious puritanism and political radicalism that had been so destructive in England and Scotland during the Civil Wars. Hunter and other British Whigs of the eighteenth century had rejected religious and political extremes as destructive in themselves and no longer necessary in postrevolutionary, Protestant, and parliamentary Great Britain. Instead they valued stability and subordination, civility and moderation.

The American colonists in the eighteenth century, however, continued to be enamored of Civil War rhetoric because it spoke to their fears of imposed social and economic immobility and imperial political and military coercion. It was indeed appropriate for the colonists to see themselves in an oppressed position comparable to Civil War parliamentarians, for the crown sought to apply in its American provinces the lessons of civil war "garrison government" by its viceroys, the governors-general. Therefore, it was also apt for Americans to find religious and political precedents for their own defiance of imperial rule in the acts and ideas of seventeenth-century opponents of divine right. Hunter rightly recognized that such defiance would lead to the rejection of royal rule in America, just as it had in England and Scotland during the civil wars.

Hunter first became aware of this potentiality for rebellion in 1711, when he was faced with an assembly in New York that refused to vote a revenue. To discipline that body and avert possible rebellion, Hunter proposed placing New York directly under parliamentary control, a half-century before such a plan was actually implemented for all the colonies. Hunter's fears of possible rebellion were shared by the Board of Trade in 1712. They supported his request for parliamentary intervention in New York's affairs. The board warned Secretary of State St. John that if the New York assembly were permitted to continue its defiance of the governor-general and the royal prerogative by refusing to vote a revenue, it would "prove a very dangerous consequence to that province, and [be] of very ill example to Her Majtys other Governts in America, who are already but too much inclined to Assume pretended rights tending to an independency on the Crown. . . . " The intricacies of colonial management that implementing such a program of direct parliamentary control would entail were beyond the capabilities of the Parliament of Great Britain at that time. The failure of Parliament to act until 1763, however, ensured that Robert Hunter's prediction of rebellion was fulfilled.[12]

Robert Hunter's lifespan had brought him from the absolute monarchy of Charles II to the limited monarchy of the Hanoverian era. Geographically, Hunter had travelled throughout Europe and to the continent of North America and to the West Indies. Through his own efforts, he had risen from an obscure childhood marked by poverty to positions of power and prestige. He had indeed come a long way from the simple boyhood he had known on the quiet moors of Ayrshire. But he had not forgotten his Scottish heritage. Throughout his life, his closest friends were invariably fellow Scots. Neither did he forget his family ties. In New York, New Jersey, and Jamaica, he named a town, a county, and a plantation respectively after his family's estate of Hunterston. Hunter's attachment to his family was also seen by the terms of his will which provided that in the event of the death of all his children without heirs, his property was to pass to his cousin, Patrick Hunter the younger of Hunterston.

But Hunter's surviving son, Thomas Orby Hunter, did inherit his father's estate and passed it on to his own children. Robert Hunter would undoubtedly have been proud of his son's career. Returning to England following the death of his father in 1734, Thomas became a member of Parliament for Winchelsea, was commissioned a lord of the admiralty, and then made commissary general with the English army in Germany.

His was an easier career than, and dependant upon that of his father, Robert Hunter, a self-made man, whose triumphant life was an object lesson in self-advancement and personal aggrandizement, of elegance pursued and obtained, of intellect recognized and developed. For the student of the rise and fall of empire, Robert Hunter's career illumi-

nates the mechanics of colonial administration and illustrates the successes and failures the imperial government met in building the British Empire
in America.

For the student of mankind, Robert Hunter's life illustrates the truth
of Simonides's observation that "Any man is good while his luck is good, /
bad when bad, and for the most part they are best / whom the gods love."
Hunter was indeed fortunate. His talents were needed by the world at the
time he was living, and he possessed the intelligence to take advantage of
the opportunities offered by fate. He was far from a perfect man, but he
was a good man.

> Therefore, I will not throw away my time and life
> into unprofitable hope and emptiness, the search
> for that object which cannot possibly be,
> the Utterly Blameless Man....
> Enough for me if one is not
> bad, not too unsteady, knows
> what is right and good for his city,
> a sound man, I will not
> look out his faults. For the generation
> of fools is endless.... [13]

⚙ NOTES ⚙

Abbreviations

Add. MSS	Additional MSS, British Library, London
Cal. S. P. Col.	*Calendar of State Papers, Colonial Series, America and West Indies*
CO	Colonial Office MSS, Public Record Office, London
DAB	*Dictionary of American Biography*
DNB	*Dictionary of National Biography*
Doc. Hist. N.Y.	*Documentary History of the State of New York*
Doc. Rel. N.J.	*Documents Relating to the Colonial History of the State of New Jersey*
Doc. Rel. Col. Hist. N.Y.	*Documents Relative to the Colonial History of New York*
FDR Library	Franklin Delano Roosevelt Library, Hyde Park, New York
Hist. Soc. Pa.	Historical Society of Pennsylvania
Journal Trade & Plant.	*Journal of the Commissioners for Trade and Plantations*
NYHS	New-York Historical Society
PC	Privy Council
PRO	Public Record Office, London
Scot. PRO	Public Record Office, Edinburgh
SHR	*Scottish Historical Review*
W&MQ	*William and Mary Quarterly*

Preface—"The Government of the Plantations"

1. *The Tatler,* 2 vols. (London: 1822), 2:158–60.
2. Simonides, "The Comment," *Greek Lyrics,* trans. Richmond Lattimore (Chicago: University of Chicago Press, 1949, 1960), 55.
3. Sir Francis Bacon, *Of Plantations,* quoted in G. H. Guttridge, *The Colonial Policy of William III in America and the West Indies* (Cambridge, Mass.: Harvard University Press, 1922), 99; Marlborough to Godolphin, June 9, 1707, Blenheim Papers, British Library. I owe reference to the Blenheim Papers (formerly Marlborough Papers) to the courtesy of Stephen Saunders Webb, whose notes are here used. The papers are now in the British Library where they are being reclassified and resorted.

Introduction—"The High Road," 1666–1688

1. James Patterson, *History of the Country of Ayr With A Genealogical Account of the Families of Ayrshire,* 3 vols. (Edinburgh: 1952), 2:133.
2. Writers to the signet seal had the sole privilege of preparing crown writs, charters, and precepts to pass the royal signet seal. *The Compact Edition of the Oxford English Dictionary,* 2 vols. (Oxford: Oxford University Press, 1971, 1981), 2:3841.
3. Patterson, *History of the County of Ayr* 2:134.
4. David Ogg, *England in the Reigns of James II and William III* (Oxford: Oxford University Press, 1955, 1957), 1, 128; Robert Hunter, Last Will and Testament, January 4, 1733, Probate Office, Public Record Office, London (hereafter cited as *PRO*).
5. Ian Finlay, *The Lowlands* (New York: 1967), 21; Lord Macaulay, *The History of England,* ed. Hugh Trevor-Roper (New York: Penguin, 1848, 1968), 369–75.
6. John Clive and Bernard Bailyn, "England's Cultural Provinces: Scotland and America," *William and Mary Quarterly* 11 (April 1954):200–213 (hereafter cited as *W&MQ*).
7. Maurice Ashley, *The Greatness of Oliver Cromwell* (New York: 1957, 1966), 255–58; Charles Firth, *Oliver Cromwell and the Rule of the Puritans in England* (New York: 1900), 294; Godfrey Davies, *The Restoration of Charles II* (Oxford: 1955, 1969), 217.
8. Firth, *Oliver Cromwell,* 294, 297; Stephen Saunders Webb, *The Governors-General, The English Army and the Definition of the Empire, 1569–1681* (Chapel Hill: University of North Carolina Press, 1979), 53.
9. Daniel Defoe, *A Tour Thro' the Whole Island of Great Britain,* 2 vols., intro. G. D. H. Cole (London: 1724, 1968), 2:640–741.
10. Gilbert Burnet, *History of His Own Time,* 2 vols. (London: 1724), 1:61; Andrew Marvell, "Horation Ode Upon Cromwell's Return from Ireland," *The Selected Poetry of Marvell,* ed. Frank Kermode (New York: New American Library, 1967), 154; John Thurloe quoted in Davies, *Restoration of Charles II,* 221.
11. David Ogg, *England in the Age of Charles II,* 2nd ed. (Oxford: Oxford University Press, 1934, 1967), 402; Lauderdale quoted in Antonia Fraser, *Royal Charles* (New York: Delta, 1980), 266.
12. *Some Family Papers of the Hunters of Hunterston,* ed. M. S. Shaw (Edinburgh: 1925), 57; Session Records, Dreghorn, quoted in James Patterson, *History of the Counties of Ayr and Wigton,* 3 vols. (Edinburgh: 1866), 3:195–96.
13. Burnet, *History of His Own Time* 1:123: Ogg. *Charles II,* 413.

14. James MacKinnon, *The Union of England and Scotland* (London: 1896), 9–10; *The Commisariat Record of Glasgow, Register of Testaments, 1547–1800* (Edinburgh: 1901), 240.

15. Alexander Gray, "The Old Schools and Universities in Scotland," *Scottish Historical Review* 9 (1912):113–38 (hereafter cited as *SHR*); Margaret F. Moore, "The Education of a Scottish Nobleman's Son in the Seventeenth Century," *SHR* 31 (1952):1–15.

16. John Prebble, *Glencoe, The Story of the Massacre* (New York: 1966), 65.

17. Burnet, *History of His Own Time* 1:472–73.

18. Archibald K. Murray, *History of the Scottish Regiments in the British Army* (Glasgow: 1862), 15, 17–18.

19. Burnet, *History of His Own Time* 2:515.

20. Ian Charles Cargill, *Colonists from Scotland: Emigration to North America, 1707–1783* (Ithaca: Cornell University Press, 1956), 11.

21. Robert Hunter to Board of Trade, October 2, 1716, *Documents Relative to the Colonial History of New York*, ed. E. B. O'Callaghan, 15 vols. (Albany: 1856–1887), 5:478 (hereafter cited as *Doc. Rel. Col. Hist. N.Y.*).

22. Eric Cregeen, "The Changing Role of the House of Argyll in the Scottish Highlands," in *Scotland in the Age of Improvement, Essays in Scottish History in the Eighteenth Century*, ed. N. T. Phillipson and Rosalind Mitcheson (Edinburgh: 1970), 5–6; Burnet, *History of His Own Time* 2:519.

23. F. C. Turner, *James II* (London: 1948, 1950), 190–91; John Miller, *James II, A Study in Kingship* (East Sussex, England: 1978), 107–8.

24. On the reaction of some upper-class Scots to James II and the Revolution of 1688, see *Dictionary of National Biography*, ed. Leslie Stephen and Sidney Lee, 22 vols. (New York: Macmillan Co., 1908) (hereafter cited as *DNB*), s.v. "Campbell Archibald, 1st duke of Argyll," "Dalrymple, John, 2nd earl of Stair," and "Erskine, Henry, 3rd Baron Cardross."

25. Cadwallader Colden to Alexander Colden, September 25, 1759, quoted in William Smith, Jr., *The History of the Province of New York*, ed. Michael Kammen (Cambridge, Mass.: Harvard University Press, 1972), 299.

26. Baldesar Castiglione, *The Book of the Courtier*, intro. and trans. George Bull (New York: Penguin, 1967, 1980), 13.

27. Ibid., 57, 60, 73, 90, 115.

28. Cadwallader Colden to Alexander Colden, September 25, 1759, in Smith, *New York*, 299.

29. Webb, *Governors-General*, appendix nos. 68, 133, 135, 158, 161, 165, 203, 205, 206.

30. *DNB*, s.v. "Campbell, John, duke of Argyll," "Hamilton, George, earl of Orkney," "Hunter, Robert," "Spotswood, Alexander," "Vetch, Samuel."

31. Clive and Bailyn, "England's Cultural Provinces," 200–213; see also Bruce T. McCully, "Governor Francis Nicholson, Patron *Par Excellence* of Religion and Learning in Colonial America," *W&MQ* 39 (April 1982):310–33.

1—"The Wars' and Fortune's Son," 1688–1706

1. W. A. Speck, *Tory and Whig, The Struggle in the Constituencies, 1701–1715* (New York: 1970), 3; J. H. Plumb, *The Origins of Political Stability in England, 1675–1725* (Boston: 1967), 23, 56, 60, 62.

2. J. R. Jones, *The Revolution of 1688 in England* (New York: 1972), 11; James II quoted in John R. Western, *Monarchy and Revolution, The English State in the 1680s* (London: 1972), 35.

3. Winston S. Churchill, *Marlborough, His Life and Times*, 5 vols. (New York: 1933), 1:283, 285.

4. James II quoted in Western, *Monarchy and Revolution*, 288.

5. *Memoirs of Sarah, Duchess of Marlborough*, ed. William King (London: 1930; New York: 1969), 13.

6. *DNB*, s.v. "Compton, Henry, Bishop of London"; Cadwallader Colden to Alexander Colden, September 25, 1759, quoted in Smith, *New York*, 300; Robert Hunter to earl of Stair, June 23, 1712, Stair Muniments, 141/1/37, Scotland, Public Record Office (hereafter cited as Scot. *PRO*).

7. Churchill, *Marlborough* 1:294, 311; Jones, *Revolution of 1688*, 292, 296.

8. Plumb, *Origins of Political Stability*, 20, 33, 63, 84, 99–103.

9. Sanford Terry, "The Siege of Edinburgh Castle, 1689," *SHR* 2 (1905):163–65.

10. Charles Dalton, *English Army Lists and Commission Register*, 6 vols. (London: 1960), Pt. 1, 3:37.

11. R. E. Scouller, *The Armies of Queen Anne* (Oxford: 1966), 127–28; Stephen Saunders Webb, "Officers and Governors, The Role of the British Army in Imperial Politics and the Administration of the American Colonies, 1689–1722" (Ph.D. diss., University of Wisconsin, 1965), 6.

12. James Hayes, "Scottish Officers in the British Army, 1714–1763," *SHR* 37 (1958):22–31.

13. *DNB*, s.v. "Erskine, Henry, third Baron of Cardross," and "Erskine, John, sixth or eleventh Earl of Mar."

14. George Farquhar, *The Recruiting Officer* in *The Complete Works of George Farquhar*, 2 vols. (London: 1930), 2:43, 67; Scouller, *Armies of Queen* Anne, 267–69.

15. J. W. Fortescue, *A History of the British Army* (London: 1910), 326.

16. George Macaulay Trevelyan, *England under Queen Anne* (London: 1930), 223.

17. Dalton, *Army Lists*, Pt. 1, 5:28.

18. Jack T. Gilbert, *A Jacobite Narrative of the War in Ireland, 1688–1691*, intro. J. G. Simms (New York: 1892, 1971), 64–65, 81–84; J. G. Simms, *Jacobite Ireland, 1685–1691* (London: 1969), 96, 101–8, 112.

19. J. R. Harvey, *The History of the Fifth (Royal Irish) Regiment of Dragoons, 1689–1799, afterward The Fifth Royal Irish Lancers* (Aldershot: 1923), 2–3.

20. Dalton, *Army Lists*, Pt. 1, 3:36; *DNB*, s.v. "Erskine, Henry."

21. Cardross to Lord Melville, Edinburgh, July 30, 1689, quoted in Hugh Mackay, *Memoirs of the War Carried on in Scotland and Ireland, 1684–1691* (Edinburgh: 1933), 229.

22. Cardross to Melville, August 25, 1689, GD 26/9/229, Scot. PRO; Mackay to Melville, August 26, 1689, in Mackay, *Memoirs*, 270.

23. Melville to Hamilton, August 8, 1689, and Mackay to Melville, September 10, 1689, in Mackay, *Memoirs*, 261, 277.

24. Dalton, *Army Lists*, Pt. 1, 3:415; Webb, *Governors-General*, 53, 55.

25. Prebble, *Glencoe*, 86–88, 97, 100, 306; Cardross to [?], February 10, 1691, GD 26/9/317, Scot. PRO; Order of William III to Disband Cardross's Dragoons, December 18, 1689, in Mackay, *Memoirs*, 308–9.

26. Cardross to [?], February 10, 1691, GD 26/9/317, Scot, PRO.

27. John Murray Graham, *Annals and Correspondence of the Viscount and the First and Second Earls of Stair* 2 vols. (Edinburgh: 1875), 1:3, 115–16; Stair to Hill, January 1692, quoted in Prebble, *Glencoe*, 202; *Gallienus Redivivus, or Murder Will Out, Being a True Account of the De-Witting of Glencoe* (Edinburgh: 1695), in *The Massacre of Glencoe* (London: 1703), 5–32.

28. Hill to Tweeddale, February 14, 1692, quoted in Prebble, *Glencoe*, 307.

29. Stair to Hill, April 1692, in Graham, *Annals*, 161–62.

30. Dalton, *Army Lists*, Pt. 2, 3:277; Prebble, *Glencoe*, 267–70.

31. Hill to Tweeddale, August 8, 1692, same to same, September 17, 1692, 7014, folios 151, 163, National Library, Scotland.

32. Fraser, *Royal Charles*, 266.

33. Narcissus Luttrell, "Brief Relation of State Affairs, April 19, 1694" and "Diary of John Evelyn, April 22, 1694," quoted in *Journal of the Society for Army Historical Research* 13 (1934):61; Percy Groves, *History of the Second Dragoons, The Royal Scots Greys, 1678–1893* (Edinburgh and London: 1893), 5.

34. Ogg, *James II and William III*, 349.

35. Dalton, *Army Lists*, Pt. 1, 4:112; Edward Almack, *The History of the Second Dragoons, Royal Scots Greys* (London: n.d.), 21.

36. Webb, *Governors-General*, 66.

37. Laurence Sterne, *Tristram Shandy* (New York: 1760–1767, 1960), 69; David Thomson, *Wild Excursions, The Life and Fiction of Laurence Sterne* (New York: 1972), 53, 71.

38. Stephen B. Baxter, *William III and the Defense of European Liberty, 1650–1702* (New York: Harcourt Brace, 1966), 328–29.

39. Extracts from old newspapers containing information about military affairs, 1680–1720, compiled by Francis Buckley, 1935, from the *London Gazette*, March 10, 1698, National Army Museum, London; W. T. Willcox, *A History of the Fifth (Royal Irish) Lancers from their Foundation as Wynne's Dragoons to the Present Day* (London: 1908), 68.

40. Angus Ross, "The Hibernian Patriot's Apprenticeship," in *The Art of Jonathan Swift*, ed. Clive T. Probyn (London: Vision Press, 1978), 85.

41. W. A. Speck, *Swift* (London: 1969), 28; Ross, "Hibernian Patriot," 85; Willcox, *A History of the Fifth Lancers*, 18–20.

42. Geoffrey Holmes, *British Politics in the Age of Anne* (New York: 1967), 82.

43. J. P. Kenyon, *Stuart England* (New York: Pelican, 1978), 288.

44. Dalton, *Army Lists*, Pt. 1, 5:39, 233; *Memoirs of Sarah, Duchess of Marlborough*, 128; Churchill, *Marlborough* 3:33, 153–54.

45. Cardonnel to Hunter, Sutendae, September 19, 1702, Stair to Marlborough, November 17, 1708, Blenheim Papers.

46. Cadwallader Colden to Alexander Colden, September 25, 1759, quoted in Smith, *New York*, 300.

47. Dalton, *Army Lists*, Pt. 2, 5:111.

48. C. T. Atkinson, *Marlborough and the Rise of the British Army* (New York: 1921), 186–91.

49. Churchill, *Marlborough* 4:102–6.

50. Fortescue, *British Army*, 443–46.

51. Churchill, *Marlborough* 4:108–12.

52. Duke of Marlborough to duchess of Marlborough, quoted in Trevelyan, *Queen Anne*, 391; same to same, August 14, 1704 (New Style), Blenheim Papers, British Library.

53. Army Lists, 1728, Additional MSS 21,188, 8, British Library, London (hereafter cited as Add. MSS.); Dalton, *Army Lists*, Pt. 2, 5:27–28.

54. Marlborough to Godolphin, June 9, 1707, Blenheim Papers, British Library.

55. Robert Walcott, Jr., *English Politics in the Early Eighteenth Century* (Cambridge, Mass.: 1956), 126–27.

56. J. H. Plumb, *Robert Walpole, The Making of a Statesman*, 2 vols. (London: 1956), 1:127–28.

57. Cadwallader Colden to Alexander Colden, September 25, 1759, quoted in Smith, *New York*, 300–301.

58. Churchill, *Marlborough* 3:112–15.

59. *London Gazette*, May 16–May 20, 1706, British Library.

60. Cadwallader Colden to Alexander Colden, September 25, 1759, quoted in Smith, *New York*, 301.

61. Atkinson, *Marlborough*, 308–9.

62. Cadwallader Colden to Alexander Colden, September 25, 1759, quoted in Smith, *New York*, 301.

63. *DNB*, s.v. "Cadogan, William"; Cadwallader Colden to Alexander Colden, September 25, 1759, quoted in Smith, *New York*, 301–2.

64. Mayor of Hythe to earl of Sunderland, April 2, 1709, *Eighth Report of the Royal Commission on Historical Manuscripts*, Report and Appendix, Pt. 1, 1881 (1907), Appendix, 45b.

65. Marlborough to Godolphin, August 26, 1706 (New Style) *The Letters and Despatches of John Churchill, First Duke of Marlborough, 1702–1712*, ed. George Murray, 6 vols. (London: 1945), 3:105.

66. Cadwallader Colden to Alexander Colden, September 25, 1759, quoted in Smith, *New York*, 301.

2—"Thro' Th' Extended World," 1707–1710

1. Marlborough to Godolphin, Meldert, June 23, 1707, Blenheim Papers, British Library.

2. Commission Edward Nott, April 25, 1705, Commission Robert Hunter, April 16, 1707, Colonial Office MSS, Public Record Office, London, 5/1361, folios 45, 62, PRO (hereafter cited as CO).

3. Marlborough to Godolphin, Meldert, June 9, 1707, Orkney to Marlborough, November 10, 1707, Blenheim Papers, British Library.

4. Andre Corvisier, *Armies and Societies in Europe, 1494–1789*, trans. Abigail T. Siddall (Bloomington, Ind.: 1979), 214.

5. Lady Hay to Marquis Tweeddale, May 15, 1707, MS 7021–7022, 125, National Library, Edinburgh; John Burke, *A Genealogical and Heraldic History of the Extinct and Dormant Baronetcies of England, Ireland, and Scotland* (London: 1844), s.v. "Orby, of Croyland."

6. Agreement Sir Thomas Orby, April 14, 1681, "Manor of Crowland and diverse other Lands ... ," Cragg Deposit, 3 #57, 11/1/2, Lincolnshire Archives; *The Victoria History of the Counties of England, Surrey*, ed. H. Arthur Doubleday, 4 vols. (Westminster: 1907), 2:412.

7. Privy council meetings, March 14, 1708, August 1, 1708, Privy Council (hereafter cited as PC) 2/82, 147–48, 279–82, PRO.

8. Daniel Defoe, *Moll Flanders*, ed. James Sutherland (Boston: Signet, NAL, 1722, 1959), 60; Farquhar, *The Recruiting Officer*, 2:108.

9. Clive and Bailyn, "England's Cultural Provinces," 200–213.

10. John Gay to Jonathan Swift, February 3, 1723, in *The Correspondence of Jonathan Swift*, ed. Harold Williams, 5 vols. (Oxford: 1963), 1:447.

11. Angus Ross, "The Hibernian Patriots," 105.

12. Robert J. Allen, *The Clubs of Augustan London* (Hamden, Conn.: 1933, 1967), 33, 239; *Tatler*, April 14, 1709, 4 vols. (London: 1754), 1:25 (British Library).

13. Peter Smithers, *The Life of Joseph Addison* (Oxford: 1954, 1968), 1, 16, 95, 104, 112.

14. *Ibid.*, 103, 127; Richard Steele to Mrs. Steele, September 30, 1707, Add. MSS 5,145, British Library.

15. George A. Aitken, *Life of Richard Steele*, 2 vols. (New York: 1889, 1968), 1:155.

16. Speck, *Swift*, 11.

17. Ibid., 16.

18. Leonard Wood Labaree, *Royal Government in America, A Study of the British Colonial System Before 1783* (New Haven: Yale University Press, 1930), 93, 99, 113, 123.

19. See Hunter's commission and instructions for New York, *Doc. Rel. Col. Hist. N.Y.* 5:124–57.

20. Labaree, *Royal Government*, 134–35.

21. Alison Gilbert Olson, "Governor Robert Hunter and the Anglican Church in New York," in *Statesmen, Scholars and Merchants*, ed. Anne Whiteman, J. S. Bromley, and P. G. M. Dickson (Oxford: Oxford University Press, 1973), 44; on the church as the bulwark of the royal prerogative, see Webb, "The Strange Career of Francis Nicholson," *W&MQ* 23 (October 1966):513–48; Webb, *Governors-General*, 454.

22. Holmes, *British Politics*, 85.

23. On the importance of the union to both England and Scotland (as well as the importance of "British" rather than "English" history), see J. G. A. Pocock, "The Limits and Divisions of British History: In Search of the Unknown Subject," *The American Historical Review* 87 (April 1982):311–36; Privy council meeting, August 18, 1708, PC 2/82, 158, *PRO*.

24. Marlborough to earl of Leven, St. James's, March 12, 1708, in Murray, *Letters and Despatches of Marlborough* 3:691.

25. Sunderland to Board of Trade, April 3, 1707, same to same, July 11, 1707, *Calendar of State Papers Colonial Series, America and West Indies* (London: 1916), #849, 417; #1096, 533 (hereafter cited as *Cal. S. P. Col.*).

26. Marlborough to Mr. Secretary Hedges, November 9, 1706, in Murray, *Letters and Despatches of Marlborough* 3:212.

27. Sunderland to Commission for Exchange of Prisoners, April 22, 1707, Sunderland Letterbook, 2, 30. I owe reference to the Sunderland Papers to the courtesy of Stephen Saunders Webb, whose notes are here used. The Sunderland Papers, previously stored at Blenheim Palace, are now in the British Library as part of the Blenheim Papers.

28. Sunderland to Commission for Exchange of Prisoners, April 21, 1708, same to same, April 27, 1708, Blenheim Papers, June 22, 1708, House of Commons, Commissioners for Exchange of Prisoners Attending, quoted in *Proceedings and Debates of the British Parliaments Respecting North America, 1702–1727*, ed. Leo Francis Stock, 5 vols. (Washington, D.C.: Carnegie Institute of Washington, 1924–1941), 3:174.

29. Angus McInnes, *Robert Harley, Puritan Politician (London: 1970), 99—100, 103, 105.*

30. *Daniel Defoe, A Brief History of the Poor Palatine Refugees,* intro. John Robert Moore, The Augustan Reprint Society, no. 106 (Los Angeles: The Society, 1709, 1965), 19.

31. Lewis Morris to secretary, quoted in George Morgan Hills, *History of the Church in Burlington, New Jersey* (Trenton: 1876), 81; Elia Neau to secretary, February 27, 1709, ibid., 89.

32. Lovelace to Board of Trade, December 18, 1708, *Doc. Rel. Col. Hist. N.Y.* 5:67.

33. Plumb, *Walpole* 1:141.

34. Col. Jenings to Board of Trade, September 20, 1708, *Cal. S. P. Col.,* #137, 97.

35. Swift to Hunter, January 12, 1709, *Correspondence of Jonathan Swift* 1:119–20.

36. For Swift's attitude toward the military, see Jonathan Swift, *Gulliver's Travels,* intro. Barry Goldensohn (New York: Collier Books, 1962), Bk. 4, 214; Swift to Hunter, January 12, 1709, *Correspondence of Jonathan Swift* 1:120.

37. Ibid.

38. Ibid.

39. Ibid. 1:121–22.

40. Swift to Hunter, March 22, 1709, *Correspondence of Jonathan Swift* 1:132–33.

41. Ibid. 1:133.

42. Ibid. 1:134.

43. Mayor of Hythe to Sunderland, April 2, 1709, *Royal Commission on Historical Manuscripts,* Appendix, 45b; Sunderland to Commission for Exchange of Prisoners, Whitehall, April 25, 1709, Sunderland Letterbook, Blenheim Papers, British Library.

44. P. E. Elkin, *The Augustan Defence of Satire* (Oxford: 1973), 156.

45. *Tatler,* April 12, 1709, 1:3 (British Library); Jonathan Swift, *The Intelligencer,* 1729, quoted in J. V. Guerinot and Rodney D. Jilg, *The Beggar's Opera* (Hampden, Conn.: Archon Press, 1976), 147.

46. *Tatler,* April 12, 1709, 1:9 (British Library).

47. Aitken, *Richard Steele* 1:256; John Nichols, *Literary Anecdotes of the Eighteenth Century* 8 vols. (London: 1912), 5:5–9, 89.

48. Privy council meeting, March 31, 1709, PC 2/82, 287, PRO.

49. Cadwallader Colden to Alexander Colden, September 25, 1759, in Smith, *New York,* 302; Privy council meeting, December 18, 1710, PC 2/83, 170–71, PRO.

50. Thomas Cockerell to Mr. Popple, July 2, 1709, *Doc. Rel. Col. Hist. N.Y.* 5:81; Godolphin to Marlborough, August 17, 1709, same to same, August 18, 1709, Blenheim Papers, British Library.

51. Marlborough to Godolphin, August 22, 1709, same to same, September 7, 1709, same to same, October 3, 1709, Godolphin to Marlborough, September 6, 1709, Blenheim Papers, British Library; *Tatler* 2:158–160 (1822 edition).

52. Cadwallader Colden to Alexander Colden, September 25, 1759, in Smith, *New York,* 299.

53. Journal, June 17, 1709, Society for the Propagation of the Gospel, London; A List of the Royal Society Commencing 1664–1767, British Library.

54. Walter Allen Knittle, *Early Eighteenth Century Palatine Emigration* (Philadelphia: 1937), 4–6.

55. Minutes, August 24, 1709, *Journal of the Commissioners for Trade and Plantations* (London: 1920–1928), 65 (hereafter cited as *Journal Trade & Plant.*); William Sachse, *Lord Somers, A Political Portrait* (Wisconsin: 1975), 280.

56. Minutes, December 2, 1709, *Journal Trade & Plant.*, 98–99.

57. Covenant for the Palatines quoted in *Ecclesiastical Records of the State of New York*, prepared under supervision of Hugh Hastings, 4 vols. (Albany: 1902), 3:1814–15; Colonel Hunter's Memorial Regarding Palatines, December 17, 1709, Blenheim Papers, British Library.

58. Sunderland to Board of Trade, December 19, 1709, *Cal. S. P. Col.*, #915, 560.

59. Eleanor Louisa Lord, *Industrial Experiments in the British Colonies of North America* (Baltimore: 1898), 42.

60. Hunter to Sunderland, Humble Representation of Colonel Hunter, 1710, Blenheim Papers, British Library.

61. H. M. Warrant for Governor Hunter to be Captain of the Independent Companies at New York, May 7, 1709 [?], *Cal. S. P. Col.*, #493, 176.

62. Hunter to secretary, February 26, 1710, Letters Received, Society for the Propagation of the Gospel, London.

63. Caroline Robbins, *The Eighteenth Century Commonwealthman* (Cambridge, Mass.: Harvard University Press, 1959), 82; Isaac Kramnick, *Bolingbroke and His Circle, The Politics of Nostalgia in the Age of Walpole* (Cambridge, Mass.: Harvard University Press, 1968), 9.

64. Carl Carmer, *The Hudson* (New York: 1939), 69; Sunderland to Hunter, n.d., *Cal. S. P. Col.*, #225, 91.

3—"The Land of Canaan," June 1710–June 1711

1. *The Journal of John Fontaine, 1716–1719*, ed. Edward Porter Alexander (Williamsburg: 1972), 115.

2. I. N. Phelps-Stokes, *The Iconography of Manhattan Island 1498–1909*, 6 vols. (New York: R. H. Dodd, 1915–1928), 2:243–46, 4:389, 412, 414; "A Glance at New York in 1697, The Travel Diary of Dr. Benjamin Bullivant," ed. Wayne Andrews, *New-York Historical Society Quarterly* (January 1956):55–73.

3. John and Francis Riggs to Charles Delafaye, November 26, 1717, *Cal. S. P. Col.*, #405, 208.

4. *Minutes of the Common Council of the City of New York*, 1675–1776, June 16, 1710, 8 vols. (New York: 1905), 2:409.

5. Hunter to William Popple, June 16, 1710, *Doc. Rel. Col. Hist. N.Y.* 5:165; Hunter to Board of Trade, July 24, 1710, *The Documentary History of the State of New York*, ed. E. B. O'Callaghan, 4 vols. (Albany: 1849–1851), 3:559 (hereafter cited as *Doc. Hist. N.Y.*).

6. *Calendar of Council Minutes, 1668–1783*, Bulletin 58, June 14, 1710 (Albany: 1902), 238.

7. Conrad Weiser, *Autobiography*, quoted in Paul A. W. Wallace, *Conrad Weiser, 1696–1760* (Philadelphia: 1945), 13.

8. Georgianna C. Nammack, *Fraud, Politics, and the Dispossession of the Indian, The Iroquois Land Frontier in the Colonial Period* (Norman: 1969), 18.

9. Hunter to Board of Trade, October 3, 1710, *Doc. Rel. Col. Hist. N.Y.* 5:168–69, 171.

10. Hunter to Board of Trade, October 3, 1710, *Doc. Hist. N.Y.* 3:560.

11. Indenture Robert Livingston to Queen Anne, Livingston Family Papers, Roll 3, General Correspondence, 1708–1718, Franklin Delano Roosevelt Library, Hyde Park, New York (hereafter cited as FDR Library); Contract with Livingston to Victual Palatines, November 13, 1710, *Doc. Hist. N.Y.* 3:653–55.

12. George M. Waller, *Samuel Vetch, Colonial Enterpriser* (Chapel Hill: University of North Carolina Press, 1960), 3–4, 12, 29, 31–32, 41, 207.

13. Lawrence H. Leder, *Robert Livingston (1654–1728) and the Politics of Colonial New York* (Chapel Hill: University of North Carolina Press, 1961), 3, 7, 9, 21, 33, 35, 212; Order to the Attorney General to Prepare Draft of Letters Patent for the Manor of Livingston, October 1, 1715, Governor Hunter's Patent, *Doc. Hist. N.Y.* 3:689–90, 690–702.

14. Linda Briggs Biemer, "The Transition from Dutch to English Law: Its Impact on Women in New York," (Ph.D. diss., Syracuse University, 1979), 187–90.

15. George Clarke to Board of Trade, May 30, 1711, *Doc. Hist. N.Y.* 3:666.

16. Plumb, *Walpole* 1:156–57; Sachse, *Lord Somers,* 288.

17. Hunter to Lord Dartmouth, October 13, 1710, *Cal. S. P. Col.,* #423, 228.

18. Dixon Ryan Fox, *Yankees and Yorkers* (Port Washington: 1940, 1963), 118–19; Robert C. Ritchie, *The Duke's Province, A Study of New York Politics and Society, 1664–1691* (Chapel Hill: University of North Carolina Press, 1977), 28, 33–34; Sung Bok Kim, *Landlord and Tenant in Colonial New York, Manorial Society, 1664–1775* (Chapel Hill: University of North Carolina Press, 1978), 77–78.

19. Edgar J. McManus, *A History of Negro Slavery in New York* (Syracuse: Syracuse University Press, 1960), 7, 24, 25, 105; James G. Lydon, "New York and the Slave Trade, 1700–1744" *W&MQ* 35 (July 1978):375–94.

20. Herbert L. Osgood, *The American Colonies in the Seventeenth Century,* 3 vols. (Gloucester: 1904, 1957), 2:121–22.

21. Ibid. 2:130, 165; Ritchie, *The Duke's Province,* 60, 94, 100, 118, 124, 185.

22. Stephen Saunders Webb, "The Trials of Sir Edmund Andros," in *The Human Dimensions of Nation Making,* ed. James Kirby Martin (Madison: University of Wisconsin Press, 1976), 23–53; Charles M. Andrews, *The Colonial Period of American History,* 4 vols. (New Haven: Yale University Press, 1934), 3:116, 121.

23. Viola F. Barnes, *The Dominion of New England, A Study in British Colonial Policy* (New Haven: Yale University Press, 1923), 223, 239, 250.

24. Leder, *Livingston,* 248; Ritchie, *The Duke's Province,* 201–2, 228; Webb, "The Strange Career of Francis Nicholson," 513–48.

25. Osgood, *Seventeenth Century* 2:470.

26. Ritchie, *The Duke's Province,* 107, 237.

27. Bruce M. Wilkenfeld, "The New York City Common Council, 1689–1800," *New York History* 52 (July 1971):249–74; Nicholas Varga, "Election Procedures and Practices in Colonial New York," *New York History* 41 (1960):249–77; Patricia U. Bonomi, *A Factious People, Politics and Society in Colonial New York* (New York: Columbia University Press, 1971), 77–78. The term "party" used here and elsewhere in the text is not meant to connote a sophisticated political organization in the modern sense (which did not exist in New York or New Jersey in the early eighteenth century), but rather a group of people temporarily allied because of common interests.

28. John D. Runcie, "The Problem of Anglo-American Politics in Bellomont's New York," *W&MQ* 25 (April 1969):191–217; Cadwallader Colden to James Alexander, quoted in W. A. Whitehead, *Contributions to the Early History of Perth Amboy* (New York: 1856), 149; Carl Lotus Becker, *The History of Political Parties in the Province of New York, 1760–1776* (Madison: University of Wisconsin Press: 1909, 1968), 5–22.

29. Clarendon to Hunter, July 31, 1710, *Doc. Rel. Col. Hist. N.Y.* 5:406.

30. Jonathan Swift, *Journal to Stella*, ed. J. K. Moorhead, intro. Walter Scott (London: n.d.), September 9, 1710, September 25, 1710, 3, 14.

31. J. A. Downie, "The Conduct of the Allies: The Question of Influence," in Probyn, *Art of Jonathan Swift*, 108; Swift quoted in Speck, *Swift*, 24; John Wilmot, earl of Rochester, "A Satyr Against Reason and Mankind," in *The Complete Poems of John Wilmot, earl of Rochester*, ed. David M. Vieth (New Haven: Yale University Press, 1968, 1974), 94.

32. Swift, *Journal to Stella*, September 9, 1710, 4.

33. *Messages from the Governors, 1683–1776*, ed. Charles Z. Lincoln, (Albany: 1909), 141–43; *Colonial Laws of New York from the Year 1665 to the Revolution*, 5 vols. (Albany: James B. Lyon, 1894), 1:706–22; Hunter to Board of Trade, October 3, 1710, *Doc. Rel. Col. Hist. N.Y.* 5:170.

34. Hunter to Board of Trade, November 14, 1710, *Doc. Rel. Col. Hist. N.Y.* 5:177.

35. Hunter, Additional Instruction, December 25, 1710, Plantation Book, PC5/4, 1–2, PRO; Hunter to Board of Trade, November 14, 1710, *Doc. Rel. Col. Hist. N.Y.* 5:143.

36. New York Assembly Journal, November 8, 1710, November 9, 1710, November 10, 1710, CO 5/1186, folio 169; For Morris's speech, see CO 5/1050, folios 27–28, PRO; Hunter to Board of Trade, November 14, 1710, *Doc. Rel. Col. Hist. N.Y.* 5:178.

37. Eugene R. Sheridan, *Lewis Morris, 1671–1746, A Study in Early American Politics* (Syracuse: Syracuse University Press, 1981), 1, 5–6, 8, 15, 52, 108.

38. Hunter to Board of Trade, November 14, 1710, *Doc. Rel. Col. Hist. N.Y.* 5:179–80.

39. Ibid. 5:180.

40. Hunter to Board of Trade, November 28, 1710, *Doc. Rel. Col. Hist. N.Y.* 5:185.

41. Hunter to Board of Trade, November 28, 1710, same to same, May 7, 1711, *Doc. Rel. Col. Hist. N.Y.* 5:184, 211.

42. John E. Pomfret, *Colonial New Jersey* (New York: 1973), 7, 24, 29, 31; Herbert L. Osgood, *American Colonies in the Eighteenth Century*, 4 vols. (Gloucester: Peter Smith, 1924, 1958), 1:382.

43. Edwin P. Tanner, *The Province of New Jersey* (New York: 1908, 1967), 18, 29.

44. Donald L. Kemmerer, *Path to Freedom, The Struggle for Self-Government in Colonial New Jersey, 1703–1776* (Princeton: 1940), 11.

45. Pomfret, *Colonial New Jersey*, 83, 87.

46. John E. Pomfret, *The New Jersey Proprietors and their Lands, 1664–1776* (New York: 1964), 93–94; Statement Under Oath, Respecting Peter Sonmans, November 2, 1710, *Documents Relating to the Colonial History of the State of New Jersey*, ed. William Adee Whitehead, 10 vols. (Newark: 1880), 4:14–15 (hereafter cited as *Doc. Rel. N.J.*).

47. George DeCou, "Burlington Country Trails and Old Roads," *Mt. Holly Herald*, November 25, 1932, Burlington Historical Society; Hunter's journey across New Jersey is reconstructed from a similar four-day trip undertaken by John Fontaine, November 10th–November 14th, 1716, *Journal*, 117–18.

48. Gabriel Thomas, *An Historical and Geographical Account of the Province and Country of Pensilvania; and of West-New-Jersey in America* (London: 1698; New York: 1848), 18.

49. Old St. Mary's Church still exists and is used on special occasions; John Barclay to [?], November 1, 1710, *Doc. Rel. N.J.* 4:13.

50. Hunter to Board of Trade, May 7, 1711, *Doc. Rel. Col. Hist. N.Y.* 5:199.

51. Sonmans to Clarendon, February 12, 1711, Add. MSS 14,034, folio 130, British Library.

52. Sonmans to William Dockwra, May 27, 1711, Add. MSS 14,034, folios 137–42, British Library.

53. Representation of New Jersey Assembly to Governor Hunter relating to Cornbury, February 9, 1711, *Doc. Rel. N.J.* 4:20– 48; Samuel Smith, *The History of the Colony of Nova-Caesara, or New-Jersey* (Burlington: 1765; Trenton: 1890), 376– 77.

54. Sachse, *Lord Somers,* 293; Plumb, *Walpole* 1:159.

55. Hunter to Addison, November 8, 1714, *The Letters of Joseph Addison,* ed. Walter Graham (Oxford: Oxford University Press, 1941), 493.

56. Board of Trade to Dartmouth, January 12, 1711, Palatine Account received from DuPré, January 25, 1711, *Cal. S. P. Col.,* #598, 340, #619, 345.

57. Clarendon to Dartmouth, March 8, 1711, *Doc. Rel. Col. Hist. N.Y.* 5:196.

58. Ibid.; Petition John Champante for Hunter, March 20, 1716, *Proceedings and Debates of British Parliaments* 3:373.

59. Bridger to Board of Trade, November 10, 1710, *Doc. Rel. Col. Hist. N.Y.* 5:175–76; Hunter to Board of Trade, May 7, 1711, *Doc. Hist. N.Y.* 3:661–62.

60. Clarke to Livingston, March 5, 1711, Roll 3, General Correspondence, 1708–1718, FDR Library.

61. Cast to Hunter, May 1, 1711, *Doc. Hist. N.Y.* 3:659–60.

62. Cast to Hunter, March 27, 1711, *Doc. Hist. N.Y.* 3:658–59.

63. Board of Trade to Hunter, January 25, 1711, *Doc. Rel. Col. Hist. N.Y.* 5:186–87.

64. Hunter Address to Assembly, April 1711, Roll 11, Livingston Family Papers, 1664–1780, FDR Library.

65. Hunter to Board of Trade, May 7, 1711, *Doc. Rel. Col. Hist. N.Y.* 5:204.

66. Ibid.; DNB, s.v. "Jamison, David."

67. Sonmans to Dockwra, May 30, 1711, Add. MSS 14,034, British Library.

68. Clarke to Livingston, April 24, 1711, Roll 3, Livingston Family Papers, FDR Library.

69. Cadwallader Colden to Alexander Colden, October 15, 1759, quoted in Smith, *New York,* 303–4.

70. Clarke to Board of Trade, May 30, 1711, Minutes of Proceedings of Commissioners, June 12, 1711, *Doc. Hist. N.Y.* 3:665, 669.

71. March 22, 1711, #2776, Board of Trade Reports on Naval Stores, *Great Britain Historical Manuscripts Commission, The Manuscripts of the House of Lords (New Series), 1710–1712,* ed. Maurice F. Bond, 10 vols. (London: 1900– 1962), 9:121.

4—"*Used Like a Dog,*" June 1711–December 1712

1. Hunter to Board of Trade, September 12, 1711, *Cal. S. P. Col.,* #451, 38.

2. Hunter to earl of Stair, October 18, 1714, *Doc. Rel. Col. Hist. N.Y.* 5:451.

3. Minutes of a Council of War, New London, Connecticut, June 21, 1711, *Cal. S. P. Col.,* #893, 558.

4. Col. Richard King's Journal, June 24, 1711, *Cal. S. P. Col.,* #46, 41; Alexander Spotswood to Board of Trade, July 24, 1711, *Official Letters of Alexander Spotswood,* intro. R. A. Brock (Richmond: 1882), 90; Hunter to Jack Hill, June 25, 1711, Colonial Documents, 60:48, N.Y. State Library.

5. Council Minutes, New Jersey, July 6, 1711, CO 5/1019, folio 86, PRO; *Colonial Laws of New York* 1:723; Hunter to St. John, September 12, 1711, *Cal. S. P. Col.*, #96, 101.

6. Peter Wraxall, *An Abridgement of the Indian Affairs*, ed. Charles H. McIlwain (Cambridge, Mass.: Harvard University Press, 1915, 1968), 92; Anthony F. C. Wallace, "Origins of Iroquois Neutrality: The Grand Settlement of 1701," *Pennsylvania History* 24 (July 1957):223–35.

7. Hovenden Walker, *A Journal Or Full Account of the Late Expedition to Canada* (London: 1720), in *The Walker Expedition to Quebec, 1711*, ed. with intro. Gerald S. Graham (Toronto: 1953), 122.

8. Hunter to Clarke, August 23, 1711, Simon Gratz Autograph Collection, Case 2, Box 30, Historical Society of Pennsylvania (hereafter cited as Hist. Soc. Pa.).

9. George Lee to [Mr. Fox?], September 12, 1711, Richard King to St. John, September 11, 1711, *Cal. S. P. Col.*, #95, 97, #98, 105.

10. Waller, *Samuel Vetch*, 220–21, 226–27; Vetch to Walker, August 26, 1711, *Cal. S. P. Col.*, #175, 151–52.

11. Hunter to Dartmouth, August 25, 1711, *Doc. Rel. Col. Hist. N.Y.* 5:277–78.

12. Hunter to Hill, October 1, 1711, Colonial Documents, 60:109, N.Y. State Library; *Memoirs of Sarah, Duchess of Marlborough*, 128.

13. Swift, *Journal to Stella*, October 16, 1711, 248–49.

14. Hunter to Dartmouth, November 12, 1711, *Doc. Rel. Col. Hist. N.Y.* 5:284–85.

15. Hunter and Nicholson to earl of Oxford, October 10, 1711, United States Letters, Rutgers University Library.

16. Hunter to Nicholson, October 22, 1711, same to same, November 6, 1711, Colonial Documents, 60:396, 61:115b, N.Y. State Library.

17. Hunter to John Chamberlayne, February 25, 1712, *Doc. Rel. Col. Hist. N.Y.* 5:315.

18. Hunter to Livingston, July 30, 1712, Hunter to Cast, September 6, 1712, *Doc. Hist. N.Y.* 3:678, 683.

19. Hunter to Popple, July 26, 1720, Hunter to Cast, October 8, 1712, *Doc. Hist. N.Y.* 3:709–19.

20. Hunter to Popple, December 16, 1712, *Doc. Rel. Col. Hist. N.Y.* 5:351; H. T. Dickinson, "The Poor Palatines and the Parties," *English Historical Review* 82 (July 1967):464–85.

21. Army Lists, 1728, Add. MSS 21,188, 2,8, British Library; Swift, *Journal to Stella*, January 1, 1712, 296; Hunter to earl of Stair, February 28, 1712, same to same, June 23, 1712, Stair Muniments, GD 135/141/1/26, 141/1/37, Scot. PRO.

22. Hunter to Dartmouth, January 1, 1712, CO 5/1050, folio 416, Board of Trade to Stanhope, November 18, 1715, CO 5/1085, Pt. 1, folio 61, British Library.

23. *The Divided Society, Parties and Politics in England, 1694–1716*, eds. Geoffrey S. Holmes and W. A. Speck, (New York: 1968), 1–2.

24. Bonomi, *A Factious People*, 70–71, 79–81, 83; Osgood, *Eighteenth Century* 2:95–96; Hunter to Board of Trade, October 3, 1710, *Doc. Rel. Col. Hist. N.Y.* 5:170.

25. Bonomi, *A Factious People*, 84–85; Sheridan, *Lewis Morris*, 116.

26. Board of Trade to Hunter, June 29, 1711, Hunter to Board of Trade, January 1, 1712, *Doc. Rel. Col. Hist. N.Y.* 5:252, 298.

27. Rex M. Naylor, "The Royal Prerogative in New York, 1691–1775," *New York History* 5 (July 1924):221–55.

28. Petition of Samuel Mulford, undated, *Doc. Rel. Col. Hist. N.Y.* 5:474; Osgood, *Eighteenth Century* 2:116–17.

29. Hunter to Board of Trade, January 1, 1712, *Cal. S. P. Col.*, #251, 191–92.

30. Hunter to Board of Trade, September 12, 1711, *Cal. S. P. Col.*, #95, 97.

31. Hunter to St. John, September 12, 1711, *Doc. Rel. Col. Hist. N.Y.* 5:254–65.

32. Hunter to St. John, January 1, 1712, *Doc. Rel. Col. Hist. N.Y.* 5:296.

33. Board of Trade to Queen Anne, March 15, 1711, Board of Trade to Hunter, June 12, 1712, *Doc. Rel. Col. Hist. N.Y.* 5:197, 333.

34. *Colonial Laws New York*, November 24, 1711, June 6, 1712, 750, 753.

35. Hunter to Board of Trade, June 23, 1712, *Cal. S. P. Col.*, #454, 303; McManus, *A History of Negro Slavery*, 123–24.

36. Hunter to Board of Trade, June 23, 1712, *Doc. Rel. Col. Hist. N.Y.* 5:339.

37. Hunter to Board of Trade, June 23, 1712, *Cal. S. P. Col.*, #454, 303; Kenneth Scott, "The Slave Insurrection in New York in 1712," *New-York Historical Society Quarterly* 45 (January 1961):43–74.

38. Hunter to Board of Trade, June 23, 1712, *Doc. Rel. Col. Hist. N.Y.* 5:341; Hunter to Dartmouth, June 23, 1712, *Cal. S. P. Col.*, #456, 307.

39. *Minutes Common Council of N.Y.*, June 13, 1712, 3:8.

40. Neau to secretary, December 15, 1712, same to same, April 12, 1714, same to Mr. Taylor, December 6, 1715, same to Sharpe, November 22, 1715, Society for the Propagation of the Gospel, Letters Received, London.

41. Hunter to Board of Trade, March 14, 1713, Board of Trade to Hunter, March 15, 1716, *Doc. Rel. Col. Hist. N.Y.* 5:356, 471.

42. Hunter to Board of Trade, March 14, 1713, *Doc. Rel. Col. Hist. N.Y.* 5:356–58; Order Queen-in-Council, October 20, 1712, *Cal. S. P. Col.*, #102,71.

43. Hunter to Bishop of London, March 1, 1712, *Doc. Rel. Col. Hist. N.Y.* 5:311.

44. Runcie, "Anglo American Politics," 191–217.

45. Ibid.

46. Hunter to Chamberlayne, February 25, 1712, Hunter to earl of Stair, October 18, 1714, *Doc. Rel. Col. Hist. N.Y.* 5:315, 453.

47. Poyer to society, December 3, 1710, same to same, May 3, 1711, Memorial of the Clergy, November 13, 1771 *(sic.)*, *Ecclesiastical Records N.Y.* 3:1875–76, 1879, 1892–96.

48. Hunter to Bishop of London, March 1, 1712, Hunter to Chamberlayne, February 25, 1712, *Doc. Rel. Col. Hist. N.Y.* 5:311–12, 313.

49. Holmes and Speck, *The Divided Society*, 3, 50; Chamberlayne to Morris, June 16, 1711, Morris Papers, Box 1, Rutgers University Library; Hunter to Board of Trade, August 13, 1715, *Doc. Rel. Col. Hist. N.Y.* 5:420.

50. "Trinity Church, 1712," *Ecclesiastical Records N.Y.* 3:1924; Queen Anne to Hunter, April 4, 1714, John Jay Papers, Box 3, #16B, New-York Historical Society (hereafter cited as NYHS).

51. Hunter to Chamberlayne, February 27, 1712, *Doc. Rel. Col. Hist. N.Y.* 5:316; Hunter to Swift, November 1, 1712, Swift to Addison, May 13, 1713, *Correspondence of Jonathan Swift* 1:334–35, 347–48.

52. Hunter to Talbot, November 3, 1712, *History Church in Burlington*, 107.

53. Deputation of General Francis Nicholson, October 17, 1712, Letters Received, 91, Journal of the Society for the Propagation of the Gospel, June 17, 1720, No. 7, Society for the Propagation of the Gospel, London; Her Majesty's Commission to Colonel Francis Nicholson, October 14, 1712, Commission Francis Nicholson Governor of Nova Scotia, October 20, 1712, *Cal. S. P. Col.*, #97, 69, #105, 71.

54. William A. Speck. *Stability and Strife, England, 1714–1760* (Cambridge, Mass.: Harvard University Press, 1977), 160.

55. Beverley McAnear, *The Income of the Colonial Governors of British North America* (New York: 1967), 10, 16–19, 21–23, 24–27, 37.

5—*"Rage and Resentment,"* January 1713–July 1716

1. H. T. Dickinson, *Bolingbroke* (London: 1969), 106–9; Plumb, *Walpole* 1:150, 158.

2. Hunter to Stair, October 18, 1714, *Doc. Rel. Col. Hist. N.Y.* 5:453; Vetch to Livingston, January 25, 1715, same to same, January 27, 1714, Livingston Family Papers, General Correspondence, 1708–1718, Roll 3, FDR Library.

3. Hunter to Stair, October 18, 1714, *Doc. Rel. Col. Hist. N.Y.* 5:451–52.

4. Hunter to Swift, March 14, 1713, *Correspondence Jonathan Swift*, 363.

5. Sharpe to Swift, June 4, 1713, *Correspondence Jonathan Swift*, 362.

6. Council Minutes, February 17, 1714, Deposition Anne Drummond, February 17, 1714, Talbot to Bishop of London, October 21, 1714, *Doc. Hist. N.Y.* 3:451, 452.

7. Address of Rector and Vestry of Trinity Church in New York, *Doc. Hist. N.Y.* 3:453–55; Robert Hunter, *Androboros, A Biographical Farce in Three Acts*, ed. Lawrence H. Leder, *Bulletin of the New York Public Library* 68 (1964): 173.

8. Robert Hunter, A Proclamation, March 3, 1714, *Doc. Hist. N.Y.* 3:455–57.

9. Remarks on the Preceding Addressed to General Nicholson, *Doc. Hist. N.Y.* 3:458.

10. Leder, *Livingston*, 229, 230; Hunter to Board of Trade, March 28, 1715, *Cal. S. P. Col.*, #311, 137.

11. Robert Hunter, "To All Whom These Presents May Concern," 1713, Early American Imprints, 1639–1800, Evans No. 1641. My thanks to Stephen Saunders Webb, whose notes are here used.

12. Hunter to Board of Trade, August 27, 1714, *Doc. Rel. Col. Hist. N.Y.* 5:379.

13. *Colonial Laws New York*, June 21, 1714, 814; Hunter to Board of Trade, August 27, 1714, *Doc. Rel. Col. Hist. N.Y.* 5:379–80.

14. Leder, *Livingston*, 233–34; Hunter to Board of Trade, November 25, 1715, *Doc. Rel. Col. Hist. N.Y.* 5:390.

15. Petition Samuel Mulford, n.d., *Doc. Rel. Col. Hist. N.Y.* 5:474; Assembly's Address to Governor, August 7, 1716, *Messages Colonial Governors*, 180; Mulford to Board of Trade, August 28, 1717, *Cal. S. P. Col.*, #49, 16; Samuel Mulford's Speech to the Assembly, April 2, 1714, CO 5/1051, folio 187, PRO.

16. Board of Trade to Stanhope, August 3, 1715, *Doc. Rel. Col. Hist. N.Y.* 5:429.

17. Hunter to Board of Trade, August 27, 1714, *Cal. S. P. Col.*, #315, 168; Hunter to George Clarke, February 1, 1714, Rutherfurd Collection, NYHS.

18. Dickinson, *Bolingbroke*, 106; Holmes, *British Politics in the Age of Anne*, 83.

19. Hunter to earl of Montrose, June 10, 1714, Hunter to earl of Stair, August 27, 1714, GD 220/5/330, GD 135, 141/1/82, Scot. PRO.

20. Speck, *Stability and Strife*, 170, 175.

21. Ibid., 11.

22. Hunter's letter to Stair was read at a Board of Trade meeting on December 28, 1715, Minutes, *Journal Trade & Plant.*, 101; Hunter to Stair, October 18, 1714, Postscript, November 8, 1714, *Doc. Rel. Col. Hist. N.Y.* 5:451–55.

23. Minutes, February 1, 1715, February 4, 1715, *Journal Trade & Plant.*, 595–97.

24. Hunter to Stair, October 18, 1714, *Doc. Rel. Col. Hist. N.Y.* 5:453; Daniel and Samuel Coxe to Board of Trade, January 14, 1715, same to same, February 21, 1715, *Cal. S. P. Col.*, #164, 69, #229, 102–3; Minutes, February 21, 1715, April 1, 1715, *Journal Trade & Plant.*, 606, 15.

25. Hunter to Board of Trade, August 13, 1715, Order in Council, June 17, 1715, *Doc. Rel. Col. Hist. N.Y.* 5:420, 411.

26. Hunter to Popple, March 28, 1715, *Doc. Rel. Col. Hist. N.Y.* 5:400.

27. Hunter to Stair, March 28, 1715, GD 135, 141/4/22, Scot. PRO.

28. On naturalization bill see, for instance, Hunter to Board of Trade, March 14, 1713, *Doc. Rel. Col. Hist. N.Y.* 5:358; *Colonial Laws New York*, July 5, 1715, 1:861.

29. *Colonial Laws New York*, July 21, 1715, 1:881.

30. Hunter to Board of Trade, July 25, 1715, *Doc.Rel.Col.Hist.N.Y.* 5:416–18.

31. Ibid.

32. Instruction to Robert Hunter, 1709, *Doc. Rel. Col. Hist. N.Y.* 5:129.

33. Bonomi, *A Factious People*, Appendix C, 302.

34. Leder, *Livingston*, 236, 247.

35. Knittle, *Palatine Emigration*, 206.

36. Minutes, February 28, 1715, *Calendar of Council Minutes*, 258.

37. Order in Council, June 17, 1715, Hunter to Justices of Albany and Dutchess Counties, July 22, 1715, to arrest John Conrad Weiser, Colonial Documents, 60:9, 26, N.Y. State Library.

38. Hunter to Stair, October 18, 1714, postscript, November 8, 1714, *Doc.Rel. Col.Hist.N.Y.* 5:453–54.

39. Hunter to Board of Trade, July 25, 1715, *Doc. Rel. Col. Hist. N.Y.* 5:417.

40. On colonial elections, see Charles S. Sydnor, *American Revolutionaries in the Making, Political Practices in Washington's Virginia* (New York: The Free Press, 1952, 1962), especially Chapter 4, "Swilling the Planters with Bumbo," 44–59; Hunter to Popple, May 29, 1716; *Cal. S. P. Col.*, #176, 97.

41. Hunter to Board of Trade, June 6, 1716, Hunter to Popple, June 8, 1716, *Cal. S. P. Col.*, #192, 104, #195, 106.

42. Council Minutes, New Jersey, June 2, 1716, CO 5/1019, folios 124–25; Smith, *New Jersey*, 406.

43. Hunter to Popple, June 8, 1716, *Cal. S. P. Col.*, #195, 106.

44. Hunter to Ambrose Philips, July 27, 1717, *Cal. S. P. Col.*, #674, 355; Plumb, *Walpole* 1:217; MacKinnon, *Union of England and Scotland*, 440–41.

45. Hunter to Ambrose Philips, July 27, 1717, *Cal. S. P. Col.*, #674, 355.

46. Hunter to Popple, October 10, 1715, *Doc. Rel. Col. Hist. N.Y.* 5:450.

47. A Summary Account of the State of the Church, October 5, 1704, *Doc. Hist. N.Y.* 3:112; Talbot to Bishop of London, October 21, 1715, in Hills, *Hist. Burlington Church*, 141–42; Memorial, Rector, Churchwardens of Trinity Church, n.d., John Jay Papers, Box 3, #16B, NYHS.

48. Hunter to Popple, April 9, 1715, *Cal. S. P. Col.*, #337, 144.

49. Hunter to Popple, November 9, 1715, CO 5/971, Pt. 1, folios 26–27, PRO.

50. Talbot to bishop of London, October 21, 1715, Hills, *Hist. Burlington Church*, 141–42.

51. Board of Trade to Hunter, March 22, 1716, People to Hunter, April 16, 1716, Hunter to Board, April 30, 1716, *Doc. Rel. Col. Hist. N.Y.* 5:470–73, 477.

52. Talbot to Hunter, April 3, 1717, *Doc. Rel. N.J.* 4:301.

53. *Dictionary of American Biography*, ed. Dumas Malone, 20 vols. (New York: Charles Scribner's Sons, 1936), s.v. "Hyde, Edward, Earl of Clarendon" (hereafter cited as *DAB*).

54. Webb, "The Strange Career of Francis Nicholson," 513–48.

55. Jonathan Swift, "The First Ode of the Second Book of Horace Paraphras'd And Address'd to Richard St--le, Esq.", in *The Poems of Jonathan Swift*, ed. Harold Williams, 3 vols. (Oxford: Oxford University Press, 1937), 1:182.

56. Hunter to Addison, November 8, 1714, *Letters of Joseph Addison*, 493.

57. Swift, "An Epistle to a Lady," 2:635; Speck, *Swift*, 36; "Lord Macaulay's Essay on the Life and Writings of Addison," July 1843, in *Select Essays of Addison*, ed. Samuel Thurber (New York: 1892), 183, 266.

58. *The De Coverley Papers from The Spectator*, ed. Samuel Thurber (Boston: 1898), *Spectator* No. 1, March 1, 1711, No. 2, March 2, 1711, 1–3, 7.

59. J. H. Plumb, "The Spectator," *In the Light of History* (Boston: 1973), 52–56; *De Coverley Papers*, see *Spectator*, Nos. 6, 107, 111, 114, 119, 122, 125; Smithers, *Life of Joseph Addison*, 228, 258.

60. Richard Hurd quoted in Smithers, *Life of Joseph Addison*, 226–27.

61. P. K. Elkin, *The Augustan Defense of Satire* (Oxford: Oxford University Press, 1973), 58; *Androboros* was not the first play performed in New York. Licenses were issued in 1699 by Lieutenant Governor John Nanfan for theatrical performances. It was, however, the first play printed in New York. For the early theater in America, see John Anderson, *The American Theatre* (New York: 1938), 8–10; For the earliest surviving printed reference to *Androboros*, see David Erskine Baker, *Biographia Dramatica, or A Companion to the Playhouse*, 2 vols. (London: 1782), 1:251, 2:16.

62. Paul Leicester Ford quoted in Anderson, *The American Theatre*, 10.

63. For the character of the folk figure "Tom," see J. H. Plumb, "Bedlam," *In the Light of History*, 29.

64. Hunter, *Androboros*, 153–90.

65. Ibid., 165–67.

66. Ibid., 168, 175.

67. Ibid., 169, 170.

68. Ibid., 171.

69. Ibid., 173.

70. Ibid., 174.

71. Ibid., 176–77.

72. Ibid., 179.

73. Ibid., 181–82.

74. Ibid., 176, 177.

75. Swift, "An Epistle to a Lady," 2:635.

76. Cadwallader Colden to Alexander Colden, October 15, 1759, quoted in Smith, *New York*, 306.

6—*"God Did Never Intend Life for a Blessing,"* August 1716–July 1719

1. Last Will and Testament of Alexander Innes, July 27, 1713, *Calendar of New Jersey Wills, 1670–1730*, ed. William Nelson (Paterson: 1901), 253–54.

2. Stokes, *Iconography*, August 9, 1716, 4:485.

3. Warrant H.R.H. Prince of Wales to Hunter, 1716, *Cal. S. P. Col.*, #353 i, 186; Report of Committee of Council, August 31, 1716, Colonial Documents, 60:125, N.Y. State Library.

4. Hunter to Board of Trade, February 13, 1717, *Doc. Rel. N.J.*, 273.

5. Hunter to Board of Trade, May 3, 1718, *Doc. Rel. N.J.*, 363.

6. Hunter to Board of Trade, February 13, 1717, *Cal. S. P. Col.*, #469, 255.

7. Leder, *Livingston*, 245; Hunter to Board of Trade, February 13, 1717, *Cal. S. P. Col.*, #469, 255; Cadwallader Colden to Alexander Colden, October 15, 1759, in Smith, *New York*, 307; *New York Colonial Laws*, 960.

8. Representation of the Grand Jury of the City and County of New York to Hunter, November 29, 1717, Merchants Trading to New York to the Board of Trade, May 2, 1718, *Cal. S. P. Col.*, #516 i, 244, #516, 243; Osgood, *Eighteenth Century*, 2:114–15.

9. Leder, *Livingston*, 248.

10. Hunter Last Will and Testament, July 28, 1718, Hunter Misc. MSS, NYHS; Memorandums 1718, Colonial Documents, 60:67, N.Y. State Library.

11. Unknown colonial quoted in Frederick B. Tolles, *James Logan and the Culture of Provincial America* (Boston: 1957), 97; Cadwallader Colden to Alexander Colden, September 25, 1759, in Smith, *New York*, 300.

12. *DAB*, s.v. "Alexander, James."

13. Stanhope to Hunter, June 22, 1716, Lists of Rebel Prisoners Transported to South Carolina, Virginia, Maryland, St. Christopher's, and Jamaica, August 16, 1716, *Cal. S. P. Col.*, #227, 130, #309, 169–71.

14. For Alexander's later career, see James Alexander, *A Brief Narrative of the Case and Trial of John Peter Zenger*, ed. Stanley Nider Katz (Cambridge, Mass.: 1963).

15. Hunter to Board of Trade, November 12, 1715, Board of Trade to Hunter, March 15, 1716, Hunter to Board of Trade, October 2, 1716, *Doc. Rel. Col. Hist. N.Y.* 5:458–59, 471, 478–79.

16. Tolles, *James Logan*, 12, 25.

17. Ibid., 15; For Logan's career as an Indian trader, see Francis Jennings, "The Indian Trade of the Susquehanna Valley," *Proceedings of the American Philosophical Society* 110 (December 1966):406–24.

18. Logan to Hunter, September 20, 1712, Logan Letterbook, Hist. Soc. Pa.

19. Logan to Hunter, October 24, 1717, same to same, November 7, 1717, Logan Letterbook, Hist. Soc. Pa.; Hunter to Colden, February 18, 1720, in Cadwallader Colden, "The Letters and Papers of Cadwallader Colden," *Collections* 50–56, 67–68 (New York: New-York Historical Society, 1918–1937), 50:100.

20. Logan to Hunter, January 8, 1717, same to same, Logan Letterbook, 147–148, 173–175, same to same, February 25, 1715, Parchment Logan Letterbook, 1712–1715, 174, Hist. Soc. Pa.

21. Logan to Hunter, January 17, 1717, same to same, January 22, 1717, same to same, July 31, 1718, same to same, August 7, 1718, same to same, September 2, 1718, same to same, October 2, 1718, Logan Letterbook, 151, 152–153, 180, 181, 182, 188, Hist. Soc. Pa.

22. Cadwallader Colden published his theories on the cause of gravity in 1746. See Brook Hindle, "Cadwallader Colden's Extension of the Newtonian Principles," *W&MQ* 13 (October 1956):459–75: For scientific societies, see A. R. Hall, *The Scientific Revolution, 1500–1800* (Boston: 1954–1956), 186–216; J. H. Plumb, "Reason and Unreason in the Eighteenth Century," *In the Light of History*, 3–24.

23. Logan to Hunter, April 3, 1717, Parchment Logan Letterbook, 161, Hist. Soc. Pa.

24. Plumb, *Walpole* 1:222–23, 225–26, 231, 235.

25. Hunter to Popple, June 3, 1718, *Doc. Rel. Col. Hist. N.Y.* 5:505.

26. Hunter to Popple, May 3, 1717, *Doc. Rel. N.J.* 4:295; Samuel Bustall to Mrs. Bustall, November 1, 1716, Ambrose Philips to Board of Trade, June 16, 1717, *Cal. S. P. Col.*, #349, 183, #634 i, 338, #634, 338.

27. Samuel Bustall to Mrs. Bustall, n.d., *Cal. S. P. Col.*, #373, iv, 183–84.

28. Daniel Coxe to [?], n.d., Board of Trade to Addison, February 13, 1718, Coxe to Richard Allison, July 7, 1716, Hunter to Popple, November 16, 1716, *Cal. S. P. Col.*, #373 ii, 183, #376, 185, #392 i, 203, #392, 202.

29. Hunter to H. M. Council in New York, November 28, 1717, R. Hudson to Hunter, November 17, 1717, Simon Gratz Autograph Collection, Hist. Soc. Pa.

30. Indian Conference, June 13, 1717, *Doc. Rel. Col. Hist. N.Y.* 5:486–87; Address of General Assembly to Hunter, October 4, 1717, *Cal. S. P. Col.*, #126, 53.

31. Verner W. Crane, *The Southern Frontier, 1670–1732* (Ann Arbor: 1929, 1956), 160–61; Lewis Henry Morgan, *The League of the Iroquois* (Secaucus, N.J.: The Citadel Press, 1851, 1975), 24; Minutes, Iroquois Conference, September 25, 1714, Hunter to Board of Trade, April 30, 1716, *Doc. Rel. Col. Hist. N.Y.* 5:387, 475.

32. Address to Sachems, August 29, 1715, Livingston Family Papers, Undated MSS, Indian Affairs Papers, Roll 5, FDR Library.

33. Minutes, Iroquois Conference, August 31, 1715, *Doc. Rel. Col. Hist. N.Y.* 5:444.

34. Spotswood to Board of Trade, February 27, 1718, *Official Letters of Alexander Spotswood*, 262; Minutes, July 7, 1720, *Journal Trade & Plant.*, 181.

35. The economic explanation of the rise of the Iroquois Confederacy, first set forth by Charles H. McIlwain in 1915 and elaborated upon by George T. Hunt in 1960, was challenged in 1962 by Allen W. Trelease. While McIlwain and Hunt felt the Iroquois were motivated to achieve dominance over other tribes primarily because of a desire to control trade routes, Trelease argued that the Iroquois were motivated by cultural preconditioning which demanded vengeance or atonement. See Peter Wraxall, *An Abridgement of Indian Affairs*, lx–lxxxv; George T. Hunt, *The Wars of the Iroquois* (Madison: 1960), 37, 41, 55; Allen W. Trelease, "The Iroquois and the Western Fur Trade: A Problem in Interpretation," *Mississippi Valley Historical Review* 44 (June 1962):32–51.

36. Propositions made by Sachems, June 15, 1717, *Doc. Rel. Col. Hist. N.Y.* 5:488.

37. Hunter to Board of Trade, July 7, 1718, *Cal. S. P. Col.*, #600, 297.

38. Addison to Board of Trade, August 22, 1717, *Letters of Addison*, 372; Board of Trade to Hunter, September 4, 1717, *Cal. S. P. Col.*, #69, 28; Mr. Attorney General to Board of Trade, February 18, 1718, *Journal Trade & Plant.*, 339.

39. Richard West to Board of Trade, August 20, 1718, *Cal. S. P. Col.*, #663, 339.

40. Hunter to Board of Trade, July 7, 1718, same to same, August 7, 1718, *Doc. Rel. Col. Hist. N.Y.* 5:510, 515.

41. James Alexander to Hunter, November 8, 1733, Rutherfurd Collection, NYHS.

42. Hunter to Popple, July 7, 1718, *Cal. S. P. Col.*, #602, 298.

43. Hunter to Popple, May 18, 1719, *Doc. Rel. Col. Hist. N.Y.* 5:521; Logan to Hunter, January 6, 1719, Logan Letterbook, 200–201, Hist. Soc. Pa.

44. Hunter's Address to Assembly, *Cal. S. P. Col.*, #286 i, 150.

45. Hunter to Popple, November 22, 1717, *Doc. Rel. Col. Hist. N.Y.* 5:493.

46. *Tatler*, #69, 2:158–59; *Messages Governors*, June 24, 1719, 189.

47. Cadwallader Colden to Alexander Colden, October 15, 1759, in Smith, *New York,* 308.

48. Smith, *New Jersey,* 377; Accounts of Money Paid by Hunter for Subsistence of Palatines, December 2, 1717, *Cal. S. P. Col.,* #235, 118.

49. Captain John Riggs to Charles Delafaye, November 26, 1716, John and Frances Riggs to Delafaye, May 11, 1717, *Cal. S. P. Col.,* #405, 208, #561, 298; For Hunter's income, see Beverley McAnear, *The Income of Colonial Governors of British North America,* 19—23.

50. Logan to Hunter, July 2, 1719, same to same, July 9, 1719, Logan Letterbook, 214, 215, Hist. Soc. Pa.

7—"The Giddy Turns of State," July 1719—January 1728

1. Hunter to Popple, October 4, 1719, *Cal. S. P. Col.,* #405, 230.

2. Defoe, *A Tour Thro' Great Britain,* 303.

3. Ibid., 313—14, 321; J. H. Plumb, *The First Four Georges* (Boston and Toronto: 1975), 7—95.

4. The Hunter portrait is in the collection of the New-York Historical Society; Castiglione, *The Book of the Courtier,* 57.

5. Plumb, *Walpole* 1:268—69, 270, 289, 292.

6. Hunter to Stair, December 22, 1719, GD 135/141, vol. 23, 146, Scot. PRO.

7. Hunter to Charles Delafaye, October 25, 1719, *Cal. S. P. Col.,* #426, 241—42.

8. Hunter's Memorial to Board of Trade, December 22, 1719, Craggs to Schuyler, December 26, 1719, *Cal. S. P. Col.,* #488, 284, #496, 289; Board of Trade to Craggs, December 23, 1719, *Doc. Rel. Col. Hist. N.Y.* 5:535.

9. Keith to Colden, July 14, 1720, "Letters and Papers of Cadwallader Colden" 50:104.

10. Burnet's Representation, January 2, 1718, T11/17, 49—50, Warrant for Allowing £200 per annum to comptroller, October 25, 1720, T11/17, 301, PRO.

11. Warrant for William Congreve to be one of the undersearchers for Port London, November 3, 1714, T11/16, 10, PRO; William Sloper, Power of Attorney to Hunter, 1712, Rutherfurd Collection, NYHS; Plumb, *Walpole* 1:308; Defoe, *Great Britain,* 312.

12. Dora Mae Clark, *The Rise of the British Treasury, Colonial Administration in the Eighteenth Century* (New Haven: 1960), 17, 19, Henry Roseveare, *The Treasury, 1660—1870* (London & New York: 1973), 41, 94.

13. Customs Commissioners to Lords of privy council, November 9, 1720, T11/18, 307, PRO.

14. On Appeals Court, see A. M. Schlesinger, "Colonial Appeals to the Privy Council, *Political Science Quarterly* 28 (1913):279—97, 433—50; Privy Council Meetings, March 14, 1715, July 15, 1717, November 16, 1717, January 29, 1718, March 10, 1717, March 20, 1717, July 23, 1718, July 27, 1718, January 6, 1719, February 9, 1719, February 26, 1719, folios 101, 68—69, 84, 58, 65, 83—84, 84, 213, 114, 115, Privy Council Register, PC 2/85, PC 2/86, PRO.

15. Petition John Conrad Weiser, July 20, 1720, *Cal. S. P. Col.,* #155, 69; Condition and Grievances of Palatines, 1720, *Doc. Hist. N.Y.* 3:709—13.

16. Case of Germans in New York, July 28, 1720, Hunter to Board of Trade, July 26, 1720, *Cal. S. P. Col.,* #164, 73, #163, 73.

17. George Clarke to Horatio Walpole, November 27, 1722, *Doc. Hist. N.Y.* 3:706–7, 719; Hunter to Alexander, February 6, 1722, Rutherfurd Collection, NYHS.

18. Minutes, July 20, 1720, August 9, 1720, *Journal Trade & Plant.*, 186, 196.

19. Minutes, August 29, 1721, *Journal Trade & Plant.*, 317; Hunter's Statement to Board of Trade, August 29, 1721, *Doc. Rel. Col. Hist. N.Y.* 5:561; Michael Kammen, *Colonial New York* (Millwood, New York: Kto Press, 1975, 1978), 193–94.

20. Minutes, January 27, 1726, *Journal Trade & Plant.*, 215; Webb, *Governors-General*, Appendix #128, 158, 167, 171, 206.

21. Minutes, February 2, 1726, *Journal Trade & Plant.*, 215; Second Memorial from Mr. Gray to Board of Trade, February 10, 1726, *Doc. Rel. N.J.*, 5:113–14.

22. Hunter to Colden, July 11, 1720, Colden Papers, Box 11, #55, NYHS; Alexander Colden to Cadwallader Colden, October 3, 1721, Colden Letters, NYHS.

23. Gay to Swift, February 3, 1723, *Correspondence Jonathan Swift*, 447.

24. A. E. Richardson, *Georgian England, 1700–1820* (Freeport, N.Y.: 1931, 1967), 174, 175, 179, 181; Pope to Percival, September 22, 1722, *Correspondence of Alexander Pope*, ed. George Sherburn, 5 vols. (Oxford: 1956), 2:135.

25. A Rental of all such Copyhold Rents, 1723, Orby/Hunter Papers, Cragg 11/1/2, Lincolnshire Archives.

26. Logan to Hunter, May 8, 1728, Logan Letterbooks, Hist. Soc. Pa.; John Nichols, *Literary Anecdotes of the Eighteenth Century* 5:5–9, 89.

27. Plumb, *Walpole* 1:293–95, 300, 301.

28. Ibid., 298–300.

29. Basil Williams, *Carteret and Newcastle* (Hamden, Conn.: 1943, 1966), 51.

30. Speck, *Stability and Strife*, 235; James A. Henretta, *Salutary Neglect, Colonial Administration Under the Duke of Newcastle* (Princeton: Princeton University Press, 1972), 5.

31. Plumb, *Walpole* 2:198.

32. Ibid., 202, 232; Kramnick, *Bolingbroke and His Circle*, 4, 6.

33. Kramnick, *Bolingbroke and His Circle*, 59–60.

34. Jonathan Swift, *Gulliver's Travels*, ed. Robert A. Greenberg (New York: 1961), 21, 222.

35. Kramnick, *Bolingbroke and His Circle*, 41–42; *Daily Journal*, February 1, 1728; Jonathan Swift, *The Intelligencer*, 1728, 1729, both quoted in J. V. Guerinot and Rodney D. Jilg, *The Beggar's Opera* (Hampden, Conn.: 1976), 127, 143, 157, 160.

36. John Ayscough to Board of Trade, July 14, 1726, Newcastle to Board of Trade, February 14, 1727, *Cal. S. P. Col.*, #217, 117, #435, 216.

37. Logan to Hunter, May 8, 1728, Logan Letterbook, Hist. Soc. Pa.; Miguel de Cervantes, *The Portable Cervantes, Don Quixote*, trans., ed., and annotated by Samuel Putnam (New York: 1951), 579–80; Edward Long, *The History of Jamaica* 2 vols. (New York: 1874, 1972), 1:6–7.

38. Dalton, *Army Lists*, Pt. 2, 2:335, 351; H.M. Commission Appointing Hunter Captain, February 15, 1727, *Cal. S. P. Col.*, #437, 217.

39. Hunter to Alexander, November 4, 1727, *Doc. Rel. N.J.*, 5:179; Hunter to Alexander, August 10, 1728, Rutherfurd Collection, NYHS; Kammen, *New York*, 194.

40. Hunter, Last Will and Testament, January 5, 1733, PRO; Hunter to Alexander, November 4, 1727, Rutherfurd Collection, NYHS.

41. Hunter to Board of Trade, February 10, 1728, *Cal. S. P. Col.*, #43, 28–29.

8—"*A Never-Ceasing Wheel*," January 1728–September 1730

1. William Beckford, *A Descriptive Account of the Island of Jamaica* (London: 1790), xiii; Richard S. Dunn, *Sugar and Slaves, The Rise of the Planter Class in the English West Indies, 1624–1713* (Chapel Hill: 1972), 36; Webb, *Governors-General,* 151–52, 158–66.

2. Hunter to Board of Trade, December 15, 1731, CO 137/20, folio 35, PRO; George Metcalf, *Royal Government and Political Conflict in Jamaica, 1729–1783* (London: 1965), 8.

3. Frank Leslie quoted in Frank Cundall, *Governors of Jamaica in the First Half of the Eighteenth Century* (London: 1937), 154; Long, *History of Jamaica* 1:6–7.

4. Governor Hunter's Answers to Queries by the Board of Trade, 1730, *Cal. S. P. Col.,* #627 iii, 416.

5. Ibid.; Sheridan, *Sugar and Slavery,* 366–67.

6. On the settlement of Jews in Jamaica, see Bernard Schlesinger, "The Jews of Jamaica: A Historical View," *Caribbean Quarterly* 13 (March 1967):46–53.

7. Charles Leslie, *A New and Exact Account of Jamaica* (Edinburgh: 1739), 36–38; Lowell Joseph Ragatz, *The Fall of the Planter Class in the British Caribbean, 1763–1833* (New York: 1928), 4.

8. Address Jamaica Assembly, November 27, 1731, CO 140/12, folio 44, PRO; A Short State of Jamaica, 1730, *Cal. S. P. Col.,* #351, 222–23.

9. Governor Hunter's Answers to Queries, *Cal. S. P. Col.,* #627 iii, 416.

10. Metcalf, *Royal Government,* 3; Slave song quoted in Michael Craton, James Wolvern, and David Wright, *Slavery, Abolition and Emancipation, Black Slaves and the British Empire* (London and New York: 1976), 138.

11. Hunter Address to Assembly, July 24, 1728, *Journal of the Assembly of Jamaica* (Jamaica: 1745), 679–80, British Library; Treaty of Madrid quoted in A. P. Newton, *The European Nations in the West Indies, 1493–1688* (New York: 1933, 1967), 270.

12. Hunter to Board of Trade, May 10, 1730, same to same, March 13, 1720, *Cal. S. P. Col.,* #225, 105, #111, 53.

13. For Spanish and slave guerilla war against the English, see Webb, *Governors-General,* 176–78; On the origin of the Maroons, see "The Maroons in the Eighteenth Century: A Note on Indirect Rule in Jamaica," *Caribbean Quarterly* 8 (1962):25–27; On the ethnic composition of the Maroons, see Barbara Kopytoff, "The Development of Jamaican Maroon Ethnicity," *Caribbean Quarterly* 22 (1976):33–50; For a social history of the Maroons, see Barbara Kopytoff, "The Early Political Development of Jamaican Maroon Societies," *W&MQ* 25 (April 1978):287–307.

14. James Knight, *History of Jamaica,* Add. MSS 12,418, folio 353, British Library; *Journal Jamaica Assembly,* March 18, 1730, June 16, 1730, 702, 709.

15. Hunter to Lilly, November 13, 1727, Lilly Letterbook, Add. MSS 12,427, British Library; Newcastle to Board of Trade, February 10, 1728, CO 137/17, 34, PRO.

16. Lilly to Ashworth, September 10, 1729, Hunter to Lilly, August 23, 1729, same to same, November 16, 1729, Lilly Letterbook, 43, 42, 44, British Library.

17. Hunter to Lilly, August 23, 1729, Lilly Letterbook Add. MSS 12,427, British Library; Hunter to Allured Popple, July 20, 1731 *Cal. S. P. Col.,* #312, 196.

18. Stewart to Josiah Burchett, May 10, 1730, ADM 1/231, Pt. 1, n.p., PRO.

19. Hunter Address to Assembly, *Jamaica Assembly Journal,* 709, British Library; Wade began his career in 1690 as an ensign in the earl of Bath's regiment of foot. It is

quite possible Hunter knew Wade, who was promoted to lieutenant general in 1727, since both men had served in Flanders. Dalton quotes the well-known couplet about Wade's construction project: "Had you seen these roads before they were made, / You would lift up your hands and bless General Wade." See Dalton, *Army Lists*, Pt. 1, 3:141.

20. Hunter to Mr. Stanyan, March 20, 1728, *Cal. S. P. Col.*, #119, 68.

21. Agnes M. Whitson, *The Constitutional Development of Jamaica, 1660–1729* (n.p.: 1929), 10–11, 17, 40, 41.

22. Metcalf, *Royal Government*, 27–28; Webb, *Governors-General*, 263–92; Whitson, *Constitutional Development*, 57–59.

23. Webb, *Governors-General*, 306–7, 310; Frederick G. Spurdle, *Early West Indian Government, 1660–1783* (New Zealand: published by the author, n.d.), 31; Lord Carteret to Duke of Portland, July 17, 1722, King to Duke of Portland, August 27, 1723, *Cal. S. P. Col.*, #226, 113, #696, 335.

24. Representation of Board of Trade . . . Regarding . . . Jamaica, February 19, 1725, CO 138/17, folios 1–3, PRO.

25. Instructions Robert Hunter, #21, July 25, 1727, CO 138/17, folio 84, PRO; Hunter to Board of Trade, May 16, 1728, *Cal. S. P. Col.*, #196, 93.

26. *Journal Jamaica Assembly*, March 28, 1728, 620; Knight, *History of Jamaica*, Add. MSS 12,418, 345, 347–48, British Library.

27. Whitson, *Constitutional Development*, 156.

28. Knight, *History of Jamaica*, Add. MSS 12,418, 348, British Library; Revenue Act, passed Assembly April 6, 1728, CO 139/12, 1, PRO.

29. Hunter to Board of Trade, May 16, 1728, Board of Trade to King, May 14, 1729, *Cal. S. P. Col.*, #196, 95, #706, 374–76.

30. Francis Fane to Board of Trade, February 4, 1729, CO 137/17, folio 129, Duke of Newcastle to Board of Trade, July 11, 1727, CO 137/17, folio 4, Hunter Instructions, July 25, 1727, CO 138/17, folio 88, Order King-in-Council, May 22, 1729, CO 137/18, folio 17, PRO.

31. Knight, *History of Jamaica*, Add. MSS 12,418, 377, British Library; Scouller, *Queen Anne's Armies*, Appendix G, 376–79; Metcalf, *Royal Government*, 17–19, 25.

32. Sheridan, *Sugar and Slavery*, Appendix VI, 498; Hunter to Board of Trade, May 16, 1728, *Cal. S. P. Col.*, #196, 95.

33. *Journal Jamaica Assembly*, July 10, 1728, 641, British Library; Hunter to Popple, August 3, 1728, CO 137/17, folio 108, PRO.

34. Hunter to Newcastle, May 17, 1728, same to same, August 3, 1728, *Cal. S. P. Col.*, #197, 96, #342, 167.

35. Hunter to Board of Trade, March 8, 1729, CO 137/17, folio 135, PRO; Newcastle to Hunter, December 1728, *Cal. S. P. Col.*, #533, 288.

36. Hunter to Alexander, August 10, 1728, Rutherfurd Collection, NYHS.

37. Ibid.

38. Ibid.

39. Newcastle to Hunter, February 17, 1729, *Cal. S. P. Col.*, #604, 320.

40. Jamaica Council Minutes, April 6, 1729, CO 140/21, n.p. PRO.

41. Hunter to Newcastle, February 17, 1728, Add. MSS 32,761, folio 98, Knight, *History of Jamaica*, Add. MSS 12,418, 348, British Library.

42. Hunter to Popple, January 15, 1729, Hunter to Lord Townshend, January 15, 1729, *Cal. S. P. Col.* #556, 298, #557, 298.

43. Hunter to Charles Delafaye, July 17, 1729, Hunter to Board of Trade, September 6, 1729, CO 137/18, folio 54, PRO.

44. Knight, *History of Jamaica*, Add. MSS 12,418, 349, British Library; Hunter to Delafaye, July 17, 1729, Hunter to Board of Trade, September 6, 1729, *Cal. S. P. Col.*, #830, 450, #895, 477.

45. Hunter to Newcastle, November 13, 1731, *Cal. S. P. Col.*, #486, 339; An Act to Prevent Dangers from Disguised...Papists, August 16, 1729, CO 139/12, folio 15, PRO.

46. Burnet, *History of His Own Time*, 515, 523–24, 527.

47. Hunter to Board of Trade, March 14, 1713, *Doc. Rel. Col. Hist. N.Y.* 5:356.

48. An Act for Better Regulating Slaves..., March 28, 1730, CO 139/12, folio 22, PRO.

49. Hunter to Board of Trade, May 10, 1730, Board of Trade to King, July 13, 1731, *Cal. S. P. Co.* #225, 106, #295, 181, Order King-in-Council, November 25, 1731, CO 137/20, folio 33, PRO.

50. Mr. Morice to Newcastle, Petition of Merchants, 1729, Hunter to Newcastle, September 6, 1729, The Affair of the Jamaica Embargo, 1729, *Cal. S. P. Col.*, #775, 401, #780, 402–403, #896, 478, #1055, 579.

51. Board of Trade to Hunter, July 7, 1730, Hunter to Newcastle, February 15, 1730, *Cal. S. P. Col.*, #317, 168, #61, 31.

52. Hunter to Newcastle, October 8, 1731, same to same, November 13, 1731, Board of Trade to Hunter, July 28, 1731, *Cal. S. P. Col.*, #433, 292, #486, 339, #328, 204; Philip Wright, "War and Peace with the Maroons, 1730–1739," *Caribbean Quarterly* 16 (March 1970):5–27.

9—"Bad Spirits, and Innumerable Griefs," September 1730–March 1734

1. Plumb, *Walpole* 2:232; Newcastle to Governors, September 25, 1730, *Cal. S. P. Col.*, #452, 287.

2. A. P. Thornton, *West India Policy Under the Restoration* (Oxford: 1956), 114–15; Alan Burns, *History of the British West Indies* (London: 1954), 441–44.

3. Petition Jamaica Merchants to Admiral Charles Stewart, May 28, 1730, ADM 1/231, Pt. 1, n.p., PRO; Townshend to Hunter, September 15, 1728, *Cal. S. P. Col.*, #394, 208.

4. Hunter to Board of Trade, September 19, 1730, Hunter Proclamation, September 26, 1730, *Cal. S. P. Col.*, #445, 283–84, #465 i, 299.

5. Hunter to Board of Trade, October 1, 1730, Hunter to Newcastle, November 7, 1730, Extract of Letter from Port Royal, October 12, 1730, *Cal. S. P. Col.*, #465, 299, #519, 337, #485, 319.

6. Newcastle to Hunter, November 9, 1730, *Cal. S. P. Col.*, #520, 337–38.

7. Hunter to Board of Trade, December 24, 1730, Hunter to Newcastle, January 23, 1731, Account of Treasure, January 23, 1731, *Cal. S. P. Col.*, #627, 412, #25, 24, #25 i, 24.

8. Hunter to Newcastle, April 2, 1731, *Cal. S. P. Col.*, #116, 81.

9. Kramnick, *Bolingbroke and His Circle*, 197–205; Lewis Namier, *England in the Age of the American Revolution*, 2nd ed. (New York: 1966), 33–34.

10. Stewart to Burchett, December 29, 1730, ADM 1/231, Pt. 1, n.p., PRO.

11. Copy of Fourth Resolution Reported by Committee of House, June 19, 1730, CO 137/18, folio 96, PRO; Hunter to Board of Trade, March 12, 1730, *Cal. S. P. Col.*, #111, 53.

12. Newcastle to Hunter, October 12, 1730, *Cal. S. P. Col.*, #457, 293; Webb, *Governors-General*, 193.

13. Council Minutes, January 12, 1731, June 22, 1731, CO 140/23, PRO; *Journal Jamaica Assembly*, January 26, 1731, British Library.

14. Colonel Hayes to Newcastle, March 9, 1731, *Cal. S. P. Col.*, #79, 54; David Thomson, *Wild Excursions*, 39, 70–71; Water was also stored in lead-lined containers. See Long, *History of Jamaica* 2:315.

15. Hunter to [Newcastle?], March 20, 1731, Hunter to Newcastle, April 2, 1731, *Cal. S. P. Co.*, #95, 69, #117, 81.

16. Hunter to Board of Trade, September 8, 1733, *Cal. S. P. Col.*, #331, 181.

17. Council Minutes, February 19, 1731, March 9, 1731, CO 140/21, PRO; Col. Hayes to [Newcastle?], March 9, 1731, *Cal. S. P. Col.*, #79, 54.

18. Hunter to [Newcastle?], March 17, 1731, Hunter to Newcastle, April 21, 1731, Hunter to Sir William Strickland, May 29, 1731, Minutes Privy Council, June 21, 1731, Extracts Letters from Jamaica, 1731, *Cal. S. P. Col.*, #92, 68, #146, 94, #202 i, 115, #210, 118, #249, 140–41.

19. For assembly message, see *Journal Jamaica Assembly*, May 14, 1731, 8, British Library; Newcastle to Hunter, September 16, 1731, *Cal. S. P. Col.*, #412, 267–68.

20. Hunter to Newcastle, December 7, 1731, *Cal. S. P. Col.*, #532, 362–63.

21. Hunter to Newcastle, October 8, 1731, Captain DeLaMillier to Hunter, December 8, 1731, *Cal. S. P. Col.*, #433, 291, #550 vii, 374.

22. *Journal Jamaica Assembly*, January 3, 1732, 47, British Library; Hunter to Newcastle, January 5, 1732, *Cal. S. P. Col.*, #6, 2.

23. Hunter to Newcastle, January 16, 1732, *Cal. S. P. Col.*, #19, 8–9.

24. Newcastle to Hunter, November 30, 1730, *Cal. S. P. Col.*, #567, 375; Acts for raising several sums . . . , CO 139/13, folios 31–34, PRO.

25. Hunter to Board of Trade, February 11, 1731, same to same, April 21, 1731, *Cal. S. P. Col.*, #51, 40, #147, 95–96.

26. Hunter to Popple, February 10, 1729, Board of Trade to Hunter, July 28, 1731, *Cal. S. P. Col.*, #591, 316, #328, 204.

27. Francis Fane to Board of Trade, August 3, 1731, *Cal. S. P. Col.*, #340, 212.

28. Board of Trade to privy council, August 25, 1731, *Cal. S. P. Col.*, #383, 240–41; H.M. Additional Instruction to Hunter, November 30, 1731, Hunter to Board of Trade, February 19, 1732, *Cal. S. P. Col.*, #520 i, 357, #92, 64.

29. Memorial South Sea Company to Board of Trade, June 27, 1732, *Cal. S. P. Col.*, #285, 164; Sheridan, *Sugar and Slavery*, 427.

30. Board of Trade to Hunter, September 13, 1732, Order King-in-Council, October 13, 1732, *Cal. S. P. Col.*, #373, 208, #418, 236.

31. Hunter to Alexander, August 18, 1732, Rutherfurd Collection, NYHS.

32. H.M. Leave of Absence for Hunter, June 1, 1732, *Cal. S. P. Col.*, #250, 131.

33. Hunter to Alexander, June 13, 1732, Rutherfurd Collection, NYHS.

34. An attempt was made in May 1732, to prevent the landing in Jamaica of smallpox-infested Negroes. See *Journal Jamaica Assembly*, May 4, 1732, 37, British Library; Hunter to Newcastle, September 20, 1732, same to same, November 18, 1732, *Cal. S. P. Col.*, #389, 215, #463, 263.

35. Hunter to Alexander, September 9, 1732, October 10, 1732, October 18, 1732, Rutherfurd Collection, NYHS.

36. Hunter to Alexander, August 27, 1733, Rutherfurd Collection, NYHS.

37. Hunter Last Will and Testament, January 4, 1733, Probate Office, PRO.

38. Hunter to Alexander, August 27, 1733, Rutherfurd Collection, NYHS.

39. Alexander to Hunter, November 8, 1733, Alexander to Thomas Orby Hunter, July 12, 1734, Rutherfurd Collection, NYHS.

40. Jamaica Assembly Journal, January 14, 1732, January 20, 1732, 57, 60, British Library; Hunter to Board of Trade, January 13, 1732, Hunter to Newcastle, January 16, 1732, Hunter to Board of Trade, March 13, 1733, *Cal. S. P. Col.*, #17, 13, #19, 9, #74, 58.

41. Council Minutes, May 23, 1733, CO 137/20, folio 133; Hunter to Board of Trade, January 13, 1733, *Cal. S. P. Col.*, #17, 13.

42. Hunter to Newcastle, January 16, 1732, Hunter to Board of Trade, March 13, 1733, *Cal. S. P. Col.*, #19, 9, #74, 58.

43. Hunter to Board of Trade, March 13, 1733, *Cal. S. P. Col.*, #74, 58.

44. *Journal Jamaica Assembly*, April 7, 1733, 130–31, British Library.

45. Hunter to Newcastle, October 20, 1733, *Cal. S. P. Col.*, #366, 222.

46. Hunter to Board of Trade, October 13, 1733, same to same, December 24, 1733, *Cal. S. P. Col.*, #358, 213, #455, 273.

47. Hunter to Board of Trade, September 8, 1733, Hunter to Newcastle, December 24, 1733, *Cal. S. P. Col.*, #331, 180–81, #456, 274.

48. Hunter to Newcastle, December 29, 1733, Hunter to Board of Trade, December 29, 1733, *Cal. S. P. Col.*, #460, 275, #459, 275.

49. Hunter to Board of Trade, March 27, 1733, Hunter's Speech to Council and Assembly, March 14, 1733, *Cal. S. P. Col.*, #74, 57, #74 i, 59.

50. Hunter to Board of Trade, September 8, 1733, same to same, December 24, 1733, *Cal. S. P. Col.*, #331, 181, #455, 273.

51. James Draper to Hunter, June 27, 1733, CO 137/20, folio 150, Council Minutes, July 31, 1733, CO 140/25, n.p., PRO.

52. Minutes Council and Council in Assembly, July 6, 1733, July 21, 1733, CO 140/25, PRO.

53. Hunter to Lilly, August 20, 1733, Lilly Letterbook, Add. MSS 12,427, 100, British Library.

54. William Nedham to Ogle, July 6, 1733, CO 137/20, folio 157, Hunter to Board of Trade, August 18, 1733, CO 137/20, folio 165; Extract Letters Mr. Hals to earl of Westmoreland, October 13, 1733, CO 137/21, folio 2, PRO.

55. Extract Letter from Jamaica, September 10, 1733, CO 137/21, folio 12; Hunter to Board of Trade, October 13, 1733, CO 137/21, folio 27, PRO.

56. Hunter to Board of Trade, October 13, 1733, *Cal. S. P. Col.*, #358, 213.

57. Hunter to Newcastle, February 9, 1734, *Cal. S. P. Col.*, #35, 32; Extract Letter from Jamaica, February 15, 1734, CO 137/21, folio 44, PRO.

58. Bill for Cutting Roads, March 9, 1734, CO 139/14, no. 7; Hunter to Board of Trade, March 11, 1734, CO 137/21, folio 48, PRO; Address Governor, Council, and Assembly to King George, February 21, 1734, Hunter to Newcastle, February 27, 1734, *Cal. S. P. Col.*, #55, 42, #62, 44, #75, 49.

59. Jonathan Swift to Mrs. Moore, December 7, 1727, quoted in Bullitt, *Swift*, 11; Major Ayscough to Board of Trade, April 4, 1732, *Cal. S. P. Col.*, #119, 75; Knight, *History of Jamaica*, Pt. 3, Add. MSS 12,418, 374, British Library.

60. Long, *History of Jamaica* 1:148; Hunter's epitaph was written by the Reverend Fleming and is quoted in Cundall, *Governors of Jamaica*, 154. Cundall also quotes the original Latin text; James Alexander to Thomas Orby Hunter, July 12, 1734, Rutherfurd Collection, NYHS.

Conclusion—"*A Sound Man*"

1. Hunter to Alexander, August 18, 1732, Rutherfurd Collection, NYHS.

2. Hunter to John Chamberlayne, February 25, 1712, *Doc. Rel. Col. Hist. N.Y.* 5:312–17.

3. Hunter to William Popple, November 14, 1715, *Cal. S. P. Col.*, #674, 341.

4. Affidavit John Coe, February 12, 1712, Colonial Documents, 57:91, N.Y. State Library.

5. Cadwallader Colden to Alexander Colden, October 15, 1759, in Smith, *New York*, 308.

6. See, for instance, anonymous letter written in Jamaica in 1733, in Letters of J. Knight and Others Relating to Jamaica, 1725–1789, Add. MSS 22,677, folio 21, British Library.

7. Plumb, *Walpole* 2:232.

8. Board of Trade to Newcastle, February 22, 1734, CO 138/17, 199–200; Board of Trade to Hunter, May 23, 1734, CO 138/17, 209–10, PRO.

9. Hunter to St. John, September 12, 1711, *Doc. Rel. Col. Hist. N.Y.* 5:255–56.

10. Hunter quoted in Osgood, *Eighteenth Century* 2:106; Hunter to Board of Trade, September 8, 1733, *Cal. S. P. Col.*, #331, 180–81.

11. Thucydides, *The Peloponnesian War*, trans. Rex Warner (New York: Penguin Books, 1954, 1975), 58.

12. Board of Trade to St. John, April 23, 1712, *Doc. Rel. Col. Hist. N.Y.* 5:329–30.

13. Simonides, "The Comment," in *Greek Lyrics*, 55.

152; establishes government-controlled trading posts, 153;
Palatines: suggests taking Palatines to New York, 60; buys supplies, 61; has Palatines sign contracts, 61; sails for New York with Palatines, 63; settles Palatines, 67–68; effects of collapse of Whig ministry, 70–71; asks government for additional funds, 71; ministry decides not to provide funds, 85; rebellions quelled, 86–87, 88–89; places Palatines under military discipline, 89; recruits Palatines for regiments, 96; stops paying expenses, 97–98; threatens those who leave Hudson River sites, 98; incurs debt of over £21,000, 98; forty Palatine families leave site for Schoharie, 98; fears imprisonment for debt, 127; secures release from Livingston for debts, 144; denies Weiser's charges, 164; attempts to get statement signed, 165–66;
Administrative career, Jamaica: calls assembly, 184; secures permanent revenue, 187–88; accepts gifts, 188–89; approves taxes on South Sea Company, 189; rejects bill making sugar legal tender, 189–90; requests removal of Ayscough from council, 190; secures passage Protestant Act, 193; supports passage of act to discourage manumission of slaves, 194–95; approves repeal of Protestant Act, 195–96; asks for troops despite assembly objections, 200; imposes taxes to subsist troops, 204; Ayscough restored to council, 208–209; assembly refuses to admit provost marshall, 209; rivalry between council and assembly accelerates, 210–11; deplores scarcity of efficient men in Jamaica's government, 211;
Defense of Jamaica: hears of planned Spanish invasion, 191–92; summons council of war, 192; finds blacks more reliable than white indentured servants, 192; hears of English merchants' objections to embargo, 195;

Maroon War: employs Highland tactics, 184; additional troops sent to Jamaica, 200; blames high death rate on consumption of rum, 200–201; home government receive reports on conditions on island, 201–202; 200 soldiers remain, 203; Nanny Town taken, 203; assembly orders barracks built, 210; unable to enforce discipline, 212; secures personal loan to pay soldiers, 212; recruits seamen, 213; hears soldiers and sailors stole supplies and deserted, 213–14;
Genoesa: returns to Port Royal, 198; turns treasure over to Spanish before receiving Newcastle's instructions, 198–99;
Merchant opposition: objections to embargo, 195; objections to duties on slaves, 204–205; effects of inability to tax merchants on the island and imperial government, 206
Hunter, Thomas Orby, RH's son: commissioned captain of cadet company, 144; becomes father's principal heir, 207; returns to England, 215; mentioned, 142, 190, 229
Hunterston, Jamaica, 183
Hunterston, Scotland, 2, 229
Huy, 31
Hyde, Anne, duchess of York, 13–14
Hyde Park, London, 25
Hythe, mayor of, 54

Ingoldsby, Richard, 128
Innes, Reverend Alexander, 141
Inveraray, 23
Inverlochy, 3, 22
Inverness, 3
Ireland, x, xi, 18, 20, 22, 27, 45, 146, 168, 171, 193, 219
Iroquois (Five [later Six] Nations): agree to sell Schoharie tract, 67–68; assist with invasion of Canada, 93–94; learn expedition cancelled, 96; fear English plan to exterminate them, 151; attack Catawba, 152; refuse to meet Spotswood anywhere but Albany, 152; sym-

ROBERT HUNTER
1666–1734

was composed in 11-point Merganthaler VIP Bodoni Book and leaded one point,
with display type in Bodoni and Excelsior Script,
by Partners Composition;
printed by sheet-fed offset on 50# acid free Glatfelter Antique cream,
Smythe-sewn and bound over 80-point binders boards in Holliston Roxite C-grade Cloth
by Braun-Brumfield, Inc;
and published by

SYRACUSE UNIVERSITY PRESS
SYRACUSE, NEW YORK 13210